Rebozos de Palabras

Rebozos de Palabras

An Helena María Viramontes Critical Reader

Edited by

GABRIELLA GUTIÉRREZ Y MUHS

THE UNIVERSITY OF
ARIZONA PRESS
TUCSON

THE UNIVERSITY OF
ARIZONA PRESS

www.uapress.arizona.edu

Library of Congress Cataloging-in-Publication Data

Rebozos de palabras : an Helena María Viramontes critical reader / edited by
Gabriella Gutiérrez y Muhs.
    p.   cm.
  Includes bibliographical references and index.
  ISBN 978-0-8165-2136-4 (cloth : alk. paper)   1. Viramontes, Helena María,
1954—Criticism and interpretation.   I. Gutiérrez y Muhs, Gabriella.
  PS3572.I63Z84   2013
  813'.54—dc23   2012032387

Publication of this book is made possible in part by the proceeds of a permanent
endowment created with the assistance of a Challenge Grant from the National
Endowment for the Humanities, a federal agency.

Contents

Foreword

"Look at These Lives"

SONIA SALDÍVAR-HULL

I first heard about Helena María Viramontes in 1984, when my brother José, then an assistant professor at the University of Houston and working as an assistant editor, read her manuscript for Arte Público Press. A few months later, my new friend Sandra Cisneros began telling me about this young writer whose work was sure to take Chicana/o literature in a new direction. Subsequently, *The Moths and Other Stories* was published in 1985; I understood then exactly what José and Sandra had recognized in the work. The new direction that I detected was a defining Chicana feminist literary production that elaborated the theoretical tracts being developed by Chicana feminist theorists and philosophers. The collection of short stories articulated the previously silenced voices of girls, young women, and mature women, *las mujeres* whose unrecognized labor, quiet life work, and, often, not so quiet political positions as working-class women in the flesh exploded into the consciousness of those of us who were reading against the grain in academic settings where these new literary productions often were not welcome or considered legitimate literature.

"Look at these lives. I just want you to look at this life."[1] In an interview, Helena María Viramontes poignantly describes what drives her masterful literary production. In her typically modest manner, in two short declarative sentences, Viramontes takes on the mantle/rebozo of political chronicler. This is all that she asks of her reader: look at the lives I am offering you and take courage and faith and hope from them. Get angry. See the injustices. Ask why the people who harvest the food of the richest nation in this world are not allowed to take a bite of a peach without risking death. The images and situations are often heartbreaking, but they are also breathtaking in their unflinching insistence that we look at the violence, misogyny, and under-education that third-space dwellers of the US third world endure and at times even triumph over. These *historias* of the mid-twentieth-century Chicana presence in the United States interrupt the hegemony of the ongoing secret war, the project of colonization, and the power of domination with an acute lens that brings to focus the instantiation of what Emma Pérez calls a decolonial imaginary. Since the publication of that first short-story collection, *The Moths and Other Stories*, Viramontes has been documenting the lives of people living in the "third space": what Gloria Anzaldúa identifies as Nepantla.

So many of the characters in Viramontes's literary works negotiate deterritorialization in late twentieth-century US borderlands. We see resistance in how, out of necessity, marginalized people create sites of empowerment in the midst of a country that prefers them invisible. Petra and Estrella in *Under the Feet of Jesus*, the women in "The Moths," and women like Tranquilina and Ermila in *Their Dogs Came with Them* all learn how to survive and even transform hostile spaces into transparent and established life *sitios*.

With the advent of the publication of literary texts by Sandra Cisneros, Ana Castillo, and Cherríe Moraga alongside Helena María Viramontes, young Chicana feminist writers were elucidating a view of a world in which Chicanas lived and struggled and, at times, thrived on the margins of the United States. *The Moths and Other Stories* gave us snapshots of life in the urban US third world of the mid-twentieth century. We witnessed the mystical experience of the titular story, "The Moths," and the soul-searing, wretched lives of the women in "The Broken Web." Viramontes's unrelenting political voice comes through clearly, forthrightly asserting the genocidal impulse of US-supported right-wing dictatorships that destroy lives across borders—from the urban borderlands of East Los Angeles to a war-torn country in Central America of the 1980s. The individually published short stories "Tears on My Pillow" and "Miss Clairol" hint of the upcoming, full-fleshed novel treatment of the urban barrio world, Los Angeles's Terrace Flats in these stories, that only Viramontes has given witness to in the unsentimental mode of what the Latina Feminist Group called the *testimoniadora*.

In *Under the Feet of Jesus*, she takes us to the world of the farmworkers, those *trabajadoras* who labor harvesting the fruits and vegetables we consume but who themselves never savor the bounty of the *tierra* that devours them. While these feminist literary narratives are examples of resistance literature, with this documentation we are also forced to look closely at the subaltern people who are consumed by exploiters. We witness the mystical transformation of Estrella, who climbs the barn, symbolically crushes the serpent under her feet, and ultimately offers the possibility that she might emerge as a *nepantlera* whose lived experience will mature into a life of spiritual activism. Yet Viramontes will not allow us to look away from those who never get the opportunity to transform, the Alejos and the Petras whose lives are prematurely extinguished by the limitations of their existence under a neocolonial, neoliberal empire.

If we think through the feminist methodologies developed by such Chicana theorists as Yvonne Yarbro-Bejarano, Mary Pat Brady, Gloria Anzaldúa, Chela Sandoval, and Emma Pérez, we comprehend Viramontes's literary production as glimpses of Anzaldúan *conocimiento*, of the reinscription of Chicana histories that Pérez elaborates as the third-space feminisms we had identified as US women-of-color feminisms or US third-world feminisms in such texts as *This Bridge Called My Back* in the early 1980s. Mujeres like Estrella and the every-Chicanita narrator in "The Moths" negotiate the periphery, learning to traverse the minefields of their worlds by deploying what Sandoval calls differential consciousness.

The feminist theories developed by the Chicana philosophers of the late twentieth century come to life in the magisterial *Their Dogs Came with Them*. Just look at the masterful craft that Viramontes exhibits in this novel that gives flesh to, that is about full embodiment of, that recognizes the *gente* who walk in the shadows of the urban dystopia of mid-twentieth-century East Los Angeles. These are the people whom Yarbro-Bejarano calls phantom people. They are the incarnation of theory in the flesh. With the authority of memory, Viramontes grants the homeless their dignity; they are en-fleshed, given face as they wander in the shadows of the post-conquest city. The narrative makes us *see* the worth of dislocated peoples. She crafts their personal histories, their material realities, and, in the case of Ben and a "phantom" woman who may be his mother, their untreated mental disabilities. This complex novel brings to light the previously neglected histories that constitute these lives. While we recognize Ermila's fledgling resistance strategies that some might dismiss as typical teenage rebellion, we see her gradual coming to consciousness. But Viramontes never offers easy solutions to the power of domination and relentlessly reminds us that a new critical (mestiza) consciousness has to be recognized in conjunction with the more restricted lives of Ben, Turtle, Luis, and even the transcendent Tranquilina. Viramontes reinscribes their embodied histories so that we might possibly—no, so that we *must*—hear them and see them. In her haunting words: "Just look at these lives. I just want you to look at this life."

At this historical moment when the United States once again attempts to enact virulently anti-Mexican, anti-Latina/o legislation not only in Arizona but also in Texas, Michigan, and other states, reading Helena María Viramontes's literary interventions is urgent. From the lost children of "The Cariboo Café," who have been taught not to trust the "poli," to the brown inhabitants of an East Los Angeles who find themselves, like dogs, under a police state surveillance administered by the fictional QA (Quarantine Authority), that resembles the strategies of the current ICE (Immigration and Customs Enforcement), Viramontes's chronicles elucidate the process of colonization and what it takes to survive it with a decolonial consciousness and spiritual activism. Her point, however, is to make the reader *look* at the lives of US subaltern who are murdered daily, figuratively and literally, by the conditions of containment.

With this much-needed anthology, Gabriella Gutiérrez y Muhs gathers the latest literary and theoretical analyses by established and emergent scholars and offers two interviews that give us further insight into Viramontes's artistry and theory making. *Rebozos de Palabras*, guided by the insight of *profesora* Gutiérrez y Muhs, shows us how to look critically at these fragile, powerful, important lives.

Sonia Saldívar-Hull
San Antonio, Tejas
July 11, 2011

Note

1. From a 2003 unpublished interview with Deborah Owen Moore titled "Moments of Light: An Interview with Helena María Viramontes."

Acknowledgments

Throughout the last twenty years since I met Yvonne Yarbro-Bejarano, we have had many conversations about Helena María Viramontes. Yvonne has continuously inspired me to look further, to look beyond, to describe what is not present in Viramontes's writings and why. I wish to acknowledge and appreciate her gentle teachings, as well as the unconditional support I have received as a scholar from her, from Mujeres Activas en Letras y Cambio Social (MALCS), and from magnificent people I perhaps see only once a year: in particular, Rosalía Solórzano, Francisca James Hernández, Karen Mary Dávalos, Ana Juárez, Cecilia P. Burciaga, Deena González, Mary Pat Brady, and especially Susana Gallardo. They all have been incredibly *solidarias* with my quest to establish and produce a new type of reader that acknowledges the literature of Chicana authors as unfettered and unboxable.

I want to thank Mary Louise Pratt for her support of me as a graduate student at Stanford University. I am also grateful to Associate Provost Jacquelyn Miller at Seattle University for all the undying lessons I learned from her about academic life. I would especially like to thank Provost Isiaah Crawford, who has supported my research from his first year there to the present.

I always dedicate my work to the four most important people in my life: my mother Socorro Favela, my husband Eric C. Muhs, and my sons Eleuterio (Tello) and Enrico (Rico) Muhs. They are the reasons for all my hard work, inspiration, and satisfaction for and about life, as I have chosen to live it. The rapture and struggles of my every day come mostly from them, and I thank them for the full life they give me—Chowder too!

I also thank my lovely *comadres* and continual sources of life and motivation, who allow for me to keep at it, no matter what else is going on in life. The list is too long; I will only list the ones who lifted me through the difficult terrain of the last two years: Antonia García, Yolanda Flores Niemann, Sally Hawkridge, Patty Lally, Kathy Cook, María Bullón, Stasha McBride, Lucía Ochoa, Victoria Kill, Coco Pellerino, Kathy Asai, Lori Osato, Graciela Vega, Guadalupe McKeithen, Kerri Sinclair, Vanessa Castañeda, Kari Lerum, Shari Dworkin, Nancy Vive, Imme Bergmeier, Melyssa Jo Kelly, Melissa Morisi, Victoria Lugo, and especially Mary Antoinette-Smith, Connie Anthony, Nalini Iyer, Jodi O'Brien, Cynthia Moe-Lobeda, Carmen G. González, and Jeanette Rodriguez.

My *compadres* also have a great deal to do with supporting me: Jesús Rosales and Noé González p/v, Alex Flores, Fémi Táíwò, Saheed Adejumobi, Dan Pickard, David Ehrich, Ted Fortier, Tayyab Mahmud, Kola Abimbola, Dan Goldberg, and Perry Phillips always.

I appreciate fully the contributors who stuck to this book through thick and thin.

My students are those without whom I could not feel useful and knowledgeable. Thank you for embracing what I have attempted to teach you. I would like to thank each of you, especially those of you who helped me input changes to my papers, or made copies for me, or took something somewhere at the university, or bought a cake at the store to celebrate someone so I could continue grading or writing. *Mil gracias* for taking care of many of my needs, including coffee and poetry.

I would especially like to name and profusely thank Aldo Ulisses Reséndiz Ramírez, Noemi Peredo, Max Cubriz, Brenda Trejo, Rose Rodríguez, Gabriela Boyle, Stasha McBride, Santa María Rivera, Carlos Sibaja-García, Aaron Raj, and particularly Marianne Mork (for her political commitment to advancing the work of her friends and political allies), without whom this manuscript would have taken much longer to come to light. My inspiration truly comes from my students as I watch them evolve into people who make changes in this complicated world, despite their quotidian challenges.

I would also like to thank Isabelle Gentili, Eliane Gentili, Jean Umbert, Jean Claude Gentili, Gerard Liberto, my family in France, and all my relatives, especially my cousins Ruth, Eric, and Carlitos Gutiérrez; María Elena Reséndiz; Ofelia Favela; Cindy Ramirez; Shirley Flores Muñoz; and the other 100+. I would like to thank my cousins Olga Favela, Joel Frías, Alonzo and Jesús Rivera, and their families.

And thanks to the always muses of my existence: writers Bettina Aptheker, Rati Saxena, Seetha Narayanan, Patrice Vecchionne, Ken Weisner, Wendy Call, Catalina Cantú, Lucha Corpi, Demetria Martínez, Francisco Lomelí, Marjorie Agosín, Alicia Partnoy, Francisco Alarcón, Marisela Norte, Martín Espada, Rigoberto González, Norma Cantú, Sandra Cisneros, María Meléndez, Kathleen Alcalá, Pía Barros, Susana Sánchez Bravo, Emma Sepúlveda, Donna Miscolta, Alex Espinoza, and especially Helena María Viramontes for her wisdom and emotional wealth.

I would like to thank our healers: Winfield Hobbs, Marc Jyringi, Marc Lacambra, Rachel Torrez, Kitty Grupp, and of course my mother-in-law Deborah Muhs; and always thank you to Lady Katherine, Heidi Knickerbocker, *y especialmente* Lucy Ramírez.

To George Donovan, Annemarie Peterson, Ian, and Garrett, our *familia* in Seattle.

I would also like to thank the following colleagues: Janet Quillian, Olga Colbert, Dede Henley, Sue Secker, Robin Craggs, Paulette Kidder, Valentín Ferdinán, Bill Buckley, Richard Delgado, Steven Bender, Marianne LeBarre, Madeline Lovell, Gordon Miller, and Lauren St. Pierre. I thank Ron and Cynthia Moe-Lobeda for parenting with us, and for generously opening their home to my Tello, as if he were theirs.

In memory of César Chávez, Don Luis Leal, Lila Martín-Geldert, Delfina Favela, Jean Claude Gentili, Adriana Berchenko, and Adrienne Rich.

Rebozos de Palabras

Introduction

GABRIELLA GUTIÉRREZ Y MUHS

> I also wish to make historically marginalized theory accessible
> to undergraduates, including my own students. I see this work
> as belonging to those whom I define as my community and as
> a welcome to those who have a desire to engage in a dialogue
> about Chicana and Mexicana literature.
> —Anna Marie Sandoval, *Toward a Latina Feminism of
> the Americas: Repression and Resistance in Chicana
> and Mexicana Literature*

> For Viramontes's aesthetic is a practice of political intervention,
> carried out in literary form. Viramontes, a daughter of the work-
> ing class, transforms her class instinct into a political position.
> —Sonia Saldívar-Hull, *Feminism on the Border:
> Chicana Gender Politics and Literature*

> The Chicana is a marginalized, brown woman who, while usually
> a US citizen, is treated at first glance as a foreigner or an immi-
> grant. She is assumed to be here to work in the service class and
> should not ask or expect anything from society. While I do not
> define my work by my ethnicity or gender, giving voice to that
> woman, who is not one woman but many, whose story is not
> one, but many, in as numerous ways and to as wide a readership
> as possible has been my objective.
> —Ana Castillo, "How I Became a Genre-Jumper"

HELENA MARÍA VIRAMONTES IS A PROFESSOR, teacher, scholar,
critic, and author of fiction and nonfiction. Born in East Los Angeles in 1954, she currently serves at Cornell University as Professor of
English and Director of the Creative Writing Center. Her work has
been anthologized and read widely both in the United States and

abroad, in countries such as India and Spain. She has been invited to give hundreds of readings and speaking engagements around the world, where she often arrives wearing a rebozo (a shawl worn by Mexican and Chicana women living on both sides of the US–Mexico border). Once, when asked about her rebozo, Viramontes explained that the Mexican shawl is a "security blanket" for her. By embracing the pre-Columbian icon, she finds comfort: "While I throw it back it gives me time to think of a response" (Viramontes, 1997).

Helena María Viramontes's work functions like a rebozo, a shawl forged with words. Her oeuvre creates what writers like Viramontes, the child of Mexican parents raised in the urban working-class neighborhoods of East Los Angeles, could only envision weaving with words, with ink and pen, or, more recently, with computer and paper.

In spite of some excellent critical commentary on Helena María Viramontes's fiction in monographs such as Sonia Saldívar-Hull's *Feminism on the Border* (University of California Press, 2000) and Raúl Homero Villa's *Barrio-Logos* (University of Texas, 2000), a major void in the scholarship on Viramontes's creative writing still exists.[1] In particular, there is a monumental gap in the array of inter-pretations of Chicana literature that reaches mainstream audiences. Our project addresses this void by focusing on the problematiza-tion of the Chicana image as it has evolved through Viramontes's literature, enriching literary fiction, particularly in the area of the inscribed female body and subjectivity. The freshly produced scholarly essays and interviews that comprise this volume will add significantly to our understanding of how gendered difference and subject posi-tions affect identity and literary or cultural representations, as well as formulate everyday life dialectically for both writers and read-ers. In order to frame the intersectionality that Viramontes utilizes to engage Chican@ and non-Chican@ audiences, I will later in this introduction tell a story about a mother and her three children. The story will become a metaphor for the manner in which Viramontes subverts victimization and includes the global to situate the regional in our agency-filled consciousness for readers, writers, and critics.

Research is essential to a comprehensive understanding of subjec-tivity within Chican@, Latin@, and Latin American communities. We need to expand intersectionality by reading perspectives that amplify the regard with which Chican@ literature is read. Additionally, we need to promote enriching gazes and more in-depth views of Viramontes's work from various junctures, including the perspective of writers/critics who reflect multiple class, race, and sexuality positionalities upon mainstream readers, and readers with little exposure to Latin@ life and culture. This project began with a two-fold intention in mind: first, to fulfill the need for books for professors teaching American ethnic literature that could be truly utilized by students and, second, to underline the need for diversifying intersectional readings of the work of major Chican@ and Latin@ authors.

Rebozos de Palabras: An Helena María Viramontes Critical Reader is intended for an audience interested in the Chican@, Latin@, and Latin American literary and cultural experience, particularly in regard to gender. Subjectivity is at the crossroads of most studies about Chicanas in a variety of disciplines, including literature, history, sociology, anthropology, and religious studies (see Cindy Cruz, Rosa-Linda Fregoso, Karen Mary Dávalos, and Susana Gallardo). *Rebozos de Palabras* will also appeal to readers interested in gender, immigration, cultural studies, women's studies, spirituality, and Mexican@/Chican@, Latin@, and Latin American culture and civilization. This book is a timely production because Viramontes's second novel, *Their Dogs Came with Them*, was published in 2007 and reissued in paperback in October of 2008; however, not much criticism has of yet been directed toward this masterpiece. This novel was much awaited, given the success of her short-story collection *The Moths and Other Stories* (1985) and her first novel, *Under the Feet of Jesus* (1995), more than ten years earlier. Viramontes's entire oeuvre will be critically addressed in this collection of newly produced articles by major literary critics and emerging scholars who know her work from multiple perspectives and who wrote their academic essays specifically for this reader. At the moment, this collection represents the only reader that gathers academic essays by multiple scholars about a Chicana or Latina author's oeuvre in its entirety. We are in this manner setting a precedent for subsequent readers about other renowned Chican@/Latin@ authors.

This collection of essays is edited with a feminist intention and perspective. This book will contribute greatly not only to the analysis of this unique, exceptional, and accomplished Latina author but also to the positive paradigm shift that dictates how books by Latin@ authors could be more thoroughly analyzed and read in a college/university classroom by audiences not familiar with Latin@ culture in the United States. Helena María Viramontes has always spoken of her work with an insistence upon underlining the quotidian events that affect people, particularly women's and children's lives. In an interview with Daniel Olivas regarding *Their Dogs Came with Them*, Viramontes states, "I set the novel in this decade [1960 to 1970] because of the radical changes happening within the nation and within the community." The political intentionality of her work emerges with agendas that are communal, that project the individual in relation to the group—oftentimes the family, or the cultural or ethnic group that is at the center of her multifaceted work.

Helena María Viramontes's work has developed within the growing body of Chican@ literature. Almost twenty years ago, in their 1991 introductory essay to *Criticism in the Borderlands*, Héctor Calderón and José David Saldívar unearthed various established realities about the trajectory of Chican@ literature. They stated that African American Studies and Women's Studies had obtained attention and "benefitted from the widening of the literary canon," underlining that Chican@ literature and other ethnic groups had not advanced as much. They also highlighted two other points that are essential in understanding the foundation of the work Chicana feminists have established in the twenty-first century: (1) They have awoken international interest in Chican@ literature through their established linguistic and creative precedence, and (2) they have commented on the fact that Chican@ scholarship should be dissociated from critical thought that emphasizes a Spanish past and disregards "mestizaje" as an essential ingredient of Chican@ literature.

Since these seminal observations, the work of several Chicana authors has been translated into at least two languages in the new millennium (and Helena María's work into at least four), and it is no longer necessary for books by Chican@ authors to first appear and succeed in sales in English in order for the book to appear simultaneously in Spanish, as used to be the case prior to Sandra Cisneros's *Caramelo* (2002). Every year, there are conferences in Europe that are organized to discuss, analyze, and centralize Chican@ literature in the world canon, by including it into both the Latin American and the American mainstream canons. For example, the recent launching and publication of *Camino Real* (2009), a critical literary journal out of the Universidad de Alcalá de Henares, Spain, features the work of major Chican@ authors and critics, and this comes as no surprise, given the expanding interest in Chican@ literature in Europe.

The notion, discussed by Calderón and Saldívar, that Chican@s are judged as "anglicized inauthentic Mexicans" by Mexicans has been left in the past, at least in academic settings. Nonetheless, much of what people in diverse disciplines read about Chican@/Latin@ life and culture is usually still from the perspective of voyeurs of culture, be they non-Latin@ or Latin@. Unfortunately, this "voyeuristic" critic has sometimes been unfamiliar even with American multiethnic or immigrant populations. As Julio Cortázar, Argentinean author, would put it: someone not in the picture, but outside the picture, observing it.

A result of this type of scholarship is, in part, that many assumptions and false stereotypes about Chican@ life have yet to be dispelled at all levels, including in academia. Some years ago, a few months after receiving my tenure at my home institution in the state of Washington, I was asked to participate in an interdisciplinary retreat with other professors from across the university. During the event, I was disappointed to find myself in the middle of a retrograde heated discussion about Latin@ immigrants living in the United States. We had been asked to read a piece by an English male travel writer about Latin@ immigrants in California in which the author compared two families, à la Alexis de Tocqueville. An openly conservative man from the School of Law faculty was alternately leading the discussions on assigned readings. The conservative professor was in charge of the California article. Ironically, after a lunch featuring asparagus, he began his discussion by crunching into an apple (a triggering sound for those of us who grew up picking fruits and vegetables), most likely harvested by Mexican immigrant hands in eastern Washington. He asserted in a patriotic tone that although some people in our group probably believed in open borders and open immigration, he did not. He then synopsized the article by focusing on the two Latino families that the English writer had described, using condescending and demeaning descriptions.

However, many of my fellow professors participating in the event did not even notice that the article was riddled with negative adjectives describing the interviewed Latin@s, for example, as "stubbornly silent" when one female subject did not want to respond to the interviewer's meddling questions during her unexpected and unplanned interrogation. The subjects of the study were portrayed as peripheral and marginal immigrants, unincorporated into the fabric of US society, and although one family was financially stable, the other was allegedly on the verge of becoming a load on the state because of the inability of its members to support themselves. The father of the second family had only recently found himself in such a precarious position; a work accident in which he had been run over by a truck left him disabled and no longer able to stand up for long periods of time, let alone walk or work. In our discussion of the two families, the male professor intermittently interjected to boast about his generous food gifts to his local church to help "the needy" as well as migrant families; he underlined that although he considered himself a religious man, he was unable to consider the family head's dilemma with compassion.

Experiences like this one have made a significant impact on my academic career. As a result of my frustration with the lack of understanding about Latin@ immigrants' lives by mainstream America and American intellectuals, I decided, given that this is my area of expertise, to produce a critical reader that introduced and theorized the writings of prominent Chicana authors (this reader being the first of a long list I envision). Latin@s and Chican@s represent the millions who are the largest minority in the United States. By the year 2050, we will make up at least one-third of the US population. Chican@/Latin@ writers are one of the groups that bring us the closest into the lives of the Americans we rarely read about. This book is the beginning of the end result of my apocalypse that began at that retreat, where I truly understood the importance of literature as a vehicle of social transformation, in particular for academics and the professional middle class at large.

Notwithstanding, because we attend conferences to hear people such as ourselves speak about theories in our varied humanities disciplines, we forget that the brushstrokes with which the general population continues to paint Latin@s, and particularly Chican@s, are monumentally broad and inexact. These brushstrokes are almost whitewashing the real profile of characterizations in the proverbial American imaginary. Moreover, literary portrayals of Latin@s continue to be stereotypical, even among intelligentsia and in spite of our increasingly technologically globalized world, where becoming informed is relatively easy. Hollywood has eagerly (re)produced the stereotypes mainstream America wanted to see on the screen. Books are, in fact, one of the only and few elements that bring American life under the microscope, allowing for the voices of silenced minorities, ethnicities, youth, and women to fully project into our minds and evolving selves. Literature—our most needed eyeglasses—helps us see history, our community, and ourselves more clearly. Writers are the scientists who keep a hand on the pulse of an evolving Latin@ community through their manuscripts. In gratitude to Latin@ authors and readers, I attempt to provide for all of you the inspiration Viramontes has brought to the keen eye of critics, philosophers, and artists, fully reflected and inscribed in the criticism brought to us by the line of critics and scholars who analyze her work, ingeniously and proactively, in this collected volume.

This manuscript consists of four sections. World-renowned scholar Sonia Saldívar-Hull, who acknowledges the value of Viramontes's work in one chapter of her book *Feminism on the Border*, has written the foreword for this collection. Saldívar-Hull's perspective and contribution are essential to our book because she has already laid the path as to how we should understand Viramontes's timely oeuvre in her invaluable scholarship. Following her foreword, the introduction describes the project and the central metaphors of the rebozo elicited by the richness of this compilation, especially in regard to the title of this book.

The next section consists of scholarly papers on Viramontes's fiction organized in three parts: Latin American Perspectives; The Body; and Ethics and Aesthetics. Included in this section are several essays by renowned scholars in the field of Chicana literary studies. Some of these critics are Barbara Brinson Curiel (the author of multiple critical chapters), Yvonne Yarbro-Bejarano (*The Wounded Heart: Writing on Cherríe Moraga*, 2001), Mary Pat Brady (*Extinct Lands, Temporal Geographies*, 2002), and Juanita Heredia (*Transnational Latina Narratives in the Twenty-first Century*, 2009). Alongside the work of these established theorists and authors are compelling research projects by emerging academics such as Margarita T. Barceló, R. Joyce Z. L. Garay, and philosopher and Chican@ Studies scholar Juan D. Mah y Busch, and also the promising young scholars Aldo Ulisses Reséndiz Ramírez and Raelene Wyse. The fourth section (Part Four) consists of two interviews—both unpublished and newly updated.

As we attempt to weave a rebozo of words about Helena María Viramontes, we find that the weave will be striped and mottled, dappled and intertwined with various interpretations of Viramontes's work. We are pleased to feature the critical work of major Chicana scholars as mentioned earlier, including Yvonne Yarbro-Bejarano, Mary Pat Brady, and others, who wrote their papers for this anthology. Helena María Viramontes is a Chicana feminist writer who does not present the reader with idealized representations of Chicana femininity, as Yvonne Yarbro-Bejarano explains in her introduction to *The Moths and Other Stories*: "Viramontes creates female characters who are a contradictory blend of strengths and weaknesses, struggling against lives of unfulfilled potential and restrictions forced upon them because of their sex. These women are conscious that something is wrong with their lives, and that what is wrong is linked to the rigid gender roles imposed on them by their men and their culture" (10). Helena María Viramontes, an urban product of Los Angeles, encapsulates through her work and life the principles of the Chican@ movement of the 1960s and 1970s, which is especially significant, recognizing that most other well-known Chicano authors focus on Texas, Chicago, and other centers of Chicano communities. Growing up in and writing about Los Angeles, Viramontes is the holder of values that pour into various generations. Her work is foundational, in a literal manner, as well as politically and socially. She exudes the political agendas of the Chican@ movement: after a physical war in the streets of Los Angeles demanded rights in the 1960s and representation by Chican@s in the academic and educational world of the United States, her work and the work of other authors sprang forth, politically bringing color to particular literary denominations.

In the early stages of the Chicano movement, however, there were also many gender struggles and intra-cultural battles within the Chicano community, and against established mainstream feminism, which had excluded the voices of Chicanas in its decision-making process. In her book *From Out of the Shadows: Mexican Women in Twentieth-Century America*, historian Vicki L. Ruiz provides the first full study of Mexican American women in the twentieth century and recounts in detail from leaders and feminists what occurred in the early stages of Chicana feminism.

According to historiographical inscriptions of Chicana feminist history, wide representation by multiple groups began in 1968. However, according to scholar activist and oral historian Maylei Blackwell, who researched Anna Nieto Gómez's archives, and Las Hijas de Cuauhtémoc, an important feminist group in Los Angeles, mainstream American and Chicano scholars established its beginnings only during the 1980s. Chicana scholar Karen Mary Dávalos situates Chicana feminism upon various planes and waves by 1971. According to her, there are first, second, and third waves of Chicana feminism. This was first documented by Alma M. García in "The Development of Chicana Feminist Discourse, 1970–1980" and verified by historian Vicki Ruiz, who states: "By 1971, in Houston, Texas, at La Conferencia de Mujeres por la Raza, the first national Chicana conference, women spoke out with a distinctly feminist platform. The resolutions called for 'free legal abortions and birth control in the Chicano community to be provided and controlled by Chicanas.' In addition they called for higher education, for acknowledgment of the Catholic church as an instrument of oppression, for compassionate equalitarian marriage ('Marriage-Chicana Style'), and for child care arrangements to ensure women's involvement in the movement" (108).

In the 1990s, Chicana activism was problematized as a response to issues such as the simplistic interpretations of La Malinche, Hernán Córtes's translator and partner, who has been blamed for the Spanish Conquest of Mexico for five hundred years, to the point of even having an adjective in Spanish derived from her name, translated as "betrayer." Cultural issues such as this one were reinterpreted by Chicanas and imbued in a political deconstruction and rewriting of meanings by valorizing characteristics from their communities that had been traditionally interpreted as transitional or temporary.

While scholar Paula Moya establishes that Chicana feminism emerged in response to sexism and defines the Chicana as a woman of Mexican ancestry born and/or raised in the United States "who possesses a radical political consciousness," I would like to initially challenge her definition of Chicana by adding that in the last ten years the Chicana nation has grown tremendously with nonbiological Chicana-identified women of a new generation. Are we to exclude nonbiological Chicanas, or what I call "cultural Chicanas," from the Chicana realm? Inclusionary practices have been achieved by many authors; nonetheless, Viramontes is one of these writers at the fore-front of Chicana feminist literary inclusion. We see this particularly in *Their Dogs Came with Them*, where we experience the lives of biracial Chican@s who live in a Chican@ barrio.

I would also add that Chicana feminism did not merely emerge as a solidified group "in response to sexism," but out of the need for communal feminism, a legacy of women of Latin American and indigenous extraction, that is, mestizas. Yes, there was an initial struggle to attain gender equality among their own ethnic group (Chicano) because many of the benefits were received along gender lines: the men got to publish, speak, and write, and the women got to make the meals and clean up, as well as write up the speeches behind the counter during the Movimiento. But it would be sim-plistic not to revise our history as a group and underline the impor-tance of meeting in groups with other women in order to talk, read poetry, cook, and speak about society and personal goals—that is, the verb "convivir" that has been a legacy of being Latin@ and Latin American. We must not forget that Chicanas' oral culture is a legacy of both indigenous and colonial societies, in both of which women came together to share, speak, strategize and sing together.

Chicana feminism has been articulated in multiple manners. Major Chicana author and cultural worker Ana Castillo's definition of a Chicana in her latest presentation, "How I Became a Genre-Jumper," quoted at the beginning of this introduction, states essential issues of gender, race, and class. In her presentation, she elaborates on the fact that Chicanas are a multiethnic and racially diverse lot. What she does not state in her definition is that sexual preference and sexuality have been central to the Chicana struggle for equality and justice in the present and recent past. Queer Studies has been one of the most prolific fields in Chicana critical production in the last ten years.

The themes that have been consistent throughout time, whether we say that Chicana feminism began in the 1960s or the 1970s, deal with issues of justice and equality with regard to race, class, gender, education, ecology, and sexuality, particularly in the last twenty years. The Chicana feminist seeks justice and resists against an established, oftentimes stereotypical vision of Mexican American women, or women of Mexican ancestry. She is continuously seen as subaltern to mainstream people at her employment, in school, and in society at large. It is only in the recent past that feminist scholars like Rosa-Linda Fregoso in her various books and articles, including *The Bronze Screen*, have underlined the unidimensionality with which Chicanas have been represented in film and culture in US society.

As Castillo stated in the quote referenced above, the Chicana is also seen as an intruder who has to push back and resist continuously all the pre-established notions about her identity and to support other oppressed peoples in the United States and, lately, specifically outside of the United States. What has occurred with Chicana leaders in the twenty-first century is that they have become the transnational voice of the oppressed, whether it be for women in Palestine or in Latin America, such as the recently disappeared women in maquiladoras (factory workers of the border who have been killed and tortured, as well as buried, in the Ciudad Juárez desert, the border city across from El Paso, Texas). But Chicanas are interested in all the needs of the subjugated: persecuted Puerto Rican *independentistas*, indigenous peoples of the Americas or throughout the continent, water rights for people in various parts of the world, and particularly women's rights to personal safety, choice, and agency. The Chicana academic and activist has always sought to speak with her own voice and echo that of her community, both locally and globally, in a dignified manner. She has also addressed issues of ecological equality with regard to human life (agricultural pesticides, water rights, etc.) and aims to raise world consciousness in the political arena, whether it be for identified or unidentified survivors. Yet, the stereotypical battles for the rights of the farmworkers, while important, have not been central for Chicana feminism in the last ten years, with the exception of authors Cherríe Moraga and Demetria Martínez.

Among Chicana feminists there is a resistance to binary oppositions or facile explanations about the behavior of the subaltern, and

in particular about the people in their community. According to Tey
Diana Rebolledo in *Women Singing in the Snow*, "Chicana writers
place the individual and her concerns against the backdrop of the
greater social and cultural picture" (6). But it is also essential to say
that for the Chicana, the group oftentimes is more important than
the individual, and that there is a profound concern with theorizing a space for Chicanas, including a specific Aztlán or philosophical homeland. In *Communal Feminisms: Chicanas, Chilenas, and
Cultural Exile*, I have attempted to recover a designated space for a
Chicana homeland that genderizes Chicanahood into collective communal and plural feminisms. I have coined the term "Maztlán" for
the Chicana mythic homeland that unites us to womanhood; that
is, a homeland for feminists that is gender specific. I invite others
to proceed in adding to the fleshing of this term that could serve as
a space for Chicana feminist and white feminist discourse in evolution (xxv).[2] Literary and cultural critics like Mary Pat Brady, Yvonne
Yarbro-Bejarano, Sonia Saldívar-Hull, and Norma Cantú have dealt
with issues of space, aesthetics, and the border in a much more layered manner than simple border studies scholars have. Viramontes
and Lorna Dee Cervantes, in particular, have looked at how spaces
like the freeway have divided and colonized Mexican American barrios, othering and dividing Chicano communities both from each
other and from historical and regional ties to the land and its richness, as well as their regional connection to the land itself, with similar
ties to those of the indigenous ancestors. Helena María is especially
important as someone who has written about both the urban and the
rural Chican@, and especially about the stereotypical Chican@: the
gang member, the farmworker, the immigrant, the Central American
woman with a mental disorder given her war-filled past, all due to
American colonization.

The Chicana feminist has concentrated on multiplying subjectivity for and about her, clarifying misunderstandings inscribed in history about the border and the relationships with the nation-state,
the establishment, institutions, etc. Some of the most prolific and
important feminist scholars and cultural workers have assisted in
reconstructing an acceptable image of the Chicana, at least in academic environments. Chicana feminist scholarship is only one part
of the immense theory based on a methodological project known

as US third-world feminism, which aligns itself with other coalitions for women of color, ethnic groups, and groups dealing with social-class issues and sexual preference. What is of particular importance is that Chicana feminism underlines collaboration and transdisciplinarity and that it is preoccupied with working in an interdisciplinary manner across racial/social-class lines with other feminists, something that was not part of its initial goal in the 1970s. Coalition politics are essential to Chicana feminists, as is the recognition of their often-groundbreaking articulations in their particular fields about race, class, gender, sexuality, and ethnicity.

Viramontes is important to us today in the twenty-first century because she brings with her a rich history of reformulating Chicana feminism with her cohort of feminists and writers. In this construction of Chicana feminism, as implemented in *The Moths and Other Stories*, the young women characterized in her short stories exemplify a certain agency that patterns a new feminism, not underlined as feminism before writers like Viramontes. After claiming it as such, Chicana feminism, it can be weaved and practiced in massive multidisciplinary practices by a highly united academic mechanism that establishes a counter-hegemonical united front of Chicana academics and writers.

Some mainstream feminists of the 1950s and 1960s had coined certain spaces, including the kitchen and the bedroom, as spaces of oppression. While in some cases these spaces are spaces to beware of, as women and as feminists, oftentimes they are not equally spaces of specific oppression for Chicanas; they are also spaces of liberation. Viramontes talks about the barn and the fields, or the river, as sexual spaces that young women are limited in exploring because they have been obscure spaces for women, but these spaces are also spaces for liberation. For example, the kitchen as a space for cooking, a symbol of oppression in mainstream feminist theory, is oftentimes identified as a space of accomplishment and empowerment for Chicanas. In Barbara Brinson Curiel's poem "Recipe: Chorizo con Huevo Made in the Microwave," the microwave represents a space of evolution, not oppression. The kitchen allows for creativity, nurturing, and experimentation, as well as empowerment and balance.

Tranquilina, one of the four main female characters in *Their Dogs Came with Them*, has the utmost objective of feeding the poor and homeless at the inner city mission that her aging parents have begun. She begs the butcher for a bone to make soup for the poor—food is then a liberating force combined with religious choice. Viramontes brings us choice—a choice that is put on feminist agendas, signify-ing freedom. Multiple (plural) feminisms and multiple agendas are added to the menu by Chicana authors in the last part of the twen-tieth century and in the twenty-first century. The literary kitchen, bathroom, and bedroom have been remodeled by Chicanas. Unlike mainstream feminist agendas, where caring for others is oftentimes considered a victimizing characteristic for the caregiver, alternative feminisms for Chicana characters are able to multiply these subjec-tivities as liberatory. Here I am speaking of Viramontes and other Chicana authors' feminism. Cooking and caring for others, specifi-cally within the family but also outside the family, are possibilities for feminism. Cooking and caring are assets not to be reneged on: they can be tools of emancipation from home, community, country—sometimes exterior and sometimes interior. Viramontes particularly constructs female characters who are genuinely influenced by Ameri-can society and culture, yet do not assimilate. She exemplifies combi-nations of women from the first, second, and third waves of feminisms that are all interweaved into a fabric that is both multigenerational and intersectional.

Some Chicana writers address issues that seem insignificant, yet perhaps have not been specifically theorized from a Chicana feminist perspective. An example would be that not all women necessarily wish to be liberated from their families and domestic chores; mostly they want to perform them in their own ideologically charged sce-narios that yet allow them to feel accepted and valued as well as vin-dicated for their work and contributions to the family, community, and country. This is especially true for elderly women. This pleasure in liberating not only the self but also other women is something mainstream American women did not originally perceive as power-ful during the civil rights movement. In the 1970s and 1980s, when the gap between women of color and white feminists grew, when women of color voiced the differences in their feminisms, is when Viramontes writes *The Moths and Other Stories*, which I consider an internationalist collection of short stories, then finishes *Under the Feet of Jesus* in Ithaca, after living in Canada and raising her children on the two coasts, which makes for a globalizing novel that regionalizes a specific type of life in a specific period.

Viramontes, a staunch and sophisticated feminist, patches the wound that several waves of exclusionary feminisms have left upon Latin@ authors, with biracial Latinos, monolingual Chicanos from East Los Angeles, loving white women, and Protestant missionaries in the inner city. The emergence of her biracial characters in *Their Dogs Came with Them* is not gratuitous—neither is Turtle, the androgynous character, who is also a gang member and traverses gender definitions as well as barrios with her multiple subjectivities, out of necessity, but also choice. Viramontes is part of a quorum of feminist Chicana writers that fully revolutionizes and digitizes feminism as multisensory, multigenerational, multicultural, and, above all, communal. Various invaluable contributions to feminism emerge from salient Chicana authors who are also professors and critics, and who catapult a series of consciousness-raising issues that are put forth by their continuous research about both their unique feminism and their ancestral and cultural feminisms.

Viramontes is fully representative of the Chicana feminist scholar who breathes feminism in her academic career and professional life, as well as in her personal life. She treads not so slowly in a converted writing world—with authors like Sandra Cisneros, Ana Castillo, Denise Chávez, Cherríe Moraga, Demetria Martínez, Norma E. Cantú, Pat Mora, Lorna Dee Cervantes, and Lucha Corpi—to where there is no going back in the agenda of representativity of the Chicana/Mexicana woman and young woman. Their agency-filled characters will not revert to the untold story. Along with critics Diana Tey Rebolledo, Deena González, and Eliana Rivero, the fields of Chicana feminism are plowed only to sow the new seeds of Chicana feminism that current and upcoming Chicana writers will tend.

In the Chicana literary arena, Viramontes's oeuvre is parallel in its success to the work of her contemporary Sandra Cisneros. In Cisneros's latest novel, *Caramelo*, the rebozo becomes a personified object with a voice, holding great cultural and ancestral significance, just as it does for Viramontes.[3] We are tempted to compare them continuously because their time line as authors is similar. For example, both of their short stories and first books were published and became successful at relatively the same time; initially, they were primarily known as short-story writers. Also, both published first with Arte Público Press, a Chican@ press in the United States. Viramontes and Cisneros are writers that came about in the same exciting era of the early to mid-1980s, and they both studied under Gabriel García Márquez, or "Gabo," as Viramontes and others affectionately call him. She was embraced by him, he who understood the uniqueness in her work and invited her, along with her children, to his workshop because she came as a package deal: her children, herself, her community.

Viramontes exemplifies the mature writer committed to family, activism, and writing, and while she solidifies the three simultaneously, the first is essential to the other two. The definition of family for her is non-translatable to Euro-American values, perhaps transcribable only through example. Her family is her children and husband and so many others: her students and her colleagues, her community, her friends, the leaders of her Chican@ community, other writers, the leaders of civil and human rights organizations, and, of course, all her other allies independent of their race, class, or gender, reformulating for the American mainstream in her literature the notion of "family."

Reminiscent of her type of Chicana feminism, where family equals community, equals literature, is that her characters sit together at the interminable table of subjectivity. Examples of this type of feminism spilling over the Chican@/Latin@ community have long prevailed among Chicana authors.[4] I first understood Viramontes's work while watching a Mexican woman at a bus station, Central Camionera in the city of Puebla in central Mexico, pull three suitcases and a basket, carry a purse and a baby in her arms, and direct her other two children, both under five, to keep persevering along to catch their bus. As her children waited for her every few meters with one of the bags, she did not ask for help—she simply used her body and technique to continue. After watching her do this a few times in front of us, although not asked, I got up with my backpack and my three-year-old holding on to my skirt to help her, and upon seeing this, another man got up, and we all helped her to her gate. We lifted and carried ourselves to support her strength because we knew she *could* make it, not because she couldn't. She was the first witness of her strength and determination, her children were also witnesses and participants, and we were the moved witnesses, participants, and students of her spirit, who would never forget her because she made us stronger.

In this story, it is obvious that the most important beings for this woman are her children, her three children, but she will not make the journey without her luggage, so the first is essential for the other two to complete their journey. This is also a metaphor for the work of Viramontes, who carries her community and her world with her to Cornell. Included in this world are *centroamerican@s*, farmworkers, single mothers, queer and heterosexual individuals, and suffering people of other nations, on her shoulders, wailing as she reads or talks about "The Cariboo Café," her internationalist *cuento*. Both Sonia Saldívar-Hull and Juanita Heredia allude to this mystic characteristic of Viramontes, which humanizes literature; I bore witness to this firsthand, both in the spring of 2009, when she visited Seattle University and conducted readings for our community, and when I first interviewed her in 1997 at Stanford University.[5]

In the interest of working as a link between both the Latin@ community and the community at large, as well as with the women's community, Helena María builds connections with larger metaphors beyond contemporary issues—her oeuvre spans from the Conquest to the present inner city. Sonia Saldívar-Hull has said it best: "For Viramontes' aesthetic is a practice of political intervention, carried out in literary form. Viramontes, a daughter of the working class, transforms her class instinct into a political position." She is not only a working-class Chicana but also an urban Chicana feminist who breaks the stereotype that still exists in the American imaginary about a "typical" Chicana. Because of this, criticism about her work is essential to understanding her oeuvre. Just like the luggage the woman in the Central Camionera needed, we need criticism. We decided to edit this much-needed reader about Viramontes's work to consolidate the luggage she has delivered to us piece by piece with dignity and commitment. Could our reader become the *carrito*, the cart that places a uniform list of her works (possessions, luggage) so that they can continue to be used in social service, anthropology discourse, literary criticism, and counseling trainings? Could we then attempt with our introduction, interviews, and research to establish where the woman was coming from, where she is going, and why the hundreds of people in the bus station sitting and waiting could not get up to help her? We believe that we can do that for Viramontes's characters by attempting to serve various interpretations of their bountiful characteristics.

Can the visionary, committed work of the new buses (theorists) about to leave the Central Camionera of this great woman author shine a path for Chican@ literature? In *Rebozos de Palabras: An Helena María Viramontes Critical Reader*, it is this question and others like it that we attempt to address.

I selected the following essays from the many abstracts submitted throughout the last few years because they span a variety of interpretations that situate the author as a Chicana/Latina feminist woman and groundbreaking author. We have three clusters—Latin American Perspectives, The Body, and Ethics and Aesthetics—to categorize the essays in this collection. Essays by Barbara Brinson Curiel and Raelene Wyse remind us that for many years Chican@ literature was placed under the umbrella of Latin American literature for scholars and students in the United States. Although I find this problematic, I understand the importance of inscribing historical literary periods in Chican@/Latin@ narrative into our lengthy literary history, while also recognizing increasingly transnational and biracial realities within the United States. Barbara Brinson Curiel's article, "Had They Been Heading for the Barn All Along? Viramontes's Chicana Feminist Revision of Steinbeck's Migrant Family," is groundbreaking, given its literary importance in denouncing poverty and highlighting Viramontes's work by paralleling it to John Steinbeck's *Grapes of Wrath*, in this manner Americanizing and canonizing Viramontes's *Under the Feet of Jesus*. Young scholar Raelene Wyse connects the work of Latin American feminists with Viramontes's fiction in "Constructing Community through Fiction in Helena María Viramontes's *Their Dogs Came with Them* and Susana Sánchez Bravo's *Espacios condenados*." She centers feminism and aesthetics as a shared visionary *latinamericanista* outcome that Chicana authors share with vibrant Latin American women's movements.

The other cluster that is essential to underline is the study of the physical body in Chican@ literature. Although this has not been entirely unearthed in this work, it has also not had the attention it merits from acknowledged critics as a Chican@ literary phenomenon that is recurring. One of the foundational aspects of Chican@ literature has been to denounce the ill treatment of the Chican@ body. We see this in early seminal texts like Tomás Rivera's *... y no se lo tragó la tierra*, Cherríe Moraga's entire oeuvre, Demetria Martinez's *Mother Tongue*, Lorna Dee Cervantes's and Francisco X. Alarcón's poetry, and lately in Rigoberto González's and Alex Espinoza's fiction. Notwithstanding, a collection of academic research detailing an analysis of a Chicana author's work had not been previously clustered together and published. Our section, The Body, is led by Yvonne Yarbro-Bejarano's "Phantoms and Patch Quilt People: Narrative Art and Migrant Collectivity in Helena María Viramontes's *Under the Feet of Jesus*." Yarbro-Bejarano's essay explores the metaphorical images Viramontes offers in her work to see the shared context of the migratory experience, especially as relating to the female reproductive body. It is followed by Juanita Heredia's eloquent reformulation of a new understanding of the Chicana body, rightfully, in East Los Angeles, through her essay "The Women in East Los Angeles: Gender and the City in *Their Dogs Came with Them*." In "Tapestries of Space-Time: Urban and Institutional Spaces in Helena María Viramontes's Short Fiction," Margarita T. Barceló indicates the value of analyzing the complex social spaces Viramontes creates in her writing, including depictions of surveillance of urban life in the barrio and the role of the Catholic Church as an institutional space that functions as a coercive force.

Chicano Studies scholar Juan D. Mah y Busch introduces the cluster on Ethics and Aesthetics and transcends a basic analysis of representation, instead theorizing Viramontes's work by studying the eminent importance of love in her fiction in "Lovingly: Ethics in Viramontes's Stories," narrativizing in this manner philosophical concepts that elevate us to the work of Mary Pat Brady and her past and present studies of space, time, and aesthetics in Chican@ literature. Her essay is entitled "Metaphors to Love By: Toward a Chicana Aesthetics in *Their Dogs Came with Them*." R. Joyce Z. L. Garay deeply theorizes the term "subaltern" and the characterization of the women in *Under the Feet of Jesus* in "Crowbars, Peaches, and Sweat: Coming to Voice through Image in *Under the Feet of Jesus*." These essays are complemented by "Our Dogs Came with Us: Viramontes Prays to Xólotl with Digna Rabia" by Millennium

Scholar and young meXicano essayist Aldo Ulisses Reséndiz Ramírez, in his deep study of the dog symbolism in *Their Dogs Came with Them*, layering with his keen eye the multiple metaphors Helena María brings to us.

This collection is foundational because it successfully traverses generations of scholars. We have among our contributors five of the most respected Chicana critics, who have prolifically opened the narrow lens of the academy in regard to gender, race, class, and sexuality. In mid-career, we have five other scholars having achieved tenure within the last six years. At the vanguard, as a professor, teacher, and scholar, I underline the importance of including new and young voices in the reading of our Chican@ texts. I invited two recent graduates from my current institution to participate in this groundbreaking book.

Conclusion

To paraphrase a line from Viramontes's critically acclaimed short story "The Cariboo Café," this project responds to the need for a "collected edition of her own." As previously mentioned, *Rebozos de Palabras* fills a void in the scholarship on her creative writing. Less positively, this collection is also the result of some frustration. Although scholars such as Raúl Homero Villa have eloquently described Viramontes's varied accomplishments, she is still viewed by some of her readers as "just" an activist, or the author of "only" a few books of fiction.

If decentered subjectivity is a central preoccupation of Viramontes's fiction, it is perhaps because she fulfills several roles at once as a creative writer, organic intellectual, college professor, co-editor of both *Chicana Creativity and Criticism* and *Chicana (W)rites: On Word and Film*, organizer of academic conferences, and public library activist, not to mention daughter, sister, wife, and mother.

Put colloquially, she is many things to many people. It is my hope that with this unique blend—or *mestizaje*—of scholarly essays and interviews, Helena María Viramontes's current and future readers will see the significance of her multiple roles and accomplishments, and that this book will represent the manner in which her writings will be read, as well as open up opportunities for others to present her work with further possibilities of interpretation. Finally, I am confident that the four sections of *Rebozos de Palabras* individually and collectively highlight this most innovative, accomplished, and important of contemporary writers.

Notes

1. In addition to the bibliographies of criticism about Helena María Viramontes compiled in this book, there are multiple independent articles about her work. However, only a couple of Chican@ authors have had a compilation of critical work published on their oeuvre—Alejandro Morales (see Gurpegui Palacios, *Alejandro Morales*) and Sandra Cisneros (see Carmen Rivera, *Border Crossings and Beyond*). Nonetheless, in the case of the Sandra Cisneros reader, the articles represent only Rivera's work and not a collection of critical essays that study and analyze the author's fiction from various perspectives as we do in *Rebozos de Palabras*. Yvonne Yarbro-Bejarano already set this trend of single authored articles on one specific Chicana writer in *The Wounded Heart: Writing on Cherríe Moraga* in 2001.

In *Toward a Latina Feminism of the Americas: Repression and Resistance in Chicana and Mexicana Literature*, Anna Marie Sandoval also dedicates an excellent chapter to Helena María Viramontes's fiction.

2. See Carroll and Naramore Maher's article "Amphibious Women: The Complexity of Class in Sandra Cisneros's *Woman Hollering Creek and Other Stories*" for an example of how the term "Maztlán" can be further theorized.

3. See "Sandra Cisneros and Her Trade of the Free Word" and "Rebozos, Our Cultural Blankets," both by Gabriella Gutiérrez y Muhs, in order to fully understand the significance of the rebozo in Chican@ life and culture. Also see Juanita Heredia's chapter "Sandra Cisnero's *Caramelo* (2002)" in her book *Transnational Latina Narrative in the Twenty-first Century* for an expanded discussion of the rebozo in Chicana literature.

4. In the case of Sandra Cisneros, the preeminent example would be the annual Macondo Writers' Workshop. In regard to author/professor Helena María Viramontes, we need to acknowledge that a large number of trained authors has passed through her classroom, including Pulitzer Prize winner Junot Díaz as well as Estrella Gonzáles, Brian Roley, Manuel Muñoz, H.G. Carrillo, Jennine Capo Crucet, Jon Katz, Elizabeth Tshele, Dolen Perkins-Valdez, Brian Lueng, and Aldo Alvarez. These few are counted among this impressive yet unfinished list.

5. See interview with Helena María Viramontes in *Communal Feminisms* by Gabriella Gutiérrez y Muhs.

Works Cited

Brady, Mary P. *Extinct Lands, Temporal Geographies: Chicana Literature and the Urgency of Space.* Durham, NC: Duke University Press, 2002.

Calderón, Héctor, and José David Saldívar, eds. *Criticism in the Borderlands: Studies in Chicano Literature, Culture and Ideology.* Durham, NC: Duke University Press, 1991.

Carroll, Michael, and Susan Naramore Maher. "Amphibious Women: The Complexity of Class in Sandra Cisneros's *Woman Hollering Creek and Other Stories.*" In *Sandra Cisneros's Woman Hollering Creek*, edited by Cecilia Donohue, 1–16. Amsterdam: Rodopi, 2010.

Castillo, Ana. "How I Became a Genre-Jumper." [TV broadcast of a lecture]. Santa Barbara, California: UCTV Channel 17.

Cisneros, Sandra. *Caramelo, o, Puro Cuento.* New York: Alfred Knopf, 2002.

Cortázar, Julio. *Hopscotch.* New York: Pantheon, 1987.

Curiel, Barbara Brinson. "Recipe: Chorizo con Huevo Made in the Microwave." *Speak to Me from Dreams*, 64–66. Berkeley, CA: Third Woman Press, 1989.

García, Alma M. "The Development of Chicana Feminist Discourse, 1970–1980." *Gender and Society* 3, no. 2 (1989): 217–238.

Gurpegui Palacios, José Antonio, ed. *Alejandro Morales: Fiction Past, Present, Future Perfect.* Tempe, AZ: Bilingual Review/Press, 1996.

———, ed. *Camino Real.* vol. 1, no. 0. Madrid: Universidad de Alcalá, 2009.

Gutiérrez y Muhs, Gabriella. "Rebozos, Our Cultural Blankets." *Voces: A Journal of Chicana/Latina Studies*, 3, nos. 1 and 2 (2001): 134–149.

———. "Sandra Cisneros and Her Trade of the Free Word." *RMMLA Journal, The Rocky Mountain Review of Language and Literature* 60, no. 2 (Fall 2006): 23–36.

———, ed. *Communal Feminisms: Chicanas, Chilenas and Cultural Exile: Theorizing the Space of Exile, Class, and Identity.* Lanham, MD: Lexington Books, 2007.

Heredia, Juanita. "Sandra Cisnero's *Caramelo* (2002): Translating Gender and Genealogy across the US/Mexico Borderlands." In *Transnational Latina Narratives in the Twenty-first Century: The Politics of Gender, Race, and Migrations* by Juanita Heredia, 25–60. New York: Palgrave Macmillan, 2009.

———. *Transnational Latina Narratives in the Twenty-first Century: The Politics of Gender, Race, and Migrations.* New York: Palgrave Macmillan, 2009.

Martinez, Demetria. *Mother Tongue.* New York: One World, 1987.

Olivas, Daniel. "Interview with Helena María Viramontes." *La Bloga.* April 2, 2007, http://labloga.blogspot.com/2007/04/interview-with-helena-maria-viramontes.html.

Rebolledo, Tey Diana. *Women Singing in the Snow*. Tucson: University of Arizona Press, 1995.

Rebolledo, Tey Diana, and Eliana S. Rivero, eds. *Infinite Divisions: An Anthology of Chicana Literature*. Tucson: University of Arizona Press, 1993.

Rivera, Carmen Haydée. *Border Crossings and Beyond: The Life and Works of Sandra Cisneros*. Santa Barbara, CA: Praeger, 2009.

Rivera, Tomás *. . . y no se lo tragó la tierra. (. . . And the Earth Did Not Devour Him)*. English translation by Evangelina Vigil-Piñón. Houston, TX: Arte Público Press, 1987.

Ruiz, Vicki L. *From Out of the Shadows: Mexican Women in Twentieth-Century America*. New York: Oxford University Press, 1998.

Saldívar-Hull, Sonia. *Feminism on the Border: Chicana Gender Politics and Literature*. Berkeley: University of California Press, 2000.

Sandoval, Anna Marie. *Toward a Latina Feminism of the Americas: Repression and Resistance in Chicana and Mexicana Literature*. Austin: University of Texas Press, 2008.

Villa, Raúl Homero. *Barrio-Logos: Space and Place in Urban Chicano Literature and Culture*. Austin: University of Texas, 2000.

Viramontes, Helena María. *The Moths and Other Stories*. Houston, TX: Arte Público Press, 1985.

———. Interview by Gabriella Gutiérrez y Muhs. "Emerging Subjectivities in Chicana Literature: Madres, Comadres, Madrinas y Quinceañeras Speaker Series," Stanford University, May 20, 1997.

———. "Interview: Helena María Viramontes." By Gabriella Gutiérrez y Muhs. In *Communal Feminisms: Chicanas, Chilenas, and Cultural Exile: Theorizing the Space of Exile, Class, and Identity*, edited by Gabriella Gutiérrez y Muhs, 123–137. New York: Lexington Books, 2007.

———. *Their Dogs Came with Them*. New York: Atria, 2007.

Yarbro-Bejarano, Yvonne. "Introduction." In *The Moths and Other Stories* by Helena María Viramontes, 9–21. Houston, TX: Arte Público Press, 1985.

———. *The Wounded Heart: Writing on Cherríe Moraga*. Austin: University of Texas Press, 2001.

I
Latin American Perspectives

I

"Had They Been Heading for the Barn All Along?"

Viramontes's Chicana Feminist Revision of Steinbeck's Migrant Family

BARBARA BRINSON CURIEL

IN HER 1995 NOVEL *Under the Feet of Jesus*,[1] Helena María Viramontes writes a California migrant narrative using many of the same themes and symbols popularized by John Steinbeck's *The Grapes of Wrath*.[2] She takes some of the most distinctive elements in Steinbeck's narrative—its dignified and sympathetic representation of migrant workers, its critique of the social inequity that creates their poverty and exploitation, and its description of the evolution of political consciousness—and from his blueprint writes her own distinctive tale. In her novel, Viramontes also forefronts a concern for women, and especially for mothers, in both corporate agribusiness and in the patriarchal family. As well, she also represents religious symbols as important manifestations of political consciousness, an association that is shaped by the iconic model of César Chávez and his leadership of the United Farm Workers union (UFW).

Steinbeck's Pulitzer Prize–winning 1939 novel about Dust Bowl migrants is a natural source for Viramontes's literary project. *The Grapes of Wrath* shaped the public's image of migrant workers: this controversial novel went through ten printings in the first nine months of its publication, and it was made into a successful 1940 film by Darryl Zanuck. Despite its popularity, the novel was banned in various communities in the United States in response to outcries over public decency and the text's socialist politics.[3] Nonetheless, the novel has stood witness to the tragedies of migrant life in California, and from its earliest days, it has also inspired counter-narratives of migrant experience. In 1939, Frank J. Taylor challenged the factual reliability of Steinbeck's portrait of migrant life. Using his own experience as evidence, Taylor argues: "Along three thousand miles of highways and byways, I was unable to find a single counterpart of the Joad family. Nor have I discovered one during fifteen years of residence in the Santa Clara Valley."[4] However, in spite of this debate, *The Grapes of Wrath* remains memorable because it brings to the public view— and champions—the struggles of individuals whose lives had heretofore been largely invisible. It is understandable that *The Grapes of Wrath* functions as a metanarrative for *Under the Feet of Jesus*, even as Viramontes challenges some of its central assumptions about social justice for migrant workers.

Steinbeck's portrait of migrant life is the product of his own inconsistent politics. In his introduction to the 1988 edition of Steinbeck's 1936 *The Harvest Gypsies: On the Road to the Grapes of Wrath*,[5] Charles Wollenberg writes that Steinbeck's field research for the novel led him to conclude that in addition to an expanded federal migrant camp housing program, and the creation of a state agricultural labor board to protect migrant workers' rights, federal and state authorities should resettle the Dust Bowl migrants "on small family farms, perhaps on public land" (x). However, as Wollenberg points out, this solution is incompatible with the agricultural history of California. California's agricultural output has since the 1870s been dominated not by small farms, but by corporate agribusiness. The expansion of California agribusiness since the late 1800s meant an increasing demand for labor that was met by various immigrant groups that followed seasonal crops, creating what Wollenberg calls "the nation's first modern migrant agricultural labor force" (xi). After the Chinese Exclusion Act of 1882, Chinese fieldworkers were replaced with workers from Japan, Southern Europe, and India. When the Gentlemen's Agreement of 1907 effectively closed immigration from Japan, workers from Mexico and the Philippines were recruited into California's migrant labor stream.

During the Depression of the 1930s, white Dust Bowl migrants displaced much of the nonwhite migrant labor in the state. The mass "repatriations" of 1931–1934, when three hundred thousand to five hundred thousand Chicanos and Mexicans were forcibly removed to Mexico, were a significant contributing factor to this shift.[6] Steinbeck believed that since the new migrants were white, they should not be forced to live in the same harsh conditions migrant workers of color had endured. Steinbeck stated that the Dust Bowl migrants "will refuse to accept the role of field peon, with attendant terrorism, squalor and starvation" (xii). Steinbeck repeatedly references in the novel the Joads' hoped-for final destination: their own "little white . . . [house] in among the orange trees" (*GW*, 98). The Joads' whiteness, and the fact that they are descended from landowners forced into the tenant farm system by banks and other economic institutions that Steinbeck portrays as "monsters" (*GW*, 32), justifies the political and economic solution of small-farm ownership.

Steinbeck's solutions to the migrant struggle of the 1930s rest not only in a utopian agricultural life, and in a political collectivism that is rooted in the family, but also in a rejection of conventional notions of religious faith. Steinbeck disassociates religion and political activism. When Casey, a former preacher who has experienced a crisis of faith, describes his evolving view of human collectivity and brotherhood as the only real manifestation of the divine, the protagonist Tom Joad observes, "You can't hold no church with ideas like that" (*GW*, 25). In spite of his association of political consciousness with the rejection of orthodox religion, Steinbeck nonetheless portrays the Dust Bowl migrants' nobility by comparing his characters to recognizable biblical figures. Viramontes's portrayal of a 1990s Chicano/Mexicano migrant family in *Under the Feet of Jesus* echoes Steinbeck's political project of portraying migrants in a sympathetic light, in part by comparing them to Christian icons, even as she abandons his economic solution of the small independent farm and challenges both the family as a viable social unit, particularly for women, and the hierarchical race and gender dynamics that underpin Steinbeck's earlier narrative.[7] Published only two years after the death of César Chávez in 1993, Viramontes's novel is informed by the legacy of his political strategies, which used Mexican Catholic religious practices and symbols as a basis of labor organizing. Viramontes positions *Under the Feet of Jesus* in light of Chávez's political legacy and of the saint-like status he achieved, particularly at the end of his life. Viramontes takes a more integrated view of politics and religion than Steinbeck. Though she shares his skepticism over organized religion, her novel is dedicated to her parents, and to the memory of César Chávez, and Chávez's status as both a political leader and a religious icon informs her representation of her protagonist Estrella as a manifestation of both iconic Christian and mythic figures. Like Chávez, Estrella's potential to be a leader and her political consciousness are expressed in actions that echo those of Jesus.

The Barn

Viramontes articulates the intertextual link between her novel and Steinbeck's from the first interrogatory sentence: "Had they been heading for the barn all along?" (*UFJ*, 3). Viramontes begins her novel at the precise place where Steinbeck's ends, even as she infuses the barn with new meanings.[8] *The Grapes of Wrath* culminates when the Joads take shelter from the flood that has claimed all their possessions in a barn on high ground. The family is reduced to its most defenseless members: the weakened father, the mother who has come to power only because of the disenfranchisement of the men, their minor children, and their daughter Rose of Sharon, recently abandoned by her husband and delivered of a stillborn baby. Steinbeck's barn is a beacon, which, in the words of Louis Owens, "offers to light the way out of this 'doomed paradise.'"[9] In the barn, Rose of Sharon infamously nurses a dying man with her breast milk, an action that suggests the familial bonding with non-kin upon which collectivism must be based. Steinbeck closes his novel with this example of how individual self-sacrifice, and especially feminine subordination to the welfare of the collective through the performance of traditional functions, can ensure the survival of the community. The barn echoes the site of the nativity of Jesus: like the flood, it marks the beginning of a new covenant between God and humanity, and it is part of the reoccurring reference to the Holy Family in both novels. As David Cassuto points out, in economic terms, the barn is also the emblem of the small independent farmer who is Steinbeck's solution to the problems of migrant life.[10]

In *Under the Feet of Jesus*, the barn takes on new meanings. From its first mention, Viramontes's barn is associated with symbols of feminine divinity. The barn that appears suddenly in the vista of Estrella's family as they drive into the migrant labor camp has a "cratered roof" that reminds Estrella of "the full moon," a symbol of feminine power (*UFJ*, 3). However, Viramontes's barn is off-limits to Estrella and her family. The children are warned away from it because it is on the verge of collapse. The barn is mysterious and alluring, but also dangerous. The bungalow where the migrants will live nearby is a similarly de-romanticized and ominous space: when they arrive, Perfecto Flores, Estrella's mother's partner, kills a scorpion on the porch, and he secretly disposes of a dead bird he finds inside so as not to upset Petra, Estrella's mother (*UFJ*, 8). In contrast, despite its decrepitude, the barn is full of sparrows and owls and is "a cathedral of a building" (*UFJ*, 9). While Steinbeck's barn is the site of human collectivity and economic safety, in Viramontes's migrant tale it is a forbidden space associated with mythic feminine power. Estrella's consciousness of her political agency will be made plain at the end of the novel in this important symbolic space. In Viramontes's barn, Estrella is reborn as a potential savior and leader to her family and to other migrants. However, the birth of her consciousness comes about through her own protest over injustice and is not connected, as in Steinbeck's novel, to women's performance of traditional roles.

Motherhood

Both the Joads and Estrella's family include a pregnant woman. Rose of Sharon is the pregnant married daughter of the Joad family, and

Estrella's mother Petra is pregnant by her common-law husband, Perfecto Flores. Both novels employ the trope of the Holy Family through the portrayal of poor pregnant women and their partners who travel though inhospitable lands like Mary and Joseph in the nativity story. Viramontes, however, reverses Steinbeck's mother-daughter dyad: in her novel, the mother and not the daughter is pregnant, although thirteen-year-old Estrella, foreshadowing her capacity to stand up to authority, acts with the leadership and authority of Ma Joad. When Petra crumbles under the grief of being abandoned by Estrella's father, the young girl has to restore the family's emotional stability: "Petra burst the door wide open. She clapped her hands against her ears and screamed Stop it, Stop it, Stop it! and the boys, terrified of her wailing, hid under the boxspring bellyache down, until finally Estrella . . . stood between her and the children . . . and hollered You, *you* stop it, Mama! Stop this now!" (*UFJ*, 18). Throughout Steinbeck's novel, Ma continually cajoles Rose of Sharon, who is upset over her abandonment by her husband, and who fears that her baby will be born sick or dead because of her constant deprivation. Like Estrella's actions toward Petra, Ma alternately confronts and comforts her daughter, at one point piercing her ears and giving her a pair of earrings salvaged from home, advising her, "Your baby gonna be a good baby. Very near let you have a baby without your ears was pierced. But you're safe now" (*GW*, 391). Although a pregnancy in an impoverished migrant family is a hardship in both novels, Rose of Sharon's baby represents a hope that their lives will at some future point be stable and productive. Even when the baby is born dead, its body serves as witness to the hardships of the Dust Bowl migrants. When Uncle John launches the baby's body into the reeds like the infant Moses, he says: "Go down an' tell 'em . . . That's the way you can talk. . . . Maybe they'll know then" (*GW*, 493–494). Even though Rose of Sharon's baby dies at birth, it becomes an articulate sign of the migrants' suffering.

In Viramontes's novel, however, pregnancy is catastrophic. Petra knows that her pregnancy, which she is keeping secret, will eventually be obvious and that it will lead to her abandonment by Perfecto Flores, since her elderly partner feels overwhelmed by his responsibility for Petra's family. Although Petra's is a healthy, vigorous pregnancy, in the novel migrant women worry that exposure to pesticides creates the risk of birth defects in their children. Estrella confides in her friend Maxine Devridge, "You think 'cause of the water our babies are gonna come out with no mouth or something?" (*UFJ*, 33). Estrella fears that one of the consequences of migrant life is a physical deformity that manifests itself as voicelessness. In contrast to Steinbeck's articulate dead baby, the migrants in Viramontes's novel are not optimistic about the potential for migrant children to have voice and be heard.

In *The Grapes of Wrath*, Rose of Sharon's pregnancy is part of the natural order of things, and her family members revel in her state. However, Petra is "sad" when she sees Estrella coming through the trees cradling a watermelon "like a baby," showing her reluctance to have her daughter experience the uncertainty motherhood brings to migrant women (*UFJ*, 40). In her novel Viramontes strips maternity of the romance that it holds for Steinbeck. The family and its propagation provide little comfort, particularly for women. Where Rose of Sharon has her family to protect her after her husband abandons her, Petra has no such safety net. In spite of the assurances of patriarchal cultures, nothing buffers the dire consequences when men abandon vulnerable pregnant women, even in the moment that they are reproducing the patriarchal family.

In Viramontes's novel both the maternal body and the land are misused by technology. Petra's body is described like the landscape: her varicose veins are "purple and thick . . . like vines" (*UFJ*, 61), and railroad ties remind Estrella of her mother's caesarean scar (*UFJ*, 59). Petra, whose name means "rock," is the embodiment of an abused Mother Earth. Her veins have been pruned hard, limited, and circumscribed, to maximize agricultural production. Her belly is a landscape overrun by machines and carved up by national borders. Demonstrating how her maternal body and the earth are merged, Petra tells Estrella to respond to La Migra, "Tell them que tienes una madre aquí. You are not an orphan, and she pointed a red finger to the earth, Aquí" (*UFJ*, 63).

Both novels include incidental descriptions of nursing mothers, which reveal distinct views of motherhood. In *The Grapes of Wrath*, a nursing mother is part of the idealized landscape of the government migrant camp. Tom Joad rises on his first day in camp and observes a young mother nursing her baby while preparing breakfast: "He saw a girl working about the stove, saw that she carried a baby on her crooked arm, and that the baby was nursing, its head up under the girl's shirtwaist. And the girl moved about, poking the fire . . . and all the time the baby sucked, and the mother shifted it deftly from arm to arm. The baby didn't interfere with her work or with the quick gracefulness of her movements" (*GW*, 319). In this portrayal, as in the one that closes the novel, breast-feeding is associated with women's traditional domestic roles as nurturers of family and community. In Viramontes's incidental portrayal of breast-feeding, Estrella observes a woman and her child while on a lunch break. However, in a departure from Steinbeck's scene, the mother's role as nurturer of her infant occurs simultaneously with her role as worker: "Another woman sat on the step of the pickup and nursed her baby, a diaper over her modest breast. The plump, bare feet of the baby wiggled from under the cover and Estrella touched the pealike toes and the toes curled and this made her smile" (*UFJ*, 84). Although the "pealike toes" is an affectionate image, it demonstrates motherhood's similarity to agricultural production. In the same way, Petra's pregnancy is described as a "lima bean" (*UFJ*, 125). The mother is by definition a producer as well as a nurturer, and her role as worker/ mother is a devalued one in both economic and cultural contexts. As Christa Grewe-Volpp observes about the world of Viramontes's novel: "Nature as such, primordial, ahistorial and prediscursive, does not occur in the life of the migrant workers. Natural processes, indifferent to human needs, serve economic interests."[11] Both the worker/ mother and her children/commodities are taken for granted in the economic scheme of things. Arianne Burford similarly notes: "Viramontes critiques a long history of a political economy within which mothers' labor is doubly exploited: their bodies labor in the fields but the labor of childbearing also produces children, the products and laborers of a future capitalist system."[12] The sight of the nursing mother triggers Estrella's realization and turning point. Soon after, her friend Alejo elaborates this idea for her. He tells her about the La Brea tar pits, and about how the bones of a girl were found in the process of decomposition into oil: arguably the central commodity of our time. Later, when Estrella's family takes Alejo to a clinic to be treated for pesticide poisoning, the nurse takes the last of their money, only to refer them to the hospital for treatment, leaving them without the gas money to get there. Angered, Estrella recalls the tar pits, resisting her own commodification as a migrant worker and as the child of a migrant mother: "Energy money, the fossilized bones of energy matter. How bones made oil and oil made gasoline. The oil was made of their bones and it was their bones that kept the nurse's car from not halting on some highway. . . . It was their bones that kept the air conditioning in the cars humming. . . . Why couldn't the nurse see that? Estrella had figured it out: the nurse owed *them* as much as they owed her" (*UFJ*, 148; original emphasis). Although Alejo provides Estrella with the analogy of the worker's body to oil, and her mother draws the connection between agricultural production and migrant motherhood, her observation of the nursing mother also demonstrates a consciousness of the relationship of workers and their families to the economy.

Viramontes's portrayal of the nursing mother is closer than Steinbeck's to Dorothea Lange's Dust Bowl–era portraits of troubled motherhood.[13] Viramontes's portrayal is also reminiscent of one of the six portraits Lange took in 1936 of Florence Thompson and her children in Nipomo, California, the best known of which is "Migrant Mother." One of these images, in which Thompson nurses her baby in the tent doorway, has a similarly de-romanticized view of maternity. Viramontes's work is consistently critical of the ways social and economic oppression impact women, and she often expresses this critique by appropriating images of maternal grief. For example, in her short story "The Moths,"[14] Viramontes's final image of a granddaughter cradling the body of her grandmother in the bathtub echoes both Michelangelo's *La Pietà*, and W. Eugene Smith's well-known photograph of a Japanese mother cradling her disabled daughter, "Tomoko Uemura in her Bath."[15] Visual references to the suffering of mothers are a reoccurring topic in Viramontes's work that expresses concern for the maternal suffering that comes from loss, injustice, and environmental pollution.

Liminality

In the novel, Estrella is powerful because she occupies a liminal space between girlhood and adulthood, between masculinity and femininity, and also between Mexican and US citizenship. Although Petra fears that Estrella's age, thirteen, is "unlucky" (*UFJ*, 9), it actually places her at the powerful nexus between childhood and adulthood. As Anne Shea demonstrates, the novel challenges the binary nature of social categories and especially illustrates "the inadequacy of the categories of legal and illegal as a means to describe the complexities of social, political, and economic conditions that shape workers' lives."[16] When Estrella sees the Border Patrol, she tries "to remember which side she was on and which side of the wire mesh she was safe in" (*UFJ*, 59–60). Estrella is also described as looking like a young man "except for the dress she'd pulled over her work clothes" (*UFJ*, 74). Her liminality, which expresses a precept of Chicana feminism, assumes the constructedness of rigid categories of identity.

Gloria Anzaldúa describes mestiza consciousness, which she identifies with Chicana and women of color identity. It is, she says, "*una conciencia de mujer*. It is a consciousness of the Borderlands," signaling that Chicana experience is not only gendered and the product of shifting borders but also conscious of the constructedness of gender and national boundaries.[17] Mestiza consciousness, according to Anzaldúa, allows the subject to embrace multiple identities at once and to refuse the split into opposing categories, including those of gender, "so that we are on both shores at once and at once, see through serpent and eagle eyes" (*BLF*, 78–79). The serpent and the eagle are, respectively, Anzaldúa's symbols of femininity and masculinity. Consciousness of the multiple nature of identity is an insight produced by Chicana borderlands experience. The belief in unitary exclusive identities is, for Anzaldúa, produced by colonialism and Western modes of thought. In her discussion of subjectivity in Moraga and Anzaldúa's collection *This Bridge Called My Back*, Norma Alarcón notes, "Multiple-voiced subjectivity is lived in resistance to competing notions for one's . . . self-identification. . . . The choice of one or many themes is both theoretical and a political decision."[18] José David Saldívar uses the concept of liminality in his discussion of Viramontes's short story "The Cariboo Café," noting the usages of this term both as process between states, as well as a state unto itself. Drawing from Victor Turner's notion of liminality as a "permanent condition," Saldívar concludes that the US–Mexico border—and

I would argue the liminal identity it produces—is for Viramontes "a lived socially symbolic space," a "position and not [a] . . . threshold" between nations and identities.[19] Estrella's mother Petra, as a migrant woman, also expresses a liminal identity. She works while pregnant, wearing "large man's pants with the zipper down and a shirt to cover the drumtight belly" and hauls "pounds and pounds of cotton," performing at once manhood, womanhood, and motherhood (*UFJ*, 51).

Another aspect of Estrella's liminal nature is that although she is a thirteen-year-old girl and a migrant, she is associated throughout the novel with icons of divinity. Just as Steinbeck relies on Christian imagery to indicate his characters' heroic natures—Tom Joad is compared to Jesus and Casey to John the Baptist—Viramontes illustrates Estrella's incipient political consciousness and potential for leadership by alluding to both Christian figures and to classical myths.[20] The use of Christian imagery is, for Viramontes, a product of the close relationship between religion and political activism in Chicano communities. The references to classical mythology, on the other hand, provide the novel a broader frame within which to understand the limits of Christianity as a belief system, and especially for the ways it historically rejects women's leadership. For Viramontes, religious symbolism is more valuable for expressing her political purposes than for affirming the value of religious faith.

According to Espinoza, Elizondo, and Miranda's volume, *Latino Religions and Civic Activism in the United States*, "Latino religious ideology, institutions, leaders, and symbols . . . have served as the ideological glue for some of the most important struggles in the Latino community over the past 150 years."[21] Viramontes's novel's dedication to the memory of César Chávez, and Chávez's status as a both political leader and religious icon, informs her framing of Estrella in the model of Jesus. Although the idea that Chávez used religious practices, especially fasting and the pilgrimage, for solely social activist purposes has been challenged, there has been a widespread perception in the Chicano movement that this is the case.[22] Therefore, like Chávez, the outward sign of Estrella's political consciousness is her ability to invoke key symbols of Mexican Catholicism. Indeed, Luis D. León argues that "Chávez's body . . . [is] an allegory of the passion of Christ."[23] Viramontes's simultaneous references to classical divinities, however, express her reluctance to embrace Christianity, as Chávez did, as both a spiritual path and as an organizing tool. She uses classical myths to establish the presence of a feminine divine that is outside orthodox Christianity. Viramontes illustrates Estrella's capacity to be powerful by associating her with multiple icons, without advocating for specific religious practices. A star "in the . . . presence of the full moon," Estrella swims in the moonlight and reminds the reader of the celestial Venus that accompanies the moon. At the same time, she evokes the mythical Venus who is born from the water, as well as the Virgin Mary, one of whose appellations is Star of the Sea (*UFJ*, 46). Estrella brings to mind multiple figures of feminine divinity, and she is frequently accompanied by various manifestations of the moon: she cuts grapes with her "crescent moon knife," and when she sits on a fence in the moonlight "the chalk-white disc of the full moon . . . [lights] the tips of her boots" (*UFJ*, 49, 68).

As a liminal character, Estrella encompasses references not only to feminine divinity but also to the masculine divinity of Jesus. Unlike Steinbeck's portrait of Tom Joad, some of Estrella's associations with Jesus come from the portrayal of her family. Although Perfecto Flores functions as a father to Estrella, like St. Joseph was to Jesus, he is identified from the beginning of the novel as "the man who was not her father" (*UFJ*, 3). Other elements of his character also create strong parallels to St. Joseph: he is an old man and a carpenter who is the caretaker of a pregnant woman and her remarkable progeny. Estrella's real father is a vague memory, but she does recall him peeling an orange at the side of a grove where they have stopped to urinate. In this corrupted Eden, reminiscent both of the Fall and of Steinbeck's de-idealized orange groves, Estrella's father peels an orange for her "as if . . . [he] plowed the sun" (*UFJ*, 12). He is a Zeus-like figure: celestial and powerful, but distant.

In a magical realist scene in the novel, Petra's depiction with references to the Virgin of Guadalupe, the Mexican incarnation of the Virgin Mary, gives additional credence to the associations between Estrella and Jesus. Petra and her children cross the highway to go to the store, an outing that results in her first meeting with Perfecto Flores. To get there they must cross a road that resembles a dead snake (*UFJ*, 104). The Nahuatl word "coatlaxopeuh," pronounced *quatlasupe*, is one of the sources for the name of the Virgin of Guadalupe and means "the one who crushes the serpent." In this scene, Petra also wears blue, the traditional Marian color. The store is a magical space: an unexpected combination of the banal and the celestial. The storekeeper's ledger book is "thick as a Bible" (*UFJ*, 108), and the vegetables are wilted "relics" (*UFJ*, 110). A poster of the Virgin of Guadalupe hangs in the store over a heap of garlic between posters of Elvis Presley and Marilyn Monroe. Petra's posture echoes the Virgin's when she stands among the spilled garlic bulbs, which are described as smelling like roses, a flower associated with the Virgin of Guadalupe. In this position, Petra appears to transcend the earth, just as the Virgin does when she is assumed into heaven: "It looked like she stood amidst the clouds" (*UFJ*, 111). In the store Petra meets Perfecto Flores for the first time. When Petra shakes his hand, she feels "as if splinters had remained in her fingers," which not only alludes to his profession as a carpenter but also prefigures the crucifixion, suggesting Petra's future suffering, and also the suffering of her daughter Estrella (*UFJ*, 112).

Estrella's own actions reinforce associations with Jesus. She especially invokes the aspect of Jesus as justice-seeker that informs liberation theology. When she realizes at the clinic that migrant workers deserve medical treatment because their labor makes the lives of more affluent citizens possible, she demands the nurse return the nine dollars and seven cents, the last of their money, which they have paid for Alejo's care, both because he was not tended by the nurse and they need the money to get him to the hospital. Estrella goes out to the car and returns with a crowbar, threatening the nurse, "I'll smash these windows first, then all these glass jars if you don't give us back our money." When the nurse resists, Estrella breaks the decorative items on her desk and scatters her files. This scene's portrayal of an individual pushed toward violence for the sake of justice recalls the story where Jesus chases the moneylenders from the temple, as well as the harvest of anger and frustration of the dispossessed that Steinbeck's novel's title alludes to. These actions are later explained by Petra as a consequence of Estrella being like her biological father: "How many times had her own mother warned her, pleaded with her not to get involved with a man like Estrella's real father?" (*UFJ*, 164). Estrella's father, like both Zeus and the Christian God, is a distant character who engenders powerful progeny. When the crying nurse smears her lipstick "as if she tried wiping her mouth away," we see that the consequences of injustice don't just poison migrants, but that injustice also renders others in society sick and voiceless (*UFJ*, 150).

In addition to claiming biblical references, when Estrella grabs the crowbar, Viramontes appropriates and re-imagines an element in *The Grapes of Wrath*: this scene echoes the moment when Ma Joad grabs the jack handle and threatens Pa with it to prevent the family from splitting up on the way to California. Pa tries to persuade her to let some of the travelers go ahead and look for work by appealing to her duty to "look after the family" (*GW*, 184). But Ma's revolt, for all its violent resistance, only arises from her and Pa's different views of what will best permit the continuation of the family. Even though she refuses to allow the family to split up by challenging Pa's ability to physically subdue her, she is motivated by a desire to ensure the family's continued survival. Because of Ma's efforts, the Joad family persists, albeit in a continually diminishing form. " 'On'y way you gonna get me to go is whup me.' She moved the jack handle gently again. 'An' I'll shame you, Pa. I won't take no whuppin', crying' an' a-beggin'. I'll light into you. An' you ain't so sure you can whup me anyways' " (*GW*, 184). The whole family witnesses Ma's challenge to Pa's authority, and his capitulation to her revolt. "They watched his lax hands to see the fists form. And Pa's anger did not rise, and his hands hung limply at his sides. And in a moment the group knew that Ma had won" (*GW*, 185). In Steinbeck's novel, women's revolt occurs within the family and does not challenge its centrality.

Estrella's protest, however, like Tom Joad's, occurs outside the family sphere and addresses social inequality. Shea observes that in the clinic scene "Viramontes upsets the equation of criminality with violence, and law with order. She represents law and order as violent, and potentially responsible for Alejo's death,"[24] displacing the exclusivity of important social categories.

Concientización

Helena María Viramontes's novel is hopeful because the reader sees Estrella's understanding expand to encompass a sense of her own agency in the face of the environmental and human consequences of twentieth-century agribusiness. According to the work of Brazilian educational theorist Paolo Freire, adult literacy is instrumental to the acquisition of voice and critical consciousness, or *concientización*, co-requisites to political action. Using Freire's strategies, Perfecto Flores teaches Estrella to read by teaching her to use his carpentry tools. The connection between experiential learning, literacy, and voice is clear when Perfecto opens "up the tool chest, as if bartering for her voice" (*UFJ,* 25).

> Perfecto Flores taught her the names that went with the tools: a claw hammer, he said with authority, miming its function; screwdrivers, see, holding up various heads and pointing to them; crescent wrenches, looped pliers like scissors for cutting chicken or barbed wire; old wood saw, new hacksaw, a sledgehammer, pry bar . . . names that gave meaning to the tools. Tools to build, bury, tear down, rearrange and repair, a box of reasons his hands took pride in. She lifted the pry bar in her hand, felt the coolness of iron and power of function, weighed the significance it awarded her, and soon she came to understand how essential it was to know these things. That was when she began to read. (*UFJ,* 26)

It is precisely this experiential learning and Estrella's mastery of tools that gets converted into resistant action when, once her critical consciousness has developed, she takes the crowbar and uses it to get the nurse to hear the message behind her words. Paula Moya observes, in her discussion of the novel's treatment of literacy and consciousness, that in Viramontes's concept of literacy "one's ability to 'read' is not separable from the material conditions through which one's interpretive consciousness come into being in the first place."[25] Experiential learning leads to consciousness and action: Estrella tells Alejo, "You talk and talk and talk to them and they ignore you. But you pick up a crowbar and break the pictures of their children, and all of a sudden they listen real fast" (*UFJ,* 151).

After Estrella's outburst at the clinic, her family retreats to the migrant camp, her mother dreading the inevitable confrontation with the police, a confrontation that will probably ruin them.

She reflects, "The authorities would . . . pull their hearts inside out like empty pockets" (*UFJ*, 163). For consolation, Petra prays at her home altar before a statue of Jesus "draped in blue robes and crushing a green serpent with bare feet" (*UFJ*, 165). Stepping on the snake is one image common to both Jesus and Mary, and Viramontes uses this commonality to call up Christian images of both feminine and masculine divinity. In addition, Petra's broken statue of Jesus with "blue robes" (*UFJ*, 165) is a hybrid image that portrays Jesus atypically in the traditional Marian color. While Petra is praying, the statue falls, and its head breaks off, signaling her "broken faith" (*UFJ*, 168). In the darkness, Estrella, whose actions have transformed her into a politically conscious person, begins to fully assume the symbolic position previously occupied by the broken deity, but in a hybrid fashion. She removes her dress, dons pants and a flannel shirt—the clothes of a man, but also of a worker of either gender—takes a lantern, and goes out to the barn that appears in the opening of the novel.

Inside the barn, Estrella climbs a rusted chain to the loft. She then exits the door to the roof, "climbing out of a box," as if emerging from a coffin (*UFJ*, 175). She can now see the potential of her actions to change the course of events in the world around her. By stepping onto the barn's moon-like roof, Estrella replaces Petra's broken statue, which in addition to being a place of prayer, also was the guardian of her family's documents.[26] The documents—marriage and birth certificates as well as other proof of the family's legitimacy and of their legitimate presence in the United States—are evidence of the injustice in the world against which Estrella must wage her struggle. Estrella replaces the broken statue of Jesus with her own body: feminine and masculine, earthly and symbolic of the divine, she, teenage daughter of a migrant mother, becomes the guardian of her crumbling family. The traditional site of Jesus' nativity, the barn memorializes the birth of Estrella's critical consciousness. Like the birth of Jesus, Estrella's reborn consciousness signals a new covenant, a new universal order, organized on the principle that consciousness and voice lead to resistance and social change. Her new covenant comes not through maternity but as a result of her own justice-seeking actions. Unlike Rose of Sharon who, at the end of Steinbeck's novel, is inside the barn nursing a dying stranger, Estrella ends on the roof of the barn, above the site of both Steinbeck's and Christianity's patriarchal nativity story. She revels in her capacity to create change and order in the world. Like Jesus the Good Shepard, "she believe[s] her heart powerful enough to summon home all those who strayed" (*UFJ*, 176).

At the end of the novel, the swallows fly out of the barn "from under the eaves of the cedar shakes like angry words spewing out of a mouth" (*UFJ*, 175). On the novel's final page, they come to their nests, which are near Estrella on the barn's roof. The swallow is a harbinger of spring, and in California, they are associated with the Mission San Juan Capistrano, where they return from their annual migration to Argentina on or around March 19. This cycle has been publicly celebrated in Orange County, California, near where Estrella's parents are married in the novel, since the beginning of the twentieth century (*UFJ*, 167). Estrella believes her newfound faith in herself, and in change, can unify the migrant workers, who are symbolized by the swallows. With her transformed consciousness, Estrella becomes a beacon for both the migrant workers, who can become physically and spiritually lost, and for those who have lost faith in their own power to create change.

Estrella's coming to consciousness parallels the consciousness-raising process of workers in the UFW union: awareness and articulation of individual and group rights are important precursors to organizing. Although the novel's dedication to César Chávez locates her narrative within an activist context, no organized protest takes place within the novel. In fact, the UFW is mentioned only briefly within the text in the form of "white leaflets with black eagles on them," one of which Estrella folds and puts in her pocket "for later reading" because "her eyes hurt too much" (*UFJ*, 84). Although at the beginning of the text Estrella cannot yet "see" her position, and her options for action are not yet formed, the novel tracks her shift from frustrated and powerless to active and powerful.

When Estrella stands on the roof of the barn like a beacon, she merges, like Chávez, religious iconography with her activist consciousness and actions. Unlike Chávez, she is not a pacifist. She not only performs active resistance but also echoes Jesus' clearing the temple as an argument for a more vigorous protest against injustice. The invocation of religious beliefs and practices has been critical in Chicano/Latino political and social reform movements, and

Viramontes's novel shows social reform in this light as well. The parallels between Estrella and Jesus locate her within the traditions of Chicano activism and specifically in the tradition of Chávez, whom León says was "powerfully adept at inventing, re-casting, and ordering religious and cultural symbols and infusing political struggles with ultimate value or sacred meanings."[27] Chávez's strategy, and the strategy of many Chicano political movements, unifies faith and reform. As León notes, "The UFW wove a religious matrix that decentered institutional authority, and poetically centered the authority of revolution."[28]

Louis Owens observes that the point of Steinbeck's novel is that "the old values and the old myths . . . must be discarded to clear the way for a new commitment to mankind and place, here and now. It is a depiction of and a plea for a genuine rebirth of national consciousness."[29] Viramontes's purpose is similar: she frames Estrella's transformed consciousness as rebirth, and the old idols fall and are replaced by leaders who, in the style of César Chávez, adapt the old beliefs and rituals for a political cause.

Viramontes's *Under the Feet of Jesus* imagines leadership and activism in ways that reflect the history of Chicana/o political movements. Like Steinbeck, she is committed to the sympathetic representation of agricultural workers and to a critical engagement with Judeo-Christian traditions and beliefs. *Under the Feet of Jesus* elaborates a young woman's development of political agency from the circumstances of her life. Consciousness provides Estrella with a high ground from which to strategize a response to the challenges of her own life, and the insight to see herself as a leader.

Notes

1. Viramontes, *Under the Feet of Jesus*. Further references will be cited parenthetically in the text as *UFJ*.
2. John Steinbeck, *The Grapes of Wrath*. Further references will be cited parenthetically in the text as *GW*.
3. Sillen, "Censoring *The Grapes of Wrath*," 3–7.
4. Taylor, "California's Grapes of Wrath," 8.
5. Wollenberg, Introduction in *The Harvest Gypsies*, v–xxii. Further references will be cited parenthetically in the text as *HG*.
6. Acuña, *Occupied America*, 138.

7. The historical period of Viramontes's novel is established very subtly, which, combined with its mythic elements, gives it a timeless quality. Nonetheless, as Christa Grewe-Volpp points out, most of the action of the novel takes place in the summer of 1990, "the only plausible date, as Perfecto Flores dreams of his birth year 1917." There is also an incidental reference to banda music that helps to date the story. Grewe-Volpp, "'The oil was made from their bones,'" 64.

8. Although the connection has not been fully explored, other critics have noted Viramontes's references to Steinbeck's work, and particularly to *The Grapes of Wrath.* Paula Moya, for example, argues that *Under the Feet of Jesus* falls within the tradition of American social realism that includes Steinbeck's work, and that it can be more insightfully read in that context than in the context of Chicana and women of color literary criticism. See Moya, *Learning from Experience.* Dan Latimer's discussion points out Viramontes's barn's antithetical relationship to Steinbeck's and insightfully enumerates some of her symbolic references to Pentecost. However, his argument that the barn is a secular space for Estrella's expanded consciousness of America as a land of opportunity dismisses the weight of his own examples. See Latimer, "The La Brea Tar Pits," 323.

9. Owens, *John Steinbeck's Re-vision of America,* 130.

10. Cassuto, "Turning Wine into Water," 67.

11. Grewe-Volpp, "'The oil was made from their bones,'" 66.

12. Burford, "Cartographies of a Violent Landscape."

13. Lange's 1936 "Migrant Madonna" was used for the cover of the pamphlet *Their Blood Is Strong,* a reprint of Steinbeck's journalistic articles about migrant workers originally published by the *San Francisco News,* published as a collection by the Simon J. Lubin Society in 1938 to bring attention to the need for agricultural labor reform. These same articles were published as *The Harvest Gypsies* and are considered the factual basis for *The Grapes of Wrath.*

14. Viramontes, "The Moths."

15. Another visual image referenced in *Under the Feet of Jesus* is Ester Hernández's *Sun Mad* (1982), a parody of the commercial logo for Sun-Maid Raisins which critiques the abuse of pesticides.

16. Shea, "'Don't let them make you feel you did a crime,'" 138.

17. Anzaldúa, *Borderlands,* 77. Further references will be cited parenthetically in the text as *BLF.*

18. Alarcón, "The Theoretical Subject(s) of *This Bridge Called My Back* and Anglo-American Feminism," 366.

19. Saldívar, *Border Matters,* 98–99.

20. In 1962, Charles T. Dougherty discusses some of the debate over whether Jim Casey or Tom Joad is the real Christ-figure of Steinbeck's novel. Dougherty endorses the idea that Tom is the Christ-figure. Viramontes also appropriates this ambiguity by giving Alejo Christ-like associations. Dougherty, "The Christ-Figure in *The Grapes of Wrath,*" 115.

21. Espinoza, Elizondo, and Miranda, "Introduction: U.S. Latino Religions and Faith-Based Political, Civic, and Social Action," 5.

22. Lloyd-Moffett, "The Mysticism and Social Action of César Chávez," 41.
23. León, "César Chávez and Mexican American Civil Religion," 55.
24. Shea, "'Don't let them make you feel you did a crime,'" 140.
25. Moya, *Learning from Experience*, 185.
26. Ellen McCracken notes, "The statue breaks, and Estrella herself symbolically replaces the image as she stands tall atop the barn" (*New Latina Narrative*, 183).
27. León, "César Chávez and Mexican American Civil Religion," 56.
28. León, "César Chávez and Mexican American Civil Religion," 61.
29. Owens, *John Steinbeck's Re-vision of America*, 140.

Works Cited

Acuña, Rodolfo. *Occupied America*. New York: Addison-Wesley, 1981.
Alarcón, Norma. "The Theoretical Subject(s) of *This Bridge Called My Back* and Anglo-American Feminism." In *Making Face, Making Soul*, edited by Gloria Anzaldúa, 356–369. San Francisco: Aunt Lute Foundation Books, 1990.
Anzaldúa, Gloria. *Borderlands/La Frontera: The New Mestiza*. San Francisco: Spinsters/Aunt Lute, 1987.
Burford, Arianne. "Cartographies of a Violent Landscape: Viramontes' and Moraga's Remapping of Feminisms in *Under the Feet of Jesus* and *Heroes and Saints*." *Genders OnLine Journal* 47 (2008), http://www.genders.org/g47/g47_burford.html.
Cassuto, David. "Turning Wine into Water: Water as Privileged Signifier in *The Grapes of Wrath*." *Papers on Language and Literature* 29, no. 1 (Winter 1993): 67–95.
Dougherty, Charles T. "The Christ-Figure in *The Grapes of Wrath*." In *A Casebook on* The Grapes of Wrath, edited by Agnes McNeill Donohue, 115–117. New York: Thomas Y. Crowell Co., 1968.
Espinoza, Gaston, Virgilio Elizondo, and Jesse Miranda. "Introduction: U.S. Latino Religions and Faith-Based Political, Civic, and Social Action." In *Latino Religions and Civic Activism in the United States*, edited by Gastón Espinoza, Virgilio Elizondo, and Jesse Miranda, 3–16. New York: Oxford University Press, 2005.
Grewe-Volpp, Christa. "'The oil was made from their bones': Environmental (In)Justice in Helena María Viramontes's *Under the Feet of Jesus*." *Interdisciplinary Studies in Literature and the Environment* 12, no. 1 (Winter 2005): 61–78.
Latimer, Dan. "The La Brea Tar Pits, Tongues of Fire: Helena María Viramontes's *Under the Feet of Jesus* and Its Background." *Soundings* 85, nos. 3–4 (2002): 323–346.
León, Luis D. "César Chávez and Mexican American Civil Religion." In *Latino Religions and Civic Activism in the United States*, edited by Gastón

Espinoza, Virgilio Elizondo, and Jesse Miranda, 53–64. New York: Oxford University Press, 2005.

Lloyd-Moffett, Stephen R. "The Mysticism and Social Action of César Chávez." In *Latino Religions and Civic Activism in the United States*, edited by Gastón Espinoza, Virgilio Elizondo, and Jesse Miranda, 35–51. New York: Oxford University Press, 2005.

McCracken, Ellen. *New Latina Narrative: The Feminine Space of Postmodern Ethnicity*. Tucson: University of Arizona Press, 1999.

Moraga, Cherríe, and Gloria Anzaldúa, eds. *This Bridge Called My Back: Writings by Radical Women of Color*. 3rd ed. Berkeley, CA: Third Woman Press, 2002.

Moya, Paula. *Learning from Experience: Minority Identities, Multicultural Struggles*. Berkeley: University of California Press, 2002.

Owens, Louis. *John Steinbeck's Re-vision of America*. Athens: University of Georgia Press, 1985.

Saldívar, José David. *Border Matters: Remapping American Cultural Studies*. Berkeley: University of California Press, 1997.

Shea, Anne. " 'Don't let them make you feel you did a crime': Immigration Law, Labor Rights, and Farmworker Testimony." *MELUS* 28, no. 1 (2003): 123–144.

Sillen, Samuel. "Censoring *The Grapes of Wrath*." In *A Casebook on* The Grapes of Wrath, edited by Agnes McNeill Donohue, 3–7. New York: Thomas Y. Crowell Co., 1968.

Steinbeck, John. *The Grapes of Wrath*. New York: Bantam Books, 1970.

———. *The Harvest Gypsies: On the Road to The Grapes of Wrath*. Orig. ed., 1936. Repr., Berkeley, CA: Heydey Books, 1988.

Taylor, Frank J. "California's Grapes of Wrath." In *A Casebook on* The Grapes of Wrath, edited by Agnes McNeill Donohue, 8–19. New York: Thomas Y. Crowell Co., 1968.

Viramontes, Helena María. "The Moths." In *The Moths and Other Stories*, 27–32. Houston, TX: Arte Público Press, 1985.

———. *The Moths and Other Stories*. Houston, TX: Arte Público Press, 1985.

———. *Under the Feet of Jesus*. New York: Dutton, 1995.

Wollenberg, Charles. "Introduction." In John Steinbeck, *Harvest Gypsies: On the Road to The Grapes of Wrath*. Orig. ed. 1936. Repr., Berkeley, CA: Heydey Books, 1988.

2

Constructing Community through Fiction in Helena María Viramontes's Their Dogs Came with Them *and Susana Sánchez Bravo's* Espacios condenados

RAELENE WYSE

BOTH HELENA MARÍA VIRAMONTES and Susana Sánchez Bravo use fiction as a tool with their respective novels *Their Dogs Came with Them* (2007) and *Espacios condenados* (2004) to challenge political and social repression. Both authors portray communities fractured by external and internalized forms of violence. In *Their Dogs Came with Them*, Helena María Viramontes depicts the freeway construction, city policing, and sexual violence that wore away at East LA's Chicano residents in the 1960s and 1970s. In *Espacios condenados*, Susana Sánchez Bravo exposes the realities of disappearance, murder, and exile that terrorized many Chileans in the 1970s and 1980s following General Augusto Pinochet's CIA-funded and -directed coup d'état. Their narratives are not of heroes rising above adversity or vigilantes coming together to fight evil, but of individuals and communities bearing the burdens of persecution. In their stories, as is often the case in real life, communities break down at a time when individuals need them most. Protagonists find themselves struggling to survive. Describing these trials rather than exploiting or romanticizing them, Viramontes and Sánchez Bravo recreate silenced histories. Their fiction opens up into a space for communities to connect to forgotten pasts, where the act of remembering ensures survival.

Writing into voids of erasure and silence, Viramontes and Sánchez Bravo choose to reconstruct the most painful details of Chicano and Chilean history, respectively, including how members of their own communities have turned against each other. Remembering these stories, I argue, secures their communities' existence in two ways. First, these novels offer a tool to reflect on the past. Understanding external and internalized forms of oppression allows for the possibility of constructing a better future. Second, the act of writing these stories provides a space for marginalized communities to belong, to speak, and to see themselves. No matter how much physical or psychological persecution these individuals confront and no matter how much they are marginalized, they will always exist and belong in this literary space.

To make this argument, I draw on theorizations of "internal exile" and "othering" to argue that "othering" is what leaves the members of these communities so vulnerable in these novels. I, then, compare how both novels depict external and internalized acts of "othering" as what destroys their respective communities. Lastly, I discuss Gabriella Gutiérrez y Muhs's theorization of literary homelands in conjunction with interviews with Helena María Viramontes and Susana Sánchez Bravo to argue that the act of remembering is linked to survival.

Francisco Lomelí's and Gabriella Gutiérrez y Muhs's theorizations of "internal exile," as well as Gloria Anzaldúa's analysis of "otherness," provide a critical framework for analyzing the breakdown of community in Viramontes's and Sánchez Bravo's texts. Lomelí describes internal exile as a consequence of "othering" in "Internal Exile in the Chicano Novel." By treating a person as "other," he or she is made "to feel as a 'foreigner in their native land' " (110). As a result, the person becomes an "internal exile," excluded from his or her own country, city, or home. Relegated to societal margins or worse, foreigner status, the internal exile has to struggle for his or her rights to political and social privileges. Gabriella Gutiérrez y Muhs defines "internal exile" as being "continuously on the verge of being expelled from the circle of legitimacy" (xxiv). An internal exile is a person who holds a tenuous position in society. While society causes the person to feel like an exile by treating him or her as "foreign," the individual and members of the community navigating the same position bear its consequences.

Internal exiling, as Lomelí and Gutiérrez y Muhs define it, destroys communities when members of a marginalized community marginalize others like themselves in an effort to be like or belong to mainstream society. Gloria Anzaldúa describes the consequences of othering on communities in her essay "En rapport, In Opposition." She writes that "external oppression is paralleled with our internalization of this oppression. And our acting from that oppression. They have us doing to those within our own ranks what they have done and continue to do to us—*Othering* people. That is, isolating them, pushing them out of the herd, ostracizing them. The internalization of negative images of ourselves, our own self-hatred, poor self esteem, makes our own people the Other" (143). When one member ostracizes another in an attempt to legitimize his or herself in society, the potential for a loving and supportive relationship disappears. The community falls apart. As a result, individuals that hold a tenuous position in society find themselves in an even more vulnerable position.

Helena María Viramontes's *Their Dogs Came with Them* and Susana Sánchez Bravo's *Espacios condenados* suggest that "othering" nearly destroys their respective Chicano and Chilean communities. In *Their Dogs Came with Them*, Viramontes analyzes the external and internal threats that nearly silence and erase East LA's residents in the 1960s and 1970s. Chief among these are those imposed by the city in the form of freeway construction and the Quarantine Authority (QA) that isolate the neighborhood and treat its residents as "foreigners." Residents also treat each other as "other," primarily through acts of sexual violence. As individuals bear the burdens of sexual violence, they feel even more alienated from their community.

While these East LA residents struggle to survive alone, Viramontes suggests that they need a communal response to overcome such external and internalized oppression. Even though this possibility does not exist within the novel, Viramontes suggests that it may, nonetheless, exist.

Freeway construction that enters the neighborhood is the first indication that the city may be actively trying to eliminate its East LA residents. The language Viramontes uses to describe this construction demonstrates the "othering" it represents. Grandmother Zumaya looks at the freeway and thinks "about how carnivorous life was, how indifferent machinery teeth could be" (145). She views the incoming bulldozers as just one more incidence in a "carnivorous" life—a life that eats people up, exploits them as nutrients, and, eventually, eliminates them as waste. In this case, "indifferent" machines do the eating, but they represent unnamed and unknown people who, in an act perhaps better described as cannibalistic, have chosen to "other" a group of people by treating them as something to be consumed. As a result, many residents are physically displaced, leaving almost no trace behind. Ermila Zumaya remembers walking over to the house where Chavela, an older-generation, Spanglish-speaking Chicana, lives. At first, Chavela disappears; later, her house and the entire block disappear, replaced by concrete, tar, and speeding cars. The space and people whose lives are forever changed by the building of freeways are forgotten, except by a few residents who remember.

The fictional QA that enters the neighborhood ten years later confirms the East LA residents' status to the city as internal exiles or foreigners. Initially, the city disseminates English-only pamphlets, even though the majority of residents only speak Spanish. Then, the QA sets up roadblocks where residents have to prove that they belong in their own neighborhood to go home at night. The process to supply this proof, an ID, alienates residents from their own homes.

> A neighbor's idea of validity was totally incongruent with the QA's norms or anyone else's, for that matter. Business was done differently in the Eastside. In need of a dentist? Wait for Dr. Padilla from Tijuana the first of each month, home visits with a leather bag full of clanging metal tools and novocaine

injections. What about a loan? The lending was done between
two men, one of which had a reputation for breaking bones.
Need legal status? For those without papers, legal status
became a shift in perspective, a matter of dubious demarcation,
depending on who the border belonged to. (66–67)

Residents have to not only learn the QA's standards, ones that are
externally defined and imposed and are incongruent with the residents' own norms, but also privilege them above their own. To
go home at night, they have to ask for the city's permission. Even
those who present the correct paperwork face suspicion. When
Ermila and her group of friends go through the checkpoint, "in
a suspicious tone, the QA examined the girlfriends from sneakers
to earrings, studied their IDs, long pauses of distrust to unnerve
them, to convince them of some guilt" (59). The QA treats them as
criminals, but they choose not to protest this false criminalization
to avoid risking being denied permission to go home. The inspec-
tions, humiliating at best, provide a powerful metaphor for the city's
efforts to remind residents daily of their tenuous, permission-based
status. Even though the Quarantine Authority is fictional, it makes
tangible less visible forms of repression Chicanos have faced, such as
immigration policing.

   In addition to the city-imposed freeways and the QA, this East LA
Chicano community faces threats from its own members. The most
effective of these, in terms of breaking down individuals and working against community formation, is sexual violence. Two of Viramontes's female characters—Turtle and Tranquilina—experience
explicit acts of sexual violence in which their femininity becomes an
excuse to turn them into the sexualized, objectified "other." Turtle,
"the bald-headed Gamboa brother, the other one who was really
a girl, but didn't want to be and got beaten up for it," recognizes
her femininity as a weakness and performs masculinity to protect
herself (11). Though neither Turtle nor Viramontes clearly identify
her as transgendered, queer, or lesbian, they recognize that being
a woman is dangerous and that masculinity affords her some protection. When she gets caught stealing from the grocery store, the
bagman searches her body for the stolen goods. "At first he believed
what he felt on her chest were not breasts but stolen apples, hard and

concealed, and he clamped his big man fingers on her flesh under her loose T-shirt to make sure. This boy had tits, this boy was really a braless girl with growing, firm chi-chis, her big brown nipples just there, under the shirt for him to pinch in utter disbelief" (24). Turtle's female body parts are a perverse curiosity for the bagman, who exploits the situation to explore her body even after he has recovered the stolen goods. The narrative voice situates Turtle's crime not in stealing food, but in being a woman. Initially, the bagman confuses her breasts for stolen apples, an image alluding to Eve's decision to steal the apple from the Tree of Knowledge in the Garden of Eden. Just as Eve's sex is blamed for her decision that marked humanity with the punishment of original sin, Turtle's sex is to blame for inspiring the bagman's curiosity. He gropes her a second time "to make sure" and then keeps touching her to "make himself believe." In the moment, Turtle feels her vulnerability—"Not one driver from all those cars zooming [past] . . . stopped to protest" (24). The city seems to be in accord with the bagman in assuming that Turtle, or rather her sex, has brought this abuse upon herself.

Female sexuality leads one of Viramontes's other characters, Tranquilina, to find herself vulnerable to male sexual violence. This realization continues to traumatize her long after the rape itself. A glance from a stranger as she walks through East LA reminds her of the man who raped her. She recalls, years before, walking away from a tent on the farm where her father was preaching and entering the woods nearby, where the rancher's son-in-law follows her, hits her over the head with a shovel, and "[drags] her face down by the ankles deeper into the innocence of pecan trees [where] she suffocated, grasping, coughing, her lungs weighed down by his body, the body that slammed her as hard as the shovel, and he mounted her and he thrusted and grunted and she felt his breath stale and dead until he exploded into her insurmountable pain, an inferno of excruciating wet fire" (208). The rancher's son-in-law turns Tranquilina into his sexual object by rendering her physically unable to defend herself or refuse her consent so that he can enact his wishes on her body. Viramontes counters Tranquilina's forced-object status by focusing the narration of the rape itself on Tranquilina's thoughts and feelings. Tranquilina's struggle to breathe, her body's transmission of sensations she does not want to feel, and the pain he enacts on her body become the focus of the narrative rather than his pleasure. Even still, as a result of the rape, she begins to see herself as the rancher's son-in-law did, an "other" and an object responsible for her own abuse (36). Haunted by this violent act, Tranquilina easily becomes fearful of others in her community who remind her of her vulnerability. When she speaks to Ben, a friend and someone she cares about, she is reminded of the man's smell and thinks that she "didn't want to associate Ben's scent with his . . . She knew better" (95). Tranquilina has to consciously remind herself not to be afraid.

Through Tranquilina and Turtle, Viramontes demonstrates that othering has powerful destructive consequences for psychological and communal health. Neither Tranquilina nor Turtle ever seem to overcome this sexual violence; instead, they repeatedly struggle with their own feelings of shame. Tranquilina needs to remind herself to be kind and personable, even though it requires her to fight against the urge to isolate herself. For the daughter of a preacher that sustains a soup kitchen, survival instincts that prevent close, trusting human interactions are debilitating. As a result, she questions her faith, her ability to do her work, and her ability to manage daily life. Turtle, who tries to make herself tougher and less approachable to avoid being hurt again, lands in an even more vulnerable position. Years later, she finds herself wandering East LA without a place to stay, her brother, or gang protection. Most of her time and energy, like Tranquilina's, become focused on getting by. Neither woman feels like she can trust anyone else. Sexual violence and the "othering" that enables it become permanent fixtures in these women's lives.

Through *Their Dogs Came with Them*, Viramontes indicates that the roots of these daily struggles lie with the othering that enables such violent acts. Freeway construction and the Quarantine Authority communicate the city's lack of concern for its residents, who are treated as if they never really belonged anyway. Even though Chavela, who is expelled from her home, and Ermila and her friends, who are forced to wait in line at the QA to go home, are collectively made into the socially and politically oppressed, residents do not gather together and fight against their oppression. Instead, their daily lives become consumed with trying to survive attacks from each other as well as mainstream society. As Tranquilina's and Turtle's stories indicate, the possibility of community, which requires strong and supportive relationships, withers away as suspicion and fear spread.

Susana Sánchez Bravo's *Espacios condenados* also depicts the destructive potential of "othering," which destroys individuals and families in addition to the entire national community in Chile during the Pinochet dictatorship in the 1970s and 1980s. In Sánchez Bravo's Chile, Pinochet's coup d'état turns hundreds of thousands of Chilean citizens into enemies. The military not only takes over the government but also launches a full-blown war against anyone labeled or perceived as a dissident. These *us* versus *them* dynamics divide the social and political scene and render characters either exploiting their newfound political power, running away from potential political repression, or becoming subject to the dictatorship's clandestine silencing forces. Among the perceived subversives is Sánchez Bravo's main character, Catalina, who becomes one of the disappeared. In prison, Catalina's relationships with the other inmates serve as a form of opposition to the camp's oppressive climate, even though it underlines the recent absence of familial and broader support systems. Even as she learns to resist the new dynamics of internal and external oppression around her, the narrative suggests that Catalina will never find psychological peace after what she has experienced. Similar to Viramontes's *Their Dogs Came with Them*, Sánchez Bravo's *Espacios condenados* suggests that external and internalized oppression wreak havoc on individuals and communities, where wars continue to be fought even after immediate dangers disappear.

Catalina's narrative underlines the staunch changes that take place in Chile following the coup d'état, which suddenly labels her the enemy "other" of the Pinochet dictatorship and, as a result, the subject of its overt repression. As soon as the coup d'état takes place, Catalina begins packing her kids' belongings and resolves to leave Santiago. Without knowing about the dictatorship's imminent repressive military measures, Catalina goes into hiding to protect herself and her family. Their lives become punctuated by a struggle for survival, which entails, among other changes, that they learn to speak in code. As her sister explains, "In case they tap the phones . . . if I give you a date, for example, we will see you on Wednesday at 12 o'clock in the Cathedral, I mean that the appointment is the following day, one hour later, on the sidewalk in front of the place I tell you" (46).[1] Communication is restricted, as is the family's ability to reach out to each other for love and support.

Although Catalina manages to escape detection for months, her "disappearance" underlines her status as an internal exile, foreign to her own country just for her political beliefs. Upon her return to Santiago to try to figure out what has happened to her missing loved ones, she finds herself "pushed . . . towards a vehicle with the engine running. They left her crushed on the floor of the vehicle and smothered her screams with a blow to her head and a 'shut up, shit!' while they accelerated down Compañía Street" (60). Catalina is picked up without any warning or any semblance of due process and taken to detention against her will. The anonymous "they" implicitly refuse to identify themselves or acknowledge her as anything other than "shit," an attempt to dehumanize her through language. Their use of physical violence to crush her and smother her screams further emphasizes their power over her. This type of "othering," marked by overt cruelty and indifference, becomes an underlying thread that links Sánchez Bravo's detained characters together.

Catalina's detainment highlights the dictatorship's use of extreme physical violence to break down its political prisoners. When Catalina is transferred from Cuatro Álamos, a torture and interrogation center, to Tejas Verdes, a more permanent detainment center, the transferring guards blindfold the prisoners and punish them with physical violence for perceived insubordination, including speaking up or not following orders. Even when Catalina pauses momentarily to take a breath, "they beat her kidneys with the butt of a gun" (12). Escaping punishment requires mindless and strategic performances of subordination, as the guards repeatedly call attention to their power over their prisoners. They must come to terms with their powerless "other" status and act submissive or be murdered.

Despite this compromising situation, Sánchez Bravo's characters connect. Riding in the truck to Tejas Verdes, Catalina hears "a voice, almost glued to her ear, [say], 'My name is Andrea, and you?'" (12). Even though the women remain silent afterward, for fear of being punished, they relate to each other through touch—Andrea's "cold fingers touch her face," Catalina blows on them to warm them, and both women "feel each other's lips, tie their phalanges together, touch each other's broken nails, calloused knuckles" (12, 13). Sánchez Bravo underlines both women's basic physical need to feel the love of another human being and be acknowledged as human. Even though this connection offers a moment of beauty, it also underlines the absence of the pre-dictatorship environment that offered Catalina and Andrea support through family and community.

The narrative's juxtaposition of intense, risky human connection with torture, repression, and inhumanity highlights the inmates' struggles to challenge their oppression despite insurmountable circumstances. Initially, the inmates fear opening up to each other, knowing that the military might exploit any personal information gained from torture or an inmate's willing betrayal. Trying to protect herself and her loved ones, Catalina keeps her stories to herself. As La Negra warns Catalina, "There is always . . . an enemy's ear that squeals" (17). Andrea, however, challenges the other women in arguing that "the enemy is only one: the military and the right with its thirst for power. Those who fall are humans . . . he is a poor victim like me . . . and the perversity is that they transform him into a tool to continue torturing us . . . we should forgive him" but still "be careful" (17). While the military is effectively rewarding betrayal with less torture, these women inmates choose to respond with compassion. Breaking down the fear around them, the women reach out to each other to form a kind of community. Catalina "knows that people confined to extreme circumstances tend to trust; they need to do so" (18). She begins to tell the other women her stories, personal histories, and memories, which provide a temporary escape from their lives in detainment. Catalina manages to bring glimpses of humanity, life, and joy to a world void of these qualities.

Despite these momentary escapes, the detention center's harsh repression begins to take its toll on Catalina. Catalina periodically retreats into herself in silence as she realizes the futility and danger of fighting back. During one of the many visits by foreigners to the prison, Catalina overhears that her sister might have died. Following a struggle to avoid speaking up and asking about her sister, Catalina returns to her cell, where she stays "inside herself" for two days (26). Periodically, she enters into these catatonic states. Even after she leaves the country, in exile, she finds herself facing periods of "inactivity" or "catatonia," sleeping for most of the day (117). Catalina's will to fight back withers away, and the "other" status cruelly forced on her begins to shape her life.

Catalina's will seems most compromised by her captors' use of rape, which ultimately turns Catalina against herself and inhibits her other relationships. Even though the narrative does not depict the rape, its consequences are real and lasting for Catalina. She realizes that "it's a strange feeling of shame, as if the blame were only hers. And it's something that begins in her body, a kind of indefinite ailment that locates itself in the lower abdomen and she needs to put her hand there, where the scar over her pubic area begins to pulse" (29). Not unlike the blame that Viramontes's Tranquilina feels, Catalina feels that she is to blame, even though she knows that she did not cause her own rape. Even counterintuitively, the shame and blame remain with her. Catalina sees her only redemption in trying to remember and reconstruct herself before she was raped. She only finds hope in returning to a time before she was raped, before she knew that she was carrying her rapist's baby, before the baby was taken out of her body, before she was left to deal with her trauma without any help, and before she was detained and exiled, even if this space only exists in memory. Catalina has internalized the violence enacted against her, as she comes to believe that her life after rape is worthless. She chooses to live in retreat in memories rather than in the present, a decision detrimental to her ability to live her life and maintain relationships with others.

Catalina repeatedly struggles with figuring out how to negotiate internalized feelings of shame and guilt. Whereas she typically withdraws into herself as a method of survival, Catalina is forced to openly confront her rape each time she visits the doctor and when she and her husband, Felipe, reunite. Still in the detention center, she meets with a doctor and tells him that she was raped, left pregnant, and that the "current and the poundings" let the fetus rot, which meant that it had to be removed (74).

Being raped remains forever written on her body in the scar and the infertility it leaves behind. Catalina had so wanted to have a female child before the rape, but afterward is barren. She feels as if her body has betrayed her by allowing the demon-child, her last chance to have a baby, to suck her blood and calcium. Sánchez Bravo's descriptions of the dimensions of psychological damage Catalina negotiates underline, as Viramontes does, the power of rape as a destructive and powerful weapon of war. Both Sánchez Bravo's and Viramontes's works affirm the significance of rape as a weapon that enacts significant and lasting consequences for its victims and whose recovery requires a constant struggle.[2]

As Catalina slowly recovers her desire to live in the present, Sánchez Bravo suggests that healing means coming to live with trauma, the consequences of external and internal oppression that never seem to go away. Even when she returns to Chile and reunites with her family, Catalina tells them "that each time she touches [her muscle] she feels the lash, buckle embedding itself, and the jerking tears. This revives my anger, but I push it deep down, I look for a dark place, and I leave it there" (194–195). The wounds and memories of her experiences stay with her, even as she relearns how to live her life. In this final memory, Catalina focuses on remembering being hit with a belt buckle rather than any of the other forms of torture she experienced. This personal form of violence requires two people to be close to each other, where the dominant person directly inflicts pain on the other individual and feels the resistance once the belt hits the other's body. Focusing on this "buckle" and on her "tears," Catalina highlights her vulnerability and frustrating powerlessness in this situation. She also indicates the sense of betrayal that another individual could cause another human being so much pain. Catalina still struggles to find peace after knowing and experiencing such extreme human cruelty. The narrative suggests that her only peace lies in living with the recognition of the traumas and joys that mark her life.

Through Catalina, *Espacios condenados* demonstrates how the military regime destroyed Chile's national community. By positing some of its citizens as "enemies" and treating them as "objects" to be eliminated, while pitting other citizens against them, the military regime cultivated a culture of mistrust and serious danger. Individuals treated as "enemies," as well as their families and other support systems, bore the brunt of this violence. Forced to separate, as Catalina's family does, for safety, many Chileans struggled alone for their survival. At a time when support systems were most needed, individuals could not find them. The rape Catalina experiences and her struggle to deal with its psychological consequences suggest that the military's violence has become her psychological battle. Fighting it requires not only her own psychological work but also

the rebuilding of trusting relationships and the re-creation of a supportive environment—a communal effort.

Sánchez Bravo and Viramontes suggest that fighting external and
internalized oppression—even though they are writing about very
different political, economic, and social contexts—requires community. In this way, both authors' fictions have real applications.
Advocating for a communal response, they suggest that literature
works toward rebuilding community. Gabriella Gutiérrez y Muhs's
comparison of Chicano and Chilean literatures' creations of literary
spaces of belonging demonstrates that this literature has the power
to cultivate community. Viramontes and Sánchez Bravo underline this
point in interviews in which they assert the importance of remembering. Remembering helps ensure their community's survival by
creating a literary space for its members to connect through a shared
history of collective struggle.

In her critical collection *Communal Feminisms: Chicanas, Chilenas, and Cultural Exile*, Gabriella Gutiérrez y Muhs first draws
attention to similarities between Chicana and Chilean women writers.
She argues that "both Chicanas and Chilenas have used similar tools
to survive otherness, racism, classism, and solitude: exclusion and
cultural and generational women's dilemmas" (xix). Both communities of women have faced and continue to face "exclusion" based on
gender, race, class, sexuality, politics, and other aspects of their identities that have been used to position them as "others" in their social
and political contexts. Chilean women writers of the 1970s and 1980s
faced discrimination, whether it was Pinochet's dictatorship's overt
repression or the remnants of a male-dominated literary scene. Chicana writers of the same time period have faced similar marginalization, whether by publishing presses preferring male Chicano voices
or by US popular consciousness continuing to marginalize Chicana/
os by treating them as something other than American. Rather than
letting themselves or their communities be relegated to the margins, Viramontes and Sánchez Bravo have chosen to use their writing to establish a literary existence. Gutiérrez y Muhs describes this
act as communal feminism—a form of feminism she encountered in
Chile and that is also "so particularly essential to Chicana/o survival
as a culture" (xix). "Communal feminism," she writes, is "a feminism grounded in the group and not the individual, an undressed

nationalism, an intangible nationalism, that diligently allows for securing a literary portable homeland for many groups" (xix). Through writing about Chicanas and Chilenas respectively, Viramontes and Sánchez Bravo create a place not only for themselves but also for their persecuted communities to belong, a literary space or "portable homeland" where their presence is assumed rather than questioned.

Viramontes and Sánchez Bravo describe their role as writers in relation to their respective communities, where writing functions as a means of serving the community. In an interview published in 2007, Helena María Viramontes describes the moment in which she realized that she writes because "it's not just my voice anymore, it's not just what I'm doing . . . it's not just mine" (132). She continues: "I feel that writers, especially Chicano and Chicana writers have to be visionaries, they have to, they have no other choice, we cannot afford not to use our imagination because our communities are under siege at any given time, we cannot afford to write without that as an inspiration" (132). Writing, for her, provides a means to "reimagine solutions to problems now," to support the Chicano community in facing a politically charged environment in the United States in which persecution of Chicanos continues to take on personal and institutionalized forms (132). Arizona's recent enactment of SB 1070, its anti–illegal immigration legislation that encourages criminalizing anyone who looks or sounds "non-American" by labeling them as a potential "illegal" immigrant, is one of the latest incarnations of this racism. Viramontes suggests that her writing, because it carefully presents the bleak situations that Chicanos have faced, works to envision a better future. In this vein, she identifies herself as a Chicana writer, which Chicana Alicia Gaspar de Alba suggests means envisioning herself as not just a writer but also a "historian, journalist, sociologist, teacher," and "activist" because of what it means to be Chicana (291). Viramontes's novel stands out alongside Lorna Dee Cervantes's "Beneath the Shadow of the Freeway," Alejandro Morales's *Brick People*, and Luis Rodríguez's *The Concrete River* as a novel depicting those forever changed by the freeway construction that fragmented one of the largest Spanish-speaking cities and communities in the United States.

Sánchez Bravo also connects her role as writer to her community as a form of working for the benefit of future generations. She developed her craft within a generation of writers for whom being a Chilean writer meant having witnessed the repression of a military government and having lost loved ones for being labeled a threat to the government. Sánchez Bravo's career as a writer took shape within this context and the fifteen years she spent in exile in Mexico, Germany, and Norway. In an interview published in 2007, Sánchez Bravo states that during her exile, her literature became "something fundamental because if you took yourself too seriously, you would fall apart. It became a necessity and as a result, I think my writing became something permanent. Fundamentally, it was more a form of therapy than a form of attaining glory. I started to write things to Chile so that my children could hear them" (40). She continues by saying, "The coup provided impetus or determined in one way or another the manner of writing in order to not lose anything that had occurred" (47). Having lost friends and family, having witnessed and experienced the dictatorship's multifarious modes of silencing and disappearing people, she sees fiction as a means of ensuring that loved ones are not forgotten.

Even though both authors seek to serve their communities, neither one presents a satisfyingly positive conclusion for her literary subjects. Instead, they identify the painful struggles that women in their communities have had to face. By recognizing rather than ignoring these pains, depicting how they were inflicted, naming those who are to blame, and honoring the struggles of people who chose to fight back even if only by choosing life over death, both authors write their communities' histories into existence. This act of remembering, first, offers the tools to recognize and fight oppression in the future. Second, it encourages other Chicana and Chilean women to keep struggling, like those who came before them. Sánchez Bravo's and Viramontes's fiction bring together Chicanos and Chileans, respectively, based on these shared histories. Both authors work for their communities' survival by inscribing into literature the complexities of what it means to be Chicana/o and Chilean so that they cannot be forgotten.

Notes

1. All quotes from *Espacios condenados* are my own translations.

2. This novel was published in 1994, the same year that rape was declared an act of war, after trying the first cases in 1993 in the former Yugoslavia ("Alien," 1).

This ruling took place only a few years before the publication of *Their Dogs Came with Them*. Before 1994, rape was considered one of the many unfortunate consequences of war, not something for which its perpetrators could be tried or punished.

Works Cited

"Alien Tort Claims Act-Classifying Peacetime Rape as an International, Human Rights Violation." *Houston Journal of International Law* 22 (2000): 451–479.

Anzaldúa, Gloria. "En rapport, In Opposition: Cobrando cuentas a las nuestras." In *Making Face, Making Soul/Haciendo Caras: Creative and Critical Perspectives by Women of Color*, edited by Gloria Anzaldúa, 142–148. San Francisco: Aunt Lute Foundation Books, 1990.

Cervantes, Lorna Dee. "Beneath the Shadow of the Freeway." In *Infinite Divisions: An Anthology of Chicana Literature*, edited by Tey Diana Rebolledo and Eliana S. Rivero, 116–118. Tucson: University of Arizona Press, 1993.

Gaspar de Alba, Alicia. "Literary Wetback." In *Infinite Divisions: An Anthology of Chicana Literature*, edited by Tey Diana Rebolledo and Eliana S. Rivero, 288–292. Tucson: University of Arizona Press, 1993.

Gutiérrez y Muhs, Gabriella, ed. *Communal Feminisms: Chicanas, Chilenas, and Cultural Exile: Theorizing the Space of Exile, Class, and Identity*. Lanham, MD: Lexington Books, 2007.

Lomelí, Francisco A. "Internal Exile in the Chicano Novel: Structure and Paradigms." In *European Perspectives on Hispanic Literature in the United States*, edited by Genvieve Fabre, 107–117. Houston, TX: Arte Público Press, 1988.

Morales, Alejandro. *The Brick People*. Houston, TX: Arte Público Press, 1988.

Rodriguez, Luis J. *The Concrete River*. Willimantic, CT: Curbstone, 1991.

Sánchez Bravo, Susana. *Espacios condenados*. Santiago: Cuarto Propio, 2004.

———. "Interview: Susana Sánchez Bravo." In *Communal Feminisms: Chicanas, Chilenas, and Cultural Exile: Theorizing the Space of Exile, Class, and Identity*, edited by Gabriella Gutiérrez y Muhs, 39–52. Lanham, MD: Lexington Books, 2007.

Viramontes, Helena María. "Interview: Helena María Viramontes." By Gabriella Gutiérrez y Muhs. In *Communal Feminisms: Chicanas, Chilenas, and Cultural Exile: Theorizing the Space of Exile, Class, and Identity*, edited by Gabriella Gutiérrez y Muhs, 123–137. Lanham, MD: Lexington Books, 2007.

———. *Their Dogs Came with Them*. New York: Atria, 2007.

II
The Body

3

Phantoms and Patch Quilt People

Narrative Art and Migrant Collectivity in Helena María Viramontes's *Under the Feet of Jesus*

YVONNE YARBRO-BEJARANO

IN AN INTERVIEW WITH GABRIELLA GUTIÉRREZ Y MUHS, novelist Helena María Viramontes remarked that Proposition 187 passed the very day she sent the finished manuscript of *Under the Feet of Jesus* to her publisher in November 1994 (127).[1] Viramontes's public gesture informs my reading of the novel, linking her story of a Mexican-origin migrant farmworker family with the virulent anti-immigrant climate that accompanied the unprecedented buildup of the US–Mexico boundary in the early 1990s (Nevins, 2).[2] We twenty-first-century readers are more prone than ever to treasure texts like *Under the Feet of Jesus* that convey migrants' humanity and subjectivity, witnesses as we are to the continuing militarization of the border, the deaths of thousands of migrants in the aftermath of deterrence strategies like Operation Gatekeeper, and the raging drug wars darkly linked to the gender slaughter known as feminicide.

Many critics of Viramontes's novel have made fruitful use of the critical and theoretical frameworks produced by Chicana feminist thought.[3] My analysis also owes a great debt to these approaches, in particular the transnational analytical frameworks of Alicia Schmidt Camacho's "migrant imaginaries" and Sonia Saldívar-Hull's "feminism on the border."[4] For Schmidt Camacho, migrant narratives such as *Under the Feet of Jesus* are "world-making" in that they "speak for a new order of citizenship and shared interest, an order that follows from the struggles of people who move" (17). Saldívar-Hull's assessment of Viramontes as a writer who "deconstructs geopolitical boundaries" (211) stems chiefly from her reading of the story "The Cariboo Café," but the interpretive power of feminism on the border also illuminates *Under the Feet of Jesus*. It furnishes a transnational reading strategy we can use to interpret the representation of gender and sexuality in the novel, particularly the female body in relation to labor and reproduction. Diverging from a Chicano nationalist imaginary, Viramontes's feminist critique, wedded to the critique of the racialized exploitation of migrants' labor, registers transborder mobility and the presence of noncitizens, erodes the value of citizenship as the principal avenue for demanding rights, and completely recasts the "race as family" narrative (Schmidt Camacho, 169) in the exploration of motherhood and the instability of "home."[5]

In her postpositivist realist interpretation of *Under the Feet of Jesus*, Paula Moya notes the radical contribution to American literature made by Viramontes's novel, "focalized entirely from the perspective of Mexican-origin migrant farmworkers" (190).[6] I propose to look at the first three sections of Part Two, a portion of the novel that brings to the fore the transnational, transethnic, and interracial components of this farmworker perspective. The migrant collective imagined in *Under the Feet of Jesus* is internally diverse and thus distinct from the cultural nationalist concept of "community" predicated on ethnoracial unity (Schmidt Camacho, 157). In the novel, Mexican-origin residents in the United States appear as parts of what Schmidt Camacho calls "a single transnational population composed of both Mexican and US citizens" (163), a population that takes in white and Asian American migrants as well. My use of the term "migrant" accommodates migratory circuits that are internal to the United States as well as transborder.[7] All the farmworkers in the novel embody Schmidt Camacho's theorization of "migrant" as "a subordinate position with respect to that of citizen" (5). Migrant farm laborers' lack of rights, regardless of legal status, pervades the representation of collectivity in the novel. Critics have paid a great deal of attention to these passages at the beginning of Part Two, highlighting the social contexts that structure the themes of migrant labor, the Border Patrol, and national belonging. My particular interest lies in examining the aesthetic texture of Viramontes's work, with a focus on certain literary features that foster a sense of migrant collectivity. To this end, I consider key metaphors such as the patch quilt, as well as strands of recurring imagery such as the peach, the female reproductive body, and the phantom. I also scrutinize variations in Viramontes's favored narrative technique of variable character-bound focalization that bring the shared context of migrant experience to the foreground,[8] namely the use of a collective focalizer and relatively bold interventions by the covert narrator.

Besides considering imagery and narrative techniques, my analysis also attends to the aesthetic effects Viramontes creates by dividing her narrative into units of varying lengths separated from each other by white spaces.[9] These blank spaces between the sections can mark temporal discontinuities,[10] as when the story shifts to the family's abandonment by Estrella's father in Part One. But the first three sections of Part Two unfold in a linear fashion. At the end of the workday narrated in section one, Alejo sees Estrella walking home along the railroad tracks; at the beginning of section two, she sits on those tracks to watch a baseball game. Estrella runs in fear of the Border Patrol out of section two and into the family's camp in section three. Yet the white spaces continue to signal the need for active participation on the reader's part. The framing of each unit slows down the plot's headlong momentum and shifts attention from the story to the narrative discourse, obliging the reader to look closely at each section to determine why the author calls our attention to this particular segment, and what it contributes to the overall meaning. At the same time that Viramontes marks the stand-alone significance of the narrative units, she stitches the sections together in patchwork fashion through the repetition of images. This simultaneity of autonomy and intertwining is a rich facet of Viramontes's narrative art. The narrative pleasure offered by *Under the Feet of Jesus* derives in part from noting how the images' shifting context and meaning enhance the understanding of climactic events such as Estrella's transformation of consciousness at the clinic.[11]

Migrant Subjectivity: Labor, Surveillance, and Reciprocity

The depiction of a day's work in the grape fields that opens Part Two flows from an imaginary "shaped by the experience of laboring for the nation without the promise of inclusion into its community as bearers of rights" (Schmidt Camacho, 9). The narration of the first section quickly settles into a pattern in which Estrella and Alejo alternate as focalizers. By this point in the novel, the reader has learned to follow the transfer of the reflector function from character to character, but this section is unusual in its movement back and forth between the same two characters. This alternation serves to highlight their differences of knowledge (Estrella possesses the necessary technologies to pick the grapes; Alejo is inept and inexperienced) and ideological investments (Alejo has imbibed the American Dream from his grandmother; Estrella sees only endless cycles of work ahead of her). Their experiences are also gendered differently, with Estrella's anchored in the female reproductive laboring body. Estrella's self-perception as a migrant farmworker emerges in a memory of her pregnant mother Petra carrying her as a four-year-old child on top of her bag of cotton, just as Estrella adopts the maternal role of caring for her sun-struck brother in the fields. She is visited by a vision of her future as a migrant worker: "Her eyes fell on the flatbeds of grapes she had lined carefully, sheet after sheet of grapes down as far as she could see. Her tracks led to where she stood now. Morning, noon or night, four or fourteen or forty it was all the same" (53). At the same time, Estrella and Alejo are similarly aligned: they are both performing backbreaking labor in the scorching heat. The fact that Alejo sees himself as passing through the migrant stream on his way to further education and success does not impede his poisoning by pesticides; he, like Estrella, must endure life-threatening occupational hazards. In Alejo's last "turn" as a focalizer in this section, he is distracted by seeing Estrella in the next row and allows the paper to slip from under the frame and fly away; he sets off in pursuit of it. For her part, Estrella's last turn as focalizer consists of two marvelously subtle passages in the development of migrant subjectivity and a collective imaginary in the novel. The first moment presents the indistinct yet menacing presence of the Border Patrol; the second moment stresses the alienating effects of the harsh working conditions on the bodies and minds of the farmworkers and the need for interaction and connection across their differences to restore a sense of personhood and humanity.

Disoriented by work, heat, exhaustion, and hunger, Estrella's own shadow has become unrecognizable to her: "It was hunched and spindly and grew longer on the grapes" (56). The image of the distorted shadow captures the fragmenting force of farm labor bearing down on the workers' bodies. Then she sees another shadow she fails to understand, "loitering larger and about to engulf her" (56). She gets up and goes to see: "She went over to the vine clutching her knife" (56). Arianne Burford reads this passage as an attempted rape in the context of her argument about violence "enacted against both land and women" (12). But a close reading of narrative features across different sections of the novel favors the interpretation that what Estrella is feeling is the pervasive, almost subliminal, fear of Border Patrol raids. The presence of the knife and the shadow here and at the end of the following section reinforces this reading. Frightened by the specter of the Border Patrol at the ball game in the second section, Estrella "fisted her knife and ran, her shadow fading into the approaching night" (60).

In the grape fields, the Border Patrol hovers at the edges of Estrella's consciousness to the extent that she maps flight and pursuit onto a worker's body in movement: "She saw a piscador running down the row, as if the person was being chased by something" (56). The reader, privy to more information than the individual characters,[12] knows that it is entirely possible that the shadow Estrella sees as overwhelming hers is Alejo's, as he peeks through the vines and learns that she is in the row next to his (55–56); it is also feasible that the figure in motion is Alejo, chasing after his runaway paper. But for Estrella the sight of a running piscador triggers fear of La Migra. This delicate passage introduces the notion of the "shadow" on the fields thrown by the Border Patrol, a presence that affects them all, regardless of legal status or ideology.

Immediately following this event, Estrella's perception returns to corporeal distortion and the alienation caused by punishing working conditions. She sees only "the bend of a back, and at first could not tell if it was female or male, old or young, and Estrella called out. The back unfolded and it was Toothless Kawamoto" (56). When he straightens up and looks at her questioningly, she throws him a peach and he smiles in thanks, "but," the reader is told, "it was she who was thankful" (57). Why does Estrella call out? Why is it *she* who is thankful when she is the one who gives away the peach? I propose that she calls out because she needs to see this fragment of a body as a person, to give the "back" a gender, a name, and an age. This is the gift that Kawamoto gives Estrella, first revealing his human identity and then acknowledging hers. She gives him the peach as an afterthought, to cover the awkwardness of her involuntary cry. Importantly, the text does not restore the fragmented working body to an ideal corporeal perfection. Kawamoto is toothless, with a mouth "like a vacant hole" (57), and his fingers are crooked, but he possesses a kind of bodily integrity that connotes dignity.

Collective Focalization and Transnational Imaginaries

Having grown accustomed to the alternation between Alejo and Estrella as the organizing narratorial principle of the section, the reader then comes upon two instances of collective focalization. The first appears just before Alejo chases his runaway paper, and the second occurs just after Estrella's interaction with Kawamoto. These passages featuring a collective reflector are like bookends for the experiences narrated in between, lending a communal framing for the main character's experiences and perspectives, especially fear of Border Patrol raids and humanizing interactions of reciprocity.[13] Both instances of collective focalization, keyed in by sounds, offer a counterpoint to the monotonous and grueling labor in the fields. The first provides a respite ("The piscadores heard the bells of the railroad crossing somewhere in the distance and they stopped to listen," 54); the second indicates the end of the work day ("The honking signaled the return of the trucks and the piscadores gathered their tools and jugs and aches and bags and children and pouches and emerged from the fields," 57). As Ann Banfield points out, focalization through a group of characters "represents . . . in some cases, a collective or class consciousness . . . a single point of view held by more than one individual" (96). The group markers "piscadores" and "trabajadores" reinforce the class aspect of the collective mentality to which Banfield refers. In the passage narrating the arrival of the trucks, the collective reflector allows the actions of the "Foreman" (with a capital "F") to be narrated *as seen through* a farmworker's class perspective, distinguishing this passage from the one in which Petra thinks resentfully of the foreman's prohibition against eating fallen fruit (12): "The Foreman produced a tablet of tables and columns of numbers, scribbled rows completed, names, erased calculations while the piscadores climbed the flatbed trucks" (57). The collective viewpoint implies that the workers "see" the process and the concrete effects of capitalism's abstraction and exploitation of their labor.

Even as these collective passages signal a unified class point of view with respect to migrant farmworkers, there is still room for diversity of experiences, as captured in the attention to various individuals and subgroups that comprise the group. In the passage narrating the arrival of the trucks, the group markers mainly alternate between the group ("piscadores," "all") and subgroups ("brittle women with bandannas over their noses; young teens rinsing their faces; children bored; men so old they were thought to be dead when they slept," 57). These subgroups represent precisely the categories Estrella was so anxious to discern in the "back": age and gender and the social roles that organize migrant farmworker culture. In the train passage, group markers ("the trabajadores," "the piscadores," "all") alternate with names identifying specific members of the group.

> The trabajadores like Señora Josefina who might be thinking about what to make for dinner; Ricky . . . thinking of a Blue Bell ice cream sandwich . . . ; or Gumecindo who might be planning his Saturday night. Piscadores like Florente of the islands who might be pinching his nostrils to blow his nose;

> Perfecto Flores who might be thinking how hard this work is
> for such an old man; the children who might be pulling . . . the
> rope tied to the waists of their weary mamas . . . ; Arnulfo who
> might be afraid of the snakes . . . ; Alejo who might be search-
> ing beyond the vines, and Estrella who might be kneeling over
> the grapes with her eyes closed. (54–55)

Although individuals are singled out, they are not represented as
diverging substantially from the "single point of view" (Banfield, 96)
that constitutes the collective mentality.

While the answer to the question "who hears the train?" is clear
(the *piscadores*), it is harder to answer the question "who sees Señora
Josefina and the others?" An even more interesting question is "who
knows what they 'might' be thinking?" As Seymour Chatman notes,
"The terrain of covert narration is bewildering, and it is easy to
lose one's bearings . . . we hear a voice speaking of events, characters, and setting, but its owner remains hidden in the discursive
[*sic*] shadows. . . . Such expression implies an interpretive device
or mediator . . . we cannot tell whether his own slant does not lurk
behind the words. . . . Hence our intuition of a shadowy narrator
lurking in the wings" (197). In both of the collectively focalized
passages under consideration, this narrator appears to momentarily
step out of the shadows. By entering into each worker's mind with
the unusual verb form "might," the narrator conveys the migrants'
thoughts and memories, desires and plans, fears and aspirations, as
well as a modest projection of their subjectivities into the future.

The group focalizer returns at the end of the train passage, record-
ing a collective response to the sounds. But in the last sentence the
covert narrator advances again: "All of them stopped to listen to
the freight train rattling along the tracks swiftly, its horn sounding
like the pressing of an accordion. The lone train broke the sun and
silence with its growing thunderous roar and the train reminded the
piscadores of destinations, of arrivals and departures, of home and
not of home. For they did stop and listen" (55). The emphatic verb
form ("they did stop") and the use of the coordinating conjunction
"for" highlight the intrusion of the narrator. By deviating in this way
from the novel's normative narratorial technique, the representation of a collective migrant subjectivity gains in poignancy. Similarly,

besides adding more weight to the sentence than a simple "because" or "since," the use of "for" here introduces a strong sequential inference. It provides a reason for what comes before, affirming the fact that listening to the train offers an occasion for the piscadores to reflect upon the migratory routes that shape their lives. In addition to providing a glimpse of individual migrants' desires, the train passage conveys a collective desire "for relief," for a "different order of space and belonging" (Schmidt Camacho, 6, 5). With the emphatic form "did," the narrator appears to comment on this collective desire, or to launch a rejoinder to an interlocutor who expresses doubt that farmworkers would "stop and listen," that is, engage in this activity of remembrance and reflection. Although the train evokes experiences of displacement and loss, it is the power of memory to maintain a relationship with what has been left behind that most powerfully shapes the migrant imaginary in this passage.

Patch Quilt People: Imagining Diverse Migrant Collectivity

Despite the Spanish terms for "pickers" and "workers" that seem to posit a specific Mexican-origin ethnicity and immigration trajectory, the migrant farmworkers' diversity includes other ethnicities as well. The reciprocity between Estrella and Kawamoto, migrants who differ in age, gender, ethnicity, and racial background, is a key scenario in the creation of an internally multifaceted collective. Preceding Kawamoto's appearance, "Florente of the islands" appears in the list of individuals imagined to be engaged in some activity while listening to the train. The presence of Florente invokes a long tradition in Chicana/o cultural production honoring the initiatory role of Filipinos in the United Farm Workers strike in the mid-1960s. Luis Valdez memorialized this vanguard action in his classic movement song "Huelga en General" ("General Strike"): "El día ocho de septiembre / de los campos de Delano / salieron los Filipinos. / Y después de dos semanas / para unirse a la batalla / salieron los mejicanos."[14] But with the presence of the Japanese-origin character Kawamoto, Viramontes's text departs from the binary "filipinos/mejicanos" in Chicano movement cultural production. Florente and

Kawamoto, both raised above the ordinary by phrases or words attached to their names, complexify the collective imaginary of the novel, making a space within it for Asian Americans embodying different histories of immigration to the United States from Japan and the Philippines, or from Japan via the Philippines.[15] The weighty yet lyrical descriptor "of the islands" counters the familiar use of Florente's first name. At the beginning of Part Three, it is Florente who identifies Alejo's sickness as "daño of the fields" (93). While Christa Grewe-Volpp erroneously attributes the comment to "the other workers" and reads it ironically (71), it is my point that giving these words specifically to Florente privileges an Asian American character in a novel that places high value on knowledge of the social environment. Florente and Kawamoto, as "piscadores," provide a richer transnational interpretive context for migrant experiences such as hunger, pesticide sickness, and the shadowy presence of the Border Patrol in Estrella's consciousness. By extending the destinations and dislocations that shape (im)migrant routes along an east-west axis as well, Viramontes acknowledges other imperial and colonial histories not often referred to as a matter of course in Chicana and Chicano fiction.

These meanings of diverse migrant collectivity also come to the fore in images that expose the ordinarily elusive narrator. The reader detects the presence of the narrator in the inclusion of "aches" in the list of things the pickers gather before emerging from the fields. The powerful metaphor "a patch quilt of people charred by the sun" (57) extends the compassionate commentary implied by "aches." The hyperbolic "charred" envisions the pickers emerging from the scorching fields as survivors of a fire. As with the phrase "for they did stop and listen," in these images the narrator comes close to assuming an overarching position vis-à-vis the characters. By manifesting a "slant," as Chatman calls it, or a high degree of sympathy for the workers laboring in these conditions, the narrator elicits a similar reaction in the reader.

In the patch quilt metaphor, the temporary shift from the social and economic markers "workers" and "pickers" to "people" highlights their communal identity and evokes varied resistance and civil rights discourses.[16] Typically, Viramontes both invokes and distances herself from these discourses. Rather than refer to the pickers as "*a* people," united by ethnoracial identity, she constructs her version of collectivity through the metaphorical patch quilt, made up "of people," just as the quilt consists of different patches. The patch quilt, a working-class art form most commonly practiced by women, resonates with the main components of the author's publicly stated commitments as a Chicana feminist writer.[17] As Gordon Collier suggests, studying the metaphors in a given literary work not only provides an appreciation of the writer's handling of figurative language but also affords a guide to the writer's "rule-book" or the work's "world" (363). The metaphor "a patch quilt of people," as a way of imagining an internally diverse migrant collective, draws on readers' knowledge of the social conditions affecting transnational and US migrants at the same time that it conveys values and meanings that point to a particular way to understand those social conditions.

The aesthetic of the patch quilt works with the tension between the totality created by sewing together different pieces of cloth and the persistent distinctiveness of the fragments differing in material and origins.[18] The histories of the garments (and the people who wore them) remain inscribed on the separate pieces after they take their place in the quilt. As with Kawamoto's body, the patch quilt metaphor imagines collectivity without valorizing a flawless corporality or homogeneous communal wholeness. In fact, the visible seams of the patch quilt constitute the form's very aesthetic. As a powerful organizer of narrative meaning, the patch quilt metaphor asks the reader to imagine what could sew diverse and displaced people together. In its materiality, the patch quilt brings workers together as "people," not in relation to their race, birthplace, or nationality, but in relation to their labor. It grounds them in a collectivity that owes less to familial ties than to the shared experience of migrant farmworkers.

An All-American Sport: The Perils of Migrant Existence

In section two, Estrella stops on her way back to the migrant camp at the end of the day to watch a baseball game. Viramontes exploits this signifier of All-American identity to portray and contest migrants' subordinate position with respect to the ideal citizen of the nation.[19]

In its depiction of the perils of transnational migration and the fear of the Border Patrol that pervades migrants' lives, this critical section draws from a migrant imaginary defined by "transborder solidarity" (Schmidt Camacho, 10). In contrast to the first section, in which the Border Patrol lurks in Estrella's consciousness without being named, here it intrudes explicitly: "She startled when the sheets of high-powered lights beamed on the playing field *like headlights of cars*, blinding her. The round, sharp white lights burned her eyes and she made a feeble attempt to shield them with an arm. The Border Patrol, she thought" (59, my emphasis). This allusion to "the headlights of cars" evokes the anti-immigrant vigilante groups, such as Light Up the Border, operating in the early 1990s.[20] The associative chain leading from the baseball diamond lights to vigilantes' car headlights to the Border Patrol depicts the constant threat of INS surveillance, compounded by anti-immigrant hostility, racist xenophobia, and nativist rhetoric about national belonging. The "round, sharp white lights" that "burned her eyes," and against which Estrella feels at a loss to protect herself, portray migrants' vulnerability faced with antagonistic social actors as well as the increasing militarization and surveillance of the Border Patrol. This brief image provides a large social context for understanding the treatment of Estrella as a migrant child by the teacher and the nurse in the novel.

At no point in *Under the Feet of Jesus* are agents of the Border Patrol "physically" present; instead, Viramontes's narrative art succeeds in portraying a state of mind, ever vigilant and fearful of INS policing actions. The degree of alarm that Estrella manifests, as a US-born migrant farm laborer, indexes the Border Patrol's indiscriminate apprehensions of US citizens and noncitizens when raiding the fields or other workplaces. In spite of an apparent distinction between "legals" and "illegals," the coercive exercise of power, backed up by the threat of violence, effectively blurs these distinctions, with the result of instilling fear in all migrants. Estrella's panicked response suggests the pervasiveness and efficacy of that tactic. Estrella's racialized social class position attenuates her relative privilege of citizenship, showing that US-born migrants' lives are also pervaded by fear and anxiety.

Viramontes's subversion of the all-American game counters nativist discourses of national identity and vividly portrays the dangers that migrants face. The references to the "bleached white" uniforms and the "white" lights suggest certain racialized notions of "American" (58–59). The various elements of the baseball game provide the grounds to figuratively join Estrella's individual experiences to a broader group perspective. Key images for this bridging originate in the first section of Part Two, namely the peach Estrella throws to Kawamoto and his mouth smiling in gratitude. Even though the ball game section foregrounds south–north migration, the figure of Kawamoto continues to bolster the east–west parameters of the migrant imaginary in the novel.

Before the Border Patrol intrudes into Estrella's consciousness, the ball flying through the air reminds her of a "peach tossed out to hungry hands" (59), an association prompted by her own hunger ("Estrella wished she had not surrendered her peach," 58). The emphatic parallels between the game and her previous action continue: "One short player . . . held [the ball] up as she had done with the peach" (59). With the transmogrification of mitts into mouths, Kawamoto once again loses his bodily integrity in Estrella's eyes: "Estrella jumped to her feet to see mitts form holes like Mr. Kawamoto's mouth readied for the catch" (59). In this bizarre simile, inspired by his toothless mouth as a "vacant hole" in the first section (57), Kawamoto's smile multiplies into many open mouths, replacing his "crooked fingers" in catching the peach/ball. There is a good deal that is grotesque about this image, even shocking. Besides undoing the restoration of migrant bodily integrity and reciprocity in the first section, it visits extreme symbolic violence on an Asian American character. In this moment of renewed disintegration, however, the shift from the nickname "Toothless" to the honorific "Mr." signals respect and helps retain the cohesive potential of social relations and other humanizing, however fleeting, practices in a context of pervasive hunger linked to global social forces.

As with the image of "toothless" Kawamoto in the first section, this passage queries the Asian American character's abjection, as with Florente's to a lesser extent, imagined "pinching his nostrils to blow his nose" (55). The same, admittedly partial, answer applies here: his flawed corporeality privileges Kawamoto in the narrative creation of a diverse migrant collectivity. With his "hole" of a mouth, Kawamoto stands in for migrant hunger, a hunger not limited to the Mexican-origin migrants represented by Estrella and her family. He becomes proliferating mouths, which then superimpose themselves on the bodies and elements of the baseball game, including the youthful All-American bodies of the players in their "bleached white" uniforms. The emphasis here moves from Kawamoto's laboring body, so prominent in the first section, to a body impelled by hunger, newly fragmented in Estrella's imagination as disembodied mouths absurdly running to catch food.[21]

After the playing field lights throw Estrella into a panic fueled by her fear of the border patrol, the images of migrant bodies and experience generated by the game's sights and sounds take a more violent turn:

> A ball hit, a blunt instrument against a skull. A player ran the bases for the point. A score. Destination: home plate. Who would catch the peach, who was hungry enough to run the field in all that light? The perfect target. The lushest peach. The element of surprise. A stunned deer waiting for the bullet. (60)

The synecdochal mouths running to catch the peach now become the bodies of transnational (im)migration ("who would catch the peach?"), fleeing from the INS at the border or in the fields. The recurring image of the peach places Estrella's and Kawamoto's hunger under the sign of global economic necessity pushing migrants to undertake border crossings that put them in severe jeopardy. "In all that light" recalls the simile of the cars' headlights to stress the danger of discovery awaiting those who attempt the journey. The sound of the bat hitting the ball triggers an image of brutal aggression at the hands of Border Patrol agents or vigilantes ("a blunt instrument against a skull"). The core image of the player/migrant running after the ball/peach in a light-drenched "field" yields to starker figures of speech that veer from the ground of the baseball game into the realms of hunting and predation ("The perfect target"; "The element of surprise"). The sentence fragments match the violent images on a syntactic level and help convey Estrella's agitation. The metaphor of the stunned deer retains the visual of the car headlights, recalling migrants caught in the forty-foot high-intensity lights at the border (Nevins, 78). The deer metaphor, referencing the illegal practice of hunting deer with lights, evokes anti-immigrant vigilantes chasing down migrants from their vehicles.

Phantoms of Transnational (Im)migration

In contrast to the material and binding connotations of "a patch quilt of people," in this section Estrella conjures a metaphor of extreme insubstantiality for migrant existence: the phantom. Toward the beginning of the section, Estrella describes one of the players as "blurred in the mesh of fence" (59). In the grip of her fear of the Border Patrol, Estrella now imagines those inside the mesh border to be "phantoms" (59). As the barrier oscillates in her imagination between the fence surrounding the playing area and the fence marking out the US–Mexico border, Estrella fleetingly loses the ability to delineate who belongs on which side. The concept of "home" is unsettled in relation to the border, as in the migrants' memories of "home and not of home" (55). In this moment, one that strongly evokes the homes lost in transnational migration and the transient homes of the migrant stream, Estrella and her social group also become phantoms, a metaphoric identity suggested by the lights' ambivalent direction and the syntactic melding of the spectators' and Estrella's perceptual standpoint ("Could the spectators see her *from* where *she* stood?" 60, my emphasis): "She tried to remember which side she was on and which side of the wire mesh she was safe in. The floodlights aimed at the phantoms in the field. Or were the lights directed at her? Could the spectators see her from where she stood? Where was home?" (59–60). In mapping the border and transnational migration onto the playing field, players and spectators alike, inside and outside the fence, share in a state of uprootedness.

The phantom metaphor dissolves the patch quilt people's materiality in the context of transnational migration, true, but it also destabilizes a nativist contention insisting on an inherent distinction between the ideal citizens of the nation (players/spectators of the all-American game) and migrants like Estrella with respect to "home." The instability of self and home, this "phantom" quality, also relates to not knowing on which "side" of the fence safety lies. The phantom metaphor reveals that being on "this side," that is, on the US side, does not guarantee Estrella's safety, as her fear of the Border Patrol reveals. At this point in the text, her lack of safety weakens her sense of self just as much as her hunger does, arising from labor exploitation.

The scope of this imagery shows how Estrella's individual consciousness holds a diversity of migrant experiences. There is no explicit information in the text that Estrella has ever been at the border, but her social experience would include listening to tales of crossing. She would have imbibed the knowing humor and ironic resistance of the DJ on the radio playing in the fields, whose question exposes the absurdity of nativists' claims to primacy and authenticity: "Whose back was wetter . . . those who crossed the river, or those who crossed the ocean?" (84). The joking DJ references a world of transnational (im)migration even as he slyly deconstructs the anti-immigrant discourse of "wetbacks." Within Estrella's family, her father's failure to return brings a reference to "troubles at the border" (13). Whether this is a lie to justify or prolong his absence (there are rumored "sightings" in Ensenada and Los Angeles), the phrase introduces transborder practices into the text, including the difficulties of entry into the United States and the discontinuity of transborder family ties. Perfecto is a long-term settled migrant from Mexico; reader's assumptions about Petra's birthplace and immigrant status are formed through narrative features such as linguistic interactions and her emphasis on her children's birth certificates. These sparse details reveal that Viramontes is less interested in spelling out parameters of legality than she is in acknowledging a spectrum of experiences with respect to entry and residence in the United States, within one family and across the group of migrants in the text. Estrella's consciousness encompasses the experiences of unauthorized and authorized transnational migrants, her family's and her own. The images of hunger and violence that arise spontaneously in Estrella's mind at the mere thought of the Border Patrol capture the commonalities that unify this diverse group. The images' density and intensity in this section implicate her in the lives of other migrants, and them in hers.

The Female Reproductive Body and Migrants' Claims to Justice

When Estrella arrives in the camp, Petra advises her on how to manage her fear of the Border Patrol and how to respond if detained by INS agents. This section pivots on "the related themes of citizenship, belonging and entitlement" (Moya, 195–196). It presents different claims for migrants' presence in the United States through metaphor and the narrative feature of "scene," in which detailed description and an emphasis on dialogue converge to create an "effect of vividness and immediacy" (Rimmon-Kenan, 107). Of the two views Petra puts forth on the right of migrants to be in the United States, one is more exclusive, limited to those who possess legal documents ("you tell them the birth certificates are under the feet of Jesus"), and the other is more inclusive, based on earned entitlement through productive labor, or "nonstate claims to rights" (Schmidt Camacho, 10). This latter view is important for the novel's creation of an internally diverse migrant collective, as it encompasses both US-born and transnational migrants regardless of legal status. In her articulation of this view, Petra contests the official discourse criminalizing migrants: "Don't let them make you feel you did a crime for picking the vegetables they'll be eating for dinner" (63). While Estrella focuses on her own fear and her concern for other family members, Petra speaks within a wider purview: "It's La Migra. Everybody's feeling it" (61). Petra's collective assertion recalls the patch quilt metaphor from the first section: there migrants are drawn together by a common labor, here by a common fear.

There is much that is contradictory or impractical in Petra's advice to Estrella. Even though she asks, rhetorically, "Do we carry proof around like belly buttons?" (62), she herself carries around the birth certificates from camp to camp, though the Border Patrol is unlikely to wait for Estrella to produce her documents before they "pull [her] into the green vans" (63). Petra herself recognizes the fact that laboring many years in the United States does not translate into belonging for either authorized or unauthorized migrants: "No sense telling La Migra you've lived here all your life" (62). The INS agents are even less likely to respect migrants for putting the food they eat on their table. But what is at the heart of this exchange is

that Petra shows Estrella a path to understanding her social location and models a stance of resistance for her daughter: "Don't run
scared. You stay there and look them in the eye" (63). Petra embodies this stance in her own determination to take a stand: "Yo ya no
voy a correr. No puedo más" (62).

This conversation takes place under the sign of the female reproductive body. Petra's body is closely associated with never-ending
migrant farm work in Estrella's memory and imagination. The image
that arises when she remembers how Petra carried her on her sack
in the cotton fields entwines motherhood, the pregnant body, and
farm labor: "The sack grew larger and heavier like the swelling child
within her" (51). Watching the baseball game, Estrella's imagination
makes a similar association, seeing Petra's body in the railroad ties
extending endlessly in both directions like the rows in the fields:
"They looked like the stitches of the mother's caesarean scar as far
as her eyes could see" (59). In Estrella's mind, Petra's body represents her own future, not just as a migrant farmworker but also as a
female migrant, with the prospect of hard work in the fields doubled
by the domestic duties assigned to girls and women and, eventually,
pregnancy and childbirth.[22]

Petra continues to be anchored in her maternal body and her gendered labor in the third section. Exhausted, frightened, and hungry at
the end of a long day in the fields, Estrella knows she must help her
mother with dinner before she can rest. She finds Petra bathing her
youngest children at the end of her own long day of doing the wash.
In her love and concern for her mother's welfare, Estrella draws the
reader's attention to the sight of Petra's body inscribed by childbirth
and the varicose veins that arise and worsen with pregnancy:[23] "The
mother struggled upward, straightening one knee then the other, and
Estrella noticed how purple and thick her veins were getting. Like
vines choking the movement of her legs. Even the black straight skirt
she wore seemed tighter and her belly spilled over the belt of waist, lax
muscles of open births, her loose ponytail untidy after the laundry" (61).
For the reader, with privileged access to the perspectives of all the
character-focalizers, the tight skirt and expansive belly are additional
signs of Petra's reproductive body, signaling her new pregnancy.

The section ends with another image of the ceaseless cycles related
to gendered migrant labor, as one of the twins gets back in the water

after Petra has dried her off painstakingly. Seeing this, "Estrella closed her eyes, not wanting to open them again" (63). Given the close association between Petra's body in "labor," in the double sense of the word, and Estrella's bleak vision of her future, it is important that Petra be the one to impart knowledge about migrant belonging and resistance to her daughter, embodying Saldívar-Hull's feminism on the border.

Madre Earth and Migrant Legitimacy

Under the Feet of Jesus is a text that incessantly foregrounds the body. Characters are minutely aware of corporality, constantly registering their own sensations and being attentive to others' bodies. Within this general alertness to physicality, certain characters' bodies are privileged metaphorically and charged with symbolism. One of these is Kawamoto, whose body, cycling through reintegration and fragmentation, becomes a figure for internally diverse migration and the perils of migrant existence. Petra's maternal body also becomes the ground for a crucial metaphor in the novel, that of "madre earth." Unlike the patch quilt metaphor, enunciated through the veil of covert narration, or the vivid ball game images focalized by Estrella, the "madre earth" metaphor emerges through the section's "scenic" quality, co-produced by words spoken by Petra and descriptions of Petra through Estrella's eyes.

When Petra says to Estrella, "Tell them que tienes una madre aquí" (63), the reader might expect Petra to be referring to herself, especially since she has just invoked the birth certificates as guarantors of national belonging and safety. Estrella's perception of Petra's defining gesture produces the metaphoric transformation of "madre earth": "You are not an orphan, and she pointed a red finger to the earth. Aquí" (63). When Estrella sees Petra pointing to the earth instead of to herself, the one-on-one association of her mother's reproductive body with legality, based on birthright, visually shifts to broader interpretative possibilities. Numerous narrative features flag this crucial moment: Petra's raised voice, her emphatic repetition of the word "aquí," and her dramatic performance combining gesture and voice. The fact that Petra has her back to Estrella when

she pronounces these words and points to the ground heightens
the drama of the moment; she turns around only after the emphatic
second "aquí." Petra's first word in the novel is also "aquí," indi-
cating that the family has arrived at their destination, yet another
labor camp. That Estrella has a mother "here" contains an array of
meanings, from a specific location (the labor camp), a nation-state
(the United States), a continent (the Americas), and the multiple
symbolic resonances of the earth.[24]

The linguistic hybridity of the metaphor "madre earth" underlines its co-production by Petra as speaker/performer and Estrella
as listener/spectator, just as it captures the narrative solutions Viramontes devises to represent interactions within a family composed
of both monolingual and bilingual members. Although some of the
connotations of the cultural traditions invoked by "Mother Earth"
and "tierra madre" cling to "madre earth," the metaphor cannot
be translated solely into one language without radically altering the
specificity of the scenic interaction between Petra and Estrella and
consequently the meanings invested in the image.

Arguably, the most accessible meanings of "madre earth" derive
from Petra's insistence on citizenship as the ultimate protection
against the Border Patrol, conflating childbirth and birthplace, with
"aquí" referring to the United States. The value placed on US citizenship introduces a complex resignification of motherhood through
the interrelating and recasting of orphanhood and legitimacy. In
pointing to the earth instead of to herself when she says "tienes
una madre aquí" (for she is also "here," in the United States), there
is a displacement or transfer of meaning from the female reproductive body to the earth as legitimizing place marker. By claiming
"You are not an orphan" and pointing to the earth, Petra suggests
that having a mother who is a noncitizen is a kind of orphanhood in
the United States, signifying vulnerability to anti-immigrant legislation, enforcement, and discrimination; she protects Estrella against
the consequences of possible familial instability and rupture by giving birth to her in the United States ("aquí"). By extension, the
earth (here) is Estrella's mother (she is not an orphan). Estrella is
"not an orphan" twice over; she has two mothers, but only one is
"legal." In this way, the notion of legitimacy as a mother's legal
marital status is refigured in terms of whether the mother has legal

documents to be in the United States. In the sense of earth as mother/birthplace-conferring-legality, then, Petra almost functions as surrogate mother.

On the other hand, the shift away from Petra's body to the earth also makes room for understanding migrants' right to be in the United States based on their productive labor. This interpretation builds on Petra's refutation of official discourses criminalizing and shaming the people who harvest the nation's food ("Don't let them make you feel you did a crime for picking the vegetables they'll be eating for dinner," 63).[25] As the madre earth metaphor depicts farm-workers as offspring of the earth, in this sense the earth's (re)produc-tiveness is also the ground for the birthing of migrant "legitimacy."

The association between migrant farmworkers and the earth evokes a variety of revolutionary and cultural nationalist discourses, including Chicana/o texts such as "El Plan Espiritual de Aztlán."[26] Estrella's perception of the color of the female reproductive body strengthens this evocation: "You are not an orphan, and she pointed a *red* finger to the earth" (63, my emphasis). Why does Estrella perceive her mother as "red" at this moment? Earlier in the section, Estrella sees Petra as having "coffee skin" (61), and the description of Petra at the beginning of the novel suggests an Afro-Hispanic heritage: "Petra had deep coffee-colored skin and black, kinked hair" (7). The unique descriptor "red" in this instance bears indigenous connota-tions that resonate with the Chicana/o cultural nationalist tone of the metaphor "madre tierra" and call forth these associations. In *The Last Generation*, published in 1993, Cherríe Moraga writes from a Chicana lesbian cultural nationalist framework: "*The Earth is female.* . . . she is called 'Mother' by all peoples of all times. *Madre Tierra*" (172, original emphasis). Moraga invokes the colonization of the Americas to make the important theoretical move from the colonized "madre tierra" to the bodies of "women, lesbians, and gay men" (173), also in need of liberation. *Under the Feet of Jesus* makes a reverse move, in which the path to women's bodies is not drawn directly via the earth as female, but rather projecting Petra's specific, racialized reproduc-tive body onto the earth that then becomes Estrella's and the other migrants' "figurative mother" in the United States. The racialization of Petra's body/the earth as indigenous and the Chicana/o cultural nationalist tone seem to close down membership in the collective to Mexican-origin migrants or those born in the Americas. But as "aquí" also signifies the United States, it would include all migrant farmworkers working here, regardless of birthplace or nationality.

As with other allusions to Chicana/o cultural nationalist representations in the novel, this particular metaphor linking workers and land does not have extended resonance in the text. Viramontes seems less interested in developing migrants' relationship to the land, represented somewhat romantically in certain cultural nationalist traditions, than with their claims to justice stemming from their labor.[27] However, the novel does exploit the multiple resonances of cultural nationalist discourses to move the metaphor's significance from the individual (Estrella) to the collective level: migrants with the right to be on the earth as her offspring, and migrants as producers of wealth and goods.

The Clinic and the Crowbar: Revisiting Migrant Belonging

Petra's advice bears fruit in Estrella's thoughts and actions at the clinic, where the family seeks help for Alejo. When the nurse takes their last dime to tell them that the deathly ill young man should be taken to the hospital, Estrella smashes a crowbar down on the nurse's desk to force her to return the money. References to the Border Patrol color the novel's approaching climax with images of fear and violence that spring from the migrant imaginary. When Estrella gestures to Perfecto with two open hands that the nurse wants ten dollars for the visit, Petra contemplates how "people surrender to the police or La Migra and how they put their hands up when they see the pistols pointed at the bulls-eye of their bellies" (144). The menacing INS agents in this image, recalling Estrella's "perfect target," meld with economic hardship in Petra's outrage. She argues against taking Alejo to the hospital for fear that, lacking papers, he will be reported. Estrella's response that he and his Texas-born ancestors "belong here" clashes pointedly with Alejo's lethal exposure to pesticides, one of the many hazards of migrant farm labor.

Of the two views on migrant belonging advanced by Petra earlier in the novel, entitlement clearly trumps legality in the chain of thoughts leading to Estrella's action in the clinic, as she apprehends the exploitation of migrants' production of wealth and goods for *all*: "Estrella had figured it out: the nurse owed *them* as much as they owed her" (148, original emphasis). Moya has shown how the "trope of fuel" plays a crucial role in Estrella's "increasing ability to 'read' her social world" (200). Alejo's vital contribution to Estrella's transformation of consciousness echoes throughout the passage leading up to her key insight, through the extended metaphor of farmworkers' bones providing the fuel for others (148).[28] But it is Petra who gives Estrella explicit lessons on how to maneuver when targeted by anti-immigrant antagonism or discrimination, refusing the shame of racialized criminalization attached to migrant labor, and insisting on the need to take a stand rather than run away. The tone and language of Estrella's concluding insight are reminiscent of Petra's feisty manner of speaking. In Viramontes's border feminist writing, the mother/daughter relationship becomes the site of knowledge transmission and the will to agency. In this moment at the clinic, understanding and action come together for Estrella. She puts both Alejo's and Petra's knowledge into practice, taking a stand with the crowbar in her hand.

The crowbar appears at three decisive points in the narrative. Critics of the novel concur that Estrella's final use of the tool at the clinic stems from her growing skill in correctly interpreting her social experience. They also stress the link between the clinic scene and an earlier interaction between Estrella and Perfecto, who teaches her the names of his tools and how to use them, laying the ground for Moya's "notion of expanded literacy," in which the crowbar represents a primary vehicle for the "connection between communication, interpretation, and agency" (178).[29] The appearance of the crowbar in the conversation with Petra about the Border Patrol constitutes an intermediary moment in this process of "expanded literacy." Upon arriving at the camp, Estrella drops the knife she had clutched in her fist as she fled from the playing field and grabs the crowbar instinctually, as an instrument of self-defense against Border Patrol agents. In this moment she still lacks the social understanding behind her deliberate wielding of the crowbar as an instrument of self-assertion on behalf of Alejo and her family. But her recourse here to the knife and the crowbar does demonstrate a highly developed sense of self-preservation and a willingness to protect herself and others.[30]

Refiguring the Phantom and the Female Reproductive Body

The reappearance of the phantom draws on some of this figure's meanings from the ball game section yet retools the image according to Estrella's experiences in the clinic. Earlier, when she feels overcome by the policing of migrant routes and uncertain about where she stands in relation to home and nation, Estrella's corporeal substance and her sense of self begin to fade. After Estrella wields the crowbar to force the nurse to return their payment, "[s]he did not feel like herself holding the money. She felt like two Estrellas. One was a silent phantom who obediently marked a circle with a stick around the bungalow as the mother had requested, while the other held the crowbar and the money. The money felt wet and ugly and sweaty like the swamp between her legs" (150). In this split subjectivity, the phantom quality is assigned to a passive daughter self who obeys the mother without questioning, marking a line of faith around the transient homes of the migrant stream. This apparition contrasts with an intensely embodied self who relies on her own inner resources and understandings to question existing power relations and take a public stand when faced with need and discriminatory treatment.[31]

By marking the sex of the embodied self, Viramontes not only genders Estrella's transformation of consciousness but also anchors it in a specifically female body: "The money felt wet and ugly and sweaty like the swamp between her legs" (150).[32] The simile characterizing Estrella's sex as "ugly" recalls other non-idealizing corporeal images that condense important meanings in the novel, such as the bodies of Kawamoto and Petra. Estrella does not experience her action as heroic in this moment. She is aware of the cost to herself and potentially to her family of what she has done; hence, the money she has fought to reclaim and the embodied self who has acted are "ugly." The "swamp between her legs" references exertion and the heat of the day, but also symbolically calls menstruation into the text, linking Estrella's new social awareness with coming of age as a woman, and figuring her knowledge-made-action through a physical rite of passage.[33] The alignment of menstruation with Estrella's awakened consciousness deflects the meanings of the female reproductive body away from connotations of pregnancy and motherhood.

Conclusion: Religious Imagery and the Collective Migrant Imaginary

Coming across the title words of a work in the text is always an occasion for joyful scrutiny; in *Under the Feet of Jesus*, the title words appear twice, encouraging a side-by-side interpretation of the two passages. The repetition and reworking of the phrase "under the feet of Jesus" play out implicitly within the mother/daughter relationship and have resonance for the collective migrant imaginary. In Part Two, Petra's words "the birth certificates are under the feet of Jesus" refer to her dual reliance on the protection granted by US citizenship and her religious faith in Jesus' power to keep her children, and the documents, safe from harm. As seen in the clinic, Estrella's process of understanding-made-action decenters the discourse of legality in favor of earned entitlement ("the nurse owed *them*"). When the statue of Jesus topples and breaks near the end of the novel (167), the reliance on divine protection as promise of safety is also "broken."

At the end, the title words are secularized in Estrella's triumphant sense of self-reliance and faith in her body as she climbs to the roof of the barn. The simile in question aligns the empowered Estrella with the privileged position formerly afforded to Jesus: "The termite-softened shakes crunched beneath her bare feet like the serpent under the feet of Jesus . . . No longer did she feel her blouse damp with sweat . . . she had to trust the soles of her feet, her hands, the shovel of her back, and the pounding bells of her heart" (175). Before climbing, she works up her courage by calling upon "her other self" (172), the one who, anchored in her female body, trusts and acts out of her own knowledge ("No longer did she feel her blouse damp with sweat," 175). Gone, for now, is the whiff of self-loathing that accompanied the "sweatiness" of her violent act in the clinic.

In the final words of the novel, Estrella's sense of empowerment at having accomplished what she set out to do finds expression in another religious image, describing her heart as "powerful enough to summon home all those who strayed" (176). In this oblique reference, Estrella is aligned in the position of the Good Shepherd and the migrant farmworker collective in the metaphorical position of flock. The Good Shepherd image is milder than that of Jesus crushing the serpent, though it retains the reference to protection, and the muted allusion to migrants as sheep is certainly more benevolent than the image of "stunned deer waiting for the bullet" (60). While the metaphorical relationship between shepherd and flock remains a hierarchical one, the secularization of the religious imagery removes the moral taint of the word "stray." For the contemporary reader, it is difficult not to think about those transnational migrants who have strayed off so many paths in the deserts and mountains of the borderlands. Given Estrella's commitment to help Alejo, her sense of empowerment at the end could encompass a desire to extend herself to others, to play some role in the aid and protection of migrants as a larger group. The argument between Perfecto and Petra over helping Alejo shows that while there may be strong cultural and class traditions of mutual aid among Mexican-origin migrants, putting them into practice is a choice, not a given. There is in Estrella's exhilaration a sense of possibility, or at the very least a wish, that they all might find a safe haven.

Acknowledgments

Many thanks to my colleague Stephen Hong Sohn for his thoughtful comments, and to Vida Mía García for research assistance.

Notes

1. Proposition 187 would have denied public education, public social services, and public health care services to unauthorized immigrants (Nevins, 3).

2. According to Viramontes, she started working on *Under the Feet of Jesus* in the fall of 1991, after completing a second draft of her novel *Their Dogs Came with Them* (2008). She finished a first draft of *Under the Feet of Jesus* in early 1994 and completed the final draft in November of 1994 (e-mail communication with the author, July 21, 2008).

3. See, for example, Arianne Burford, who builds on "the anti-colonialist based feminist politics" (2) of Chela Sandoval, Mary Pat Brady, Sonia Saldívar-Hull, Emma Pérez, and other women of color to elaborate her analysis of Viramontes's and Cherríe Moraga's "remapping of feminisms." Because the novel has been so well studied, I will assume a general familiarity with the story line.

4. Burford also points to "the necessity of transnational feminist alliances" (14).

5. See Schmidt Camacho for a full discussion of the "structuring absence" of migrants in Chicano movement discourse (157), the delimitation of the Chicano nation "within the boundaries of US citizenship," and the subsequent "remasculinization of the liberation struggle" (166). See also Rosa-Linda Fregoso on the "Chicano familia romance."

6. For Anne Shea, such migrant narratives "threaten to transform not only images of the workers themselves but also the image that the United States cultivates for itself" (133).

7. Schmidt Camacho reserves the term "migrant" for "those with Mexican citizenship who cross the international boundary into the United States" (xiii).

8. See Moya for a detailed examination of variable character-bound focalization in the novel. Moya's interpretation links "the epistemic status of identity" (177) with this narrative strategy, in which the covert narrator hides behind one of the four main characters from whose perspectives the narrated events are "seen."

9. I use the flexible term "passage" to refer to an excerpt of the text ranging from a few sentences to a paragraph or more. Viramontes divides her novel into five "parts."

10. See Cecelia Lawless (quoted in Moya, 192, n. 20). For Rick Altman, the "stretch of white space separating one following-unit from the next" resembles an "implied disclaimer" for extreme temporal breaks (246).

11. The phrase is Moya's; see her book for an in-depth interpretation of Estrella's process.

12. See Moya for a discussion of the implications of the "partiality of perspective" in the novel, which places the reader in a "privileged position" (187).

13. Near the end, on the road to the clinic, another instance of collective focalization occurs, when some piscadores stop to help Perfecto and Estrella free the family's station wagon from the mud: "They briefly glanced at Alejo wrapped in his blanket, one of them even tapping the window with a scraped knuckle, but after they saw him, they averted their glances, steadied their boots, determined not to look again" (134–135). Christa Grewe-Volpp reads this passage as the group of migrants "superstitiously avoiding their glances as if that could ward off similar fates for themselves" (71). While the collective reflector here reinforces the aura of death around Alejo, as in the image "a few of the men stood like pallbearers on either side of the wagon" (134), their desire to distance themselves from Alejo does not cancel out their act of generosity, an act that recalls the exchange between Estrella and Kawamoto. The image

of the pallbearers itself reinforces the willingness to be of service to a fellow migrant, in life or in death.

14. "On the 8th of September the Filipinos walked out of the fields of Delano, and after two weeks the Mexicans walked out to join the struggle."

15. In his in-progress study of "Chicano literary orientalisms," Stephen Hong Sohn examines the implications of the Asian American figures in Viramontes's novel (personal communication). In his work on Alejandro Morales's *The Rag Doll Plagues*, Sohn also elaborates a reading practice for excavating the importance of Asian Americans in Chicano cultural production.

16. Perhaps because I have heard it so many times, I perceive echoes of Daniel Valdez's iconic Chicano movement song "Brown Eyed Children of the Sun" in Viramontes's "a patch quilt people charred by the sun." Unlike the representation of Chicano community as heteronormative family in Valdez's song, Viramontes creates a metaphor that selects difference as a defining characteristic of a collective.

17. See her essay "'Nopalitos': The Making of Fiction."

18. See Beardsley et al.

19. Lene Johannessen sees in the ball game passage a "process where the discourse of the physical landscape meets that of mental inscape" (101).

20. Joseph Nevins comments that these local groups, whether defining themselves in racist, anti-immigrant and/or national sovereignty terms, "did not exist in a national sociopolitical vacuum, but rather in a sea of sympathy" (78).

21. The theme of hunger threads throughout the novel, many times tied to the despair of parenting in poverty, as when in the wake of her father's departure Estrella "tried to feed the children with noise," drumming on the empty oatmeal box (20), or when Petra reflects that she could make tortillas in the dark, "because tortillas filled her children's stomachs and made their stomachs hungry for more" (120).

22. For Burford, by referring to Petra frequently as "the mother," Viramontes "critiques a long history of political economy within which mothers' labor is doubly exploited" (10). Future research considering focalization could explore why only Estrella uses this term.

23. See Burford on the veins-as-vines metaphor (10).

24. Johannessen discusses this passage in light of the "Janus-face of the landscape" (105).

25. Shea focuses on the criminalization of farmworkers and the reworking of justice.

26. For Shea, this passage implies a "critique of nationalist rhetorics" (141). Burford sees the novel as an "anti-pastoral" in which the land does not figure as "a romanticized space" (12), and Grewe-Volpp refers to Viramontes's strategic use of romanticized associations with "Mother Earth" as a "source of essentialized female strength and power" (67).

27. Marilyn Chandler McEntyre speaks of a "comprehensive idea of justice" in the novel that "implies solidarity among and with the poor" (102).

28. See Dan Latimer's article for another reading of the tar pits in the novel.

29. See also Shea (140).

30. For Shea, the crowbar in this scene "represents the materiality of the laborers' struggle" (140).

31. These are qualities that Petra herself has taught Estrella, but it is ironic, and typical of Viramontes's non-reductive narrative art, that by putting them into practice Estrella may become less conforming in her role as daughter in the domestic sphere.

32. Moya notes that "the entire experience for Estrella is figured in explicitly embodied, relational, and gendered terms" (208).

33. When Petra reflects that Estrella "[s]oon would begin menstruation" (120) and recalls "the absence of her own," she is struck by the realization that she cannot protect her daughter from danger and heartache stemming from female sexuality (120–121).

Works Cited

Altman, Rick. *A Theory of Narrative.* New York: Columbia University Press, 2008.

Banfield, Ann. *Unspeakable Sentences: Narration and Representation in the Language of Fiction.* London: Routledge, 1982.

Beardsley, John, William Arnett, Paul Arnett, and Jane Livingston. *Gee's Bend: The Women and Their Quilts.* Atlanta, GA: Tinwood Books, 2002.

Burford, Arianne. "Cartographies of a Violent Landscape: Viramontes' and Moraga's Remapping of Feminisms in *Under the Feet of Jesus* and *Heroes and Saints.*" *Genders OnLine Journal* 47 (2008), http://www.genders .org/g47/g47_burford.html.

Chatman, Seymour. *Story and Discourse: Narrative Structure in Fiction and Film.* Ithaca, NY: Cornell University Press, 1978.

Collier, Gordon. *The Rocks and Sticks of Words: Style, Discourse and Narrative Structure in the Fiction of Patrick White.* Amsterdam: Rodopi, 1992.

"El Plan Espiritual de Aztlán: Chicano Liberation Youth Conference." 1969. In *Aztlán: An Anthology of Mexican American Literature*, edited by Luis Valdez and Stan Steiner, 402–406. New York: Vintage Books, 1972.

Fregoso, Rosa-Linda. *meXicana Encounters: The Making of Social Identities on the Borderlands.* Berkeley: University of California Press, 2003.

Grewe-Volpp, Christa. "'The oil was made from their bones': Environmental (In)Justice in Helena María Viramontes' *Under the Feet of Jesus.*" *Interdisciplinary Studies in Literature and Environment* 12, no. 1 (Winter 2005): 61–78.

Johannessen, Lene. "The Meaning of Place in Viramontes' *Under the Feet of Jesus.*" In *Holding Their Own: Perspectives on the Multi-ethnic Literatures of the United States*, edited by Dorothea Fischer-Hornung and Heike Raphael-Hernandez, 101–109. Tübingen: Stauffenburg, 2000.

Latimer, Dan. "The La Brea Tar Pits, Tongues of Fire: Helena María Viramontes's *Under the Feet of Jesus* and Its Background." *Soundings* 85, nos. 3–4 (2002): 323–346.

Lawless, Cecelia. "Helena María Viramontes' Homing Devices in *Under the Feet of Jesus*." In *Homemaking: Women Writers and the Politics and Poetics of Home*, edited by Catherine Wiley and Fiona R. Barnes, 361–382. New York: Garland, 1996.

McEntyre, Marilyn Chandler. "Sickness in the System: The Health Costs of the Harvest." *Journal of Medical Humanities* 28, no. 2 (2007): 97–104.

Moraga, Cherríe. *The Last Generation*. Boston: South End Press, 1993.

Moya, Paula M. L. *Learning from Experience: Minority Identities, Multicultural Struggles*. Berkeley: University of California Press, 2002.

Nevins, Joseph. *Operation Gatekeeper: The Rise of the "Illegal Alien" and the Making of the U.S.–Mexico Boundary*. New York: Routledge, 2002.

Rimmon-Kenan, Shlomith. *A Glance beyond Doubt: Narration, Representation, Subjectivity*. Columbus: Ohio State University Press, 1996.

Saldívar-Hull, Sonia. *Feminism on the Border: Chicana Gender Politics and Literature*. Berkeley: University of California Press, 2000.

Schmidt Camacho, Alicia. *Migrant Imaginaries: Latino Cultural Politics in the U.S.-Mexico Borderlands*. New York: New York University Press, 2008.

Shea, Anne. "'Don't let them make you feel you did a crime': Immigration Law, Labor Rights, and Farmworker Testimony." *MELUS* 28, no. 1 (2003): 123–144.

Sohn, Stephen Hong. "Yellow Peril Cyborg: Techno-Orientalism in the Futuristic Borderlands of Alejandro Morales's *The Rag Doll Plagues*." Modern Language Association Annual Conference, Chicago, Illinois, December 2007. Author's private collection.

Viramontes, Helena María. "The Cariboo Café." In *The Moths and Other Stories*, 65–82. Houston, TX: Arte Público Press, 1985.

———. "'Nopalitos': The Making of Fiction (testimonio)." In *Breaking Boundaries: Latina Writing and Critical Readings*, edited by Asunción Horno-Delgado et al., 33–38. Amherst: University of Massachusetts Press, 1989.

———. *Under the Feet of Jesus*. New York: Dutton, 1995.

———. "Interview: Helena María Viramontes." By Gabriella Gutiérrez y Muhs. In *Communal Feminisms: Chicanas, Chilenas, and Cultural Exile: Theorizing the Space of Exile, Class, and Identity*, edited by Gabriella Gutiérrez y Muhs, 123–137. Lanham, MD: Lexington Books, 2007.

4

The Women in East Los Angeles

Gender and the City in *Their Dogs Came with Them*

JUANITA HEREDIA

AS A PIONEER AUTHOR OF CHICANA literature who emerged in the 1980s, Helena María Viramontes received critical attention for her collection of short fiction, *The Moths and Other Stories* (1985) and the novel *Under the Feet of Jesus* (1995). Although she has written about multifaceted aspects of living in the United States, in both rural and urban America, she cements her reputation as an urban feminist writer with her groundbreaking novel *Their Dogs Came with Them* (2007).[1] She represents Chicanas/os coming of age and surviving social inequalities in East Los Angeles in the 1960s in the midst of the Chicano movement, the Chicano Moratorium, and the Vietnam War. While these historical events are recorded in official discourse, Viramontes focuses on the experiences of the youth, particularly women, who must confront limitations at home as well as discrimination in society at large, owing to the racial hostility affecting their neighborhood.[2] In *Their Dogs Came with Them*, she further intervenes in the critical discourses of Chicano cultural nationalism and

metropolitan neocolonialism by recentering the urban experiences
of female adolescents to demonstrate the effects of modernization
and urban restructuring on gender.[3] She responds to the hegemonic
forces threatening the welfare of the neighborhood, East Los Angeles, in which she grew up, by probing into the race relationships
between Chicanos and Anglo-Americans who dominate the police
force, the legal system, and urban planning (real estate) to resusci-
tate the role of young women in the community. In doing so, Viramontes becomes a significant and necessary contemporary writer
who demystifies questions regarding urban crime and cultural wars
to better understand young women of color in the city. In recaptur-
ing East Los Angeles in the first decade of the twenty-first century,
this Chicana author participates in a critical dialogue with a host
of Latina/o writers who are concerned with the changing urban
demographics of their respective cities because many ethnic populations in the United States and globally are increasingly migrating *to*
and *within* cities to find a home and a sense of community that may
not be possible elsewhere.[4]

In the interview "Praying for Knowledge" (2000), Viramontes
shares initial thoughts on the writing of the novel *Their Dogs Came
with Them* by comparing the colonization of the Aztecs in Mexico
in the sixteenth century with the struggles of Chicanas/os in East
Los Angeles in the 1960s. She reflects:

> At first I wanted to write about the colonized imagination—how
> we have learned to hate ourselves as a people so much that we
> kill one another, as in gang violence. This is the basic premise.
> I felt that I had to excavate the history of colonization. The
> book starts out with an epigram from Miguel Portillo's *The Bro-
> ken Spears: The Aztec Account of the Conquest of México* and the
> whole idea of dogs, how the Spaniards have brought in these
> dogs and trained them to rip flesh. I can unravel the violence
> that perpetrates it and the ambiance that perpetrates it. I can
> go back to the sixties. It deals with a lost community divided by
> freeways. It deals with fragmentation of the self and society. (154)

In order to understand Viramontes's ideas on the "colonized imagination" and its ramifications, she appropriately refers to the colonial

legacy of the Spanish Conquest and its influence on the Aztecs, the indigenous population who ruled over a vast empire, stretching through much of what is present-day central and southern Mexico, until the sixteenth century. By alluding to the Spanish Conquest, she implies that the consequences of this invasion have continued in the *mestizaje* (hybrid ethnic and racial mixing) of the descendants, Chicanos/Mexican Americans, as they interact with Anglo-American authorities in East Los Angeles, the largest neighborhood of people of Mexican descent in the United States.[5] She astutely draws parallels between the Aztecs and Spaniards, who brought dogs to control their captives, and Chicanos and Anglo-Americans, who also use dogs to control the community of East Los Angeles during a rabies outbreak in the 1960s in the novel. Because the Spaniards used dogs to conquer the Aztecs, Viramontes is preoccupied with the psychological as well as the physical aspect of domination over a community, a phenomenon she views as leading to the "fragmentation of the self and society." In her novel, Viramontes further comments on the colonial effects of violence on the containment of women's bodies and minds in both private and public spheres to demonstrate that gender does matter as it intersects with surviving in a city plagued by injustices against Chicanas/os.

Modernity, Geography, and Los Angeles in the 1960s

In *Their Dogs Came with Them*, Viramontes reconfigures the paradigms of colonization in East Los Angeles in the 1960s to show the contradictions of modernity and "progress" as far as Chicanas/os are concerned. In an epigram at the beginning of her novel, she cites Miguel León-Portilla: "Their dogs came with them, running ahead of the column. They raised their muzzles high; they lifted their muzzles to the wind. They raced on before with saliva dripping from their jaws." While the Spanish conquerors brought dogs with them in the colonial period, Viramontes suggests that the police in Los Angeles represent the new conquerors in the 1960s who bring their dogs to control Chicanas/os. Viramontes draws attention to the powerful image of the dogs to critique the unrecognized abuse by police authority and, by extension, the legal system that the East Los Angeles community must respect and obey despite its contradictory role in using violence against them. She further unveils the hypocrisy of the law that should defend Chicanas/os and Mexicans in East Los Angeles but that in reality criminalizes rather than protects them. Thus, Viramontes insinuates that Chicanos and Mexicans must become conscientious subjects of change to empower themselves through their own grassroots organizations because institutions of authority have neglected to care about the people whom they claim to defend.[6] In the surveillance of the community, the officers use dogs to control the residents of East Los Angeles in a derogatory manner. Viramontes critiques this form of dehumanization in society because it is another form of colonizing residents in their own neighborhood.[7] Urban scholar Ed Soja notes, "Los Angeles, after a long history of racist administration, zoning, and violence, had become one of the most segregated cities in the country; its mayor, police chief, and dominant newspaper had given sufficient indications that this tradition of recalcitrant racism was still flourishing in the centers of political power" ("Los Angeles," 430). Los Angeles continues to live its violent legacy beyond the 1960s.

In the larger scheme of modernization, Los Angeles emerges as a major metropolis in the 1950s with the construction of freeways, which affects the social and economic inequalities in different ethnic neighborhoods in the city during this time. Historian Ricardo Romo states:

> In the late 1950s the massive construction of freeways linking the Anglo suburban communities with the central business core began. High overpasses and expansive six-lane freeways crisscrossed the east side. Thousands of residents from Boyle Heights, Lincoln Heights, City Terrace, and surrounding neighborhoods were relocated. The freeways divided the neighborhoods without consideration for the residents' loyalties to churches, schools, businesses, or family. (170)

Similar to the Aztecs who were exploited by the Spaniards who removed them from political power and forced them to work for their benefit in the sixteenth century, Chicanas/os had to yield their freedom by abiding by a new urban restructuring implemented by Anglo-Americans that at times resulted in a removal from their homes.[8] Like Romo, Viramontes underscores the physical impact of freeways on the Chicano community in East Los Angeles. She "excavates" the ruins of East Los Angeles by drawing attention to how larger city planners' decisions affected a marginalized community "divided by freeways." Critic Raúl Villa also illustrates how the geographical transformation of neighborhoods like East Los Angeles has converted Los Angeles into an "expressway metropolis" in the twentieth century (84).

In *Their Dogs Came with Them*, Viramontes responds to the modernizing efforts by urban developers who built freeways to make Los Angeles a premier city of the twentieth century. By transforming the geography of East Los Angeles, Chicanos/Mexicans were displaced from their homes in the barrio, a phenomenon that affected the stability of families, both immigrants and long-time residents, through historical dislocation.[9] More importantly, she considers the reasons neighborhoods such as these were targeted rather than, say, the more privileged middle-class suburban ones in Los Angeles. Viramontes captures the mood and ambience of this historical period because she exposes the contradictions of the police and the law in targeting the community of East Los Angeles that became alienated. Viramontes affirms, "The isolation bred a sense of being immigrants in our own land and a self-hatred, boiling over into a brown-on-brown violence of major and cruel proportions" (Shea, 38). If freeways were built at the expense of dividing Chicano/Mexican communities, city authorities should be held accountable for the psychological and physical disruption and chaos that in reality victimized the youth, especially women, and should help resolve the conflicts that ensue as a consequence.

In *Their Dogs Came with Them*, Viramontes illustrates how policies imposed on the East Los Angeles community by city officials limit them as well and may lead to confusing situations. For example, curfews are implemented for residents living in designated areas of East Los Angeles to search for supposed "dogs with rabies." Thus, residents are prohibited from roaming the streets freely from eight in the evening until six in the morning. When the Quarantine Authority forces the residents to carry a strict identification code, they are further inconvenienced because it is not easy accessing this form of identity card. At one point in the novel, a Spanish-surnamed officer, Rodríguez, almost arrests one of the main protagonists, Ermila, because she is roaming the streets at night past curfew time without an identification card. He also suspects erroneously that she takes drugs, unaware that she has a legitimate excuse for being out late (293).

In addition to spatial and temporal limitations, Chicanas/os did not have the freedom to enjoy their neighborhood in East Los Angeles as they wished owing to urban restructuring placed upon them in the name of modernity and "progress." At one point in the novel, the narrator fast-forwards and accelerates to the future: "Ten years later the child becomes a young woman who will recognize the invading engines of the Quarantine Authority helicopters because their whir of blades above the roof of her home, their earth-rattling explosive motors, will surpass in volume the combustion of engines driving the bulldozer tractors, slowly, methodically unspooling the six freeways" (12). Viramontes compares two kinds of noises over time in the life of one of the protagonists, emanating from helicopters for surveillance and bulldozer tractors for freeway construction, to demonstrate how these elements are the new "arms" of "modernization" in the twentieth century. Even though the invasion of freeway construction began in the 1950s, city officials have not stopped there, because they must also introduce the Quarantine Authority to disrupt the community ten years later. These modern devices not only fragment the daily lives of the residents in East Los Angeles but also catch them in the frenzy of imprisonment that does not enable them to live freely. Chicanas/os become prisoners in their own homes owing to the invasion and manipulation of modern technology by the forces of urban developers. Thus, Viramontes critiques urban restructuring as an outcome of modernization because the residents of East Los Angeles must sacrifice their time and space, let alone displacement from their homes, and undergo a process of geographical and psychological colonization. As Raúl Villa argues in *Barrio-Logos*, the process of disempowerment or "ruins" that Chicanas/os and Mexicans experienced resulted from the founding of Anglo Los Angeles that moved forward with railways and then freeways.[10]

working-class Chicanas/os of East Los Angeles.[13] However, she expands the critical conversation to include the role of young women, not necessarily the heroines nor the political activists in the Chicano movement, but rather the ordinary girls who had to follow orders at home and pay for the consequences of choices made by others in the community and society at large. Viramontes explores the cracks and crevices that often elide our attention because Chicanas' rights and agency are at stake in a city where they should feel protected, not persecuted. She probes into the other side of this social movement, the youth who are literally and symbolically lost in the community, not of their own free will, but as a result of larger machinations related to urban development placed upon them. Viramontes also considers what constitutes family, community, and gender in a moment when one's neighborhood is being invaded physically and disrupted psychologically by outsiders.

In *Their Dogs Came with Them,* Viramontes portrays the lives of four distinct females of Mexican descent coming of age in East Los Angeles from 1960 to 1970. Although she focuses on these female teenagers as protagonists, she does not abandon the rest of the Chicano and Mexican community (e.g., brothers, fathers, grandparents, friends), because they are interlinked with the main characters in important ways. Viramontes further delves into the situation of the women, who form the backbone of this community but are rarely acknowledged in relevant history, literary, and urban studies criticism. She addresses gender through questions of sexuality and poverty to understand what it means to be female and young during this period of disruptions in the 1960s. She addresses the quotidian reality of young female adolescents in the city in the present and the future rather than dwelling on the past.[14] Viramontes also includes a wide spectrum of women in the community by insisting that young Chicanas are not necessarily in all-female gang groups nor obedient daughters nor Catholic; rather, they form part of a diversity of gender identities and social groups *within* East Los Angeles. By portraying an array of female (and male) characters, Viramontes speaks to the complexity of cultural values of different women in the transforming community of East Los Angeles, even within the same generation and gender.

The narrative structure of *Their Dogs Came with Them* is divided into five main sections, each containing chapters dedicated to one or all of the four main protagonists—Turtle, Ermila, Tranquilina, and Ana—told by an omniscient narrator. Viramontes situates the narrative in the present of the 1960–1970 decade with flashbacks to the past and forwarded scenes to the future (e.g., thirty years later). Except for Ana and Tranquilina, the female characters rarely interact with one another, although they may coincide at times spatially in the novel. As Viramontes experiments with geographical fragmentations that mirror the transforming urban neighborhood of East Los Angeles in the city, she consistently shifts temporalities in the narrative to illustrate the growth of four main female characters from childhood to adolescence, from innocence to sexual awakening.

Viramontes further considers how these young female characters negotiate gender and the city when few options are available to them. She clearly shows how the neighborhood's fragmentation, "divided into freeways," may also serve as a metaphor for families' separation (divided by deaths or departures) in a rapidly changing urban environment. As seen with each main character, parents leave, dic, or become embedded in a faith that no longer protects their children. On a microcosmic scale, Viramontes traces how family breakups affect individuals to understand the motives behind the younger generation's actions (e.g., shoplifting, breaking curfew, rebellion). She provides a lens to illustrate how the main female characters experience some form of physical, psychological, or sexual harassment at the hands of strangers as well as family members. Since the narrative chronicles their teenage years in an urban environment, the young women must mature rapidly, leaving behind innocence in order to survive without the guidance of parents or with the overprotection of the elderly. Rather than present idealized models of femininity or archetypes, Viramontes prefers to explore how each female character responds to her particular urban experiences to avoid the loneliness of living in a metropolis, especially when their families no longer have a united front. Thus, the youngsters seek a sense of community. In the adolescent years of the young women, Viramontes chronicles how their lives become more complicated and entangled like freeways, owing to patriarchal and social limitations. The female protagonists may partake in sexual activities and look for other forms of independence as they search for their identity and a place to belong. Although the main characters are culturally Chicana, each female teenager contributes a different aspect of the urban experience, gender, and family values in East Los Angeles in *Their Dogs Came with Them*.

Real Women, Sex, and the City

In the character of Turtle (Antonia) Gamboa, an androgynous figure in the novel, Viramontes exemplifies how one young woman must negotiate her transgender identity because she dresses like a tomboy in order to belong to a Chicano male gang, the McBride Boys (rivals with the Lote M Boys), to project a specific public image. Yet, biologically, she is female. Because she lost her father and mother, she can only rely on her brother, Luis Lil Lizard, who is already a member of the McBride Boys. He does not have to worry about acceptance by his peers because he is male. However, Turtle must transcend the boundaries of her gender identity by following rules created by the patriarchal members of this circle to prove herself to them. She must abide by certain rituals that involve using violence to display physical strength and obedience. Rather than be protective of her, the male members, including her brother Lil Lizard, actually make her undergo physical trials like eating garbage that humiliate her. In fact, her brother teases her at one point and claims that she moves as slowly as a turtle, her symbolic nickname. Unlike the other female characters in the novel, Turtle views joining the young group of men as "unquestioned loyalty that only *familia* could understand" (158, emphasis mine). She also shaves her head to prove her unflinching commitment to the McBride Boys with whom she believes she will find comfort, solace, and a sense of community.

Because the parents are physically absent by the time Turtle and her brother Luis are teenagers, Turtle loses faith in depending on the network of a close-knit biological family, which she substitutes for with the McBride Boys. Interestingly, the names turtle and lizard refer to creatures that are amphibians, with the ability to live on land or water, mobile experiences similar to the siblings, who must move between the home and the streets of East Los Angeles in a precarious situation. In one instance, Turtle shoplifts out of necessity because there is no food at home and she is hungry. When Turtle and her brother were children, Turtle was chased by the bagman at the Val U Mini Mart. After they were caught stealing, the bagman took advantage of the situation and groped her, realizing she was a girl, after he recovered the stolen goods (24). She feels physically, if not sexually, harassed by this incident. Viramontes reconsiders the "real" crime, the hunger of the youth and police harassment of a youth as a result of an indifferent capitalist society resulting in a petty theft for the sake of survival.

The consequences of a young girl joining a male gang are not without further complications due to her gender. In order to be accepted as a *carnal* (a kind of homeboy, not just the literal meaning of brother) by the McBride Boys, Turtle must conform to their rules, including the peer pressure of taking drugs, which naturally alters her state of mind. For example, Turtle attacks Nacho with a screwdriver at the end of the novel. Unfortunately, she suffers in this instance because the male members of the McBride Boys abandon her in a time of need and allow her to take the fall for a crime, the senseless beating of an innocent boy, that was initially instigated by them. Clearly, Viramontes critiques this incident that demonstrates how women are abused physically and mentally by Chicano males at home and by the Anglo-American police in society.

As for the rebellious teenager, Ermila Zumaya represents another female character growing up in East Los Angeles whose "Communist" parents abandoned her to foster homes during childhood. Although her grandmother rescues her as a seven-year-old, Ermila must learn how to negotiate the domestic duties and obedience to the elderly at home with her desire to live and act with more freedom, like her female peers, in public. By belonging to a group of female teenagers, Mousie, Rini, and Lollie, she does not feel the pressure to confront the rituals that Turtle does in terms of a patriarchal gang. The young women bond and are loyal to one another as if they were sisters, although they are not related biologically. Unlike Turtle's situation, Ermila and her friends prove their fidelity in different ways because they look after one another in times of need. For example, when the girlfriends learn that Jan, the boyfriend of Rini's mother, abuses and molests their girlfriend Rini, who is like a sister, they meet clandestinely to plan revenge against him for taking advantage of one of their own (56, 178, 187, 196–198, 285).

The narrator says, "The girlfriends fought against their individual doubts and concentrated on one communal goal. Lollie repeated instructions and then they separated, holding two steel wool pads each, outlaw indias about to circle the wagon train" (198). Rather than humiliate one another as the McBride Boys do, the girlfriends support one another to resist patriarchal violence to survive in the city because they know that they cannot depend on adults at home or in public.

Viramontes also examines mixed feelings that Chicanas experience regarding their sexuality. Because Ermila is an adolescent in full bloom, the grandparents keep a close vigilance over her by monitoring her time outside the household. She appears to get into trouble when she meets up with her unreliable and immature boyfriend Alfonso, also a member of the McBride Boys, whose father abandoned their home when he was younger because he could not hold a job and whose mother had to work two jobs to make ends meet. Even though Ermila engages in sex with Alfonso, she reflects, "Like a border crossing, sex promised a different, uplifting life and yet all she encountered was intolerable guilt, a filthy feeling that bathing couldn't cleanse and the fear that her body would someday call for mutiny" (74). While her Catholic grandmother attempts to save her from sin by hammering a crucifix in her room, Ermila wonders why she rebels the way she does, not completely understanding her own behavior. Even though she wishes to feel liberated by having sexual relations with Alfonso, she in reality can only experience the *illusion* of such a feeling, for she is more of a trophy girlfriend, an object of his affection, than a full-fledged respected human being.

In the Zumaya household, Viramontes not only exposes the emptiness of practicing the rigid codes of traditional Catholicism by the grandmother to rescue Ermila, another "fallen woman," but also critiques the gender inequality passed down to a younger generation that leaves women further disempowered. In the character of the grandmother, Viramontes subtly alludes to the Spaniards, because the elderly lady brings a watchdog into the household *to protect* Ermila from escaping through her window at night, not realizing that the dog can "rip flesh." She does not wish that her granddaughter follow the rebellious footsteps of her mother, who could not be controlled and consequently neglected her duties as a mother. Ironically, the dog bites and hurts Ermila, who initially wonders if this dog belongs to the police. Instead of being protected, Ermila worries that she may contract an illness, which alludes to the way the Aztecs died from diseases when the Spaniards settled in the Americas. On another note, the grandmother is also critical of Ermila's black and coarse hair (similar to the Aztecs), which she inherited from the father's side, that she eventually forces her granddaughter to cut to civilize her. This violation upon Ermila's body represents a desire to control both gender and race at the expense of mutilating an individual's freedom. Interestingly, Ermila, who is apt at geography and math, works part-time by doing the accounting at Salas Used Cars, which means there is more to her than a body. She proves that she has a mind and has the potential to become financially independent as an adult, which means she will break with social and economic subjugation owing to her gender. She proves to be intelligent, even though she had undergone the humiliation of being diagnosed deaf as a child, which shows the lack of care and concern on the part of the educational system.

Viramontes does not refrain from portraying the inequality of sexual power within a family structure because she is well aware that young women can fall victim to predatory advances from older male relatives. For example, Ermila holds an unusual relationship with her peer cousin Nacho from Mexico, who appears to help her in times of need, but who also takes advantage of the fact that she is a younger woman and sometimes expects "sexual favors" in return, a harassment of gender and age. Viramontes also critiques the fact that older relatives like the grandmother are not always the best to judge how to keep close watch over female adolescents, especially if they give free rein to a male member like Nacho, turning a blind eye to his gender privilege as a male, another contradiction of the male protector in the family, which signals female autonomy and self-reliance.

In the character of Tranquilina, the daughter of missionaries, Viramontes draws attention to the changing role of cultural identity through organized religion and migrations. Tranquilina's family migrates between East Los Angeles, California, and Cuero, Texas, to work and spread the word of their Protestant religion. She remembers two things about her family's travels in her childhood: heat and prayers, which may allude to the boundary between hell and heaven. Although the novel begins with the daughter and the mother in the present asking for food and preparing it for the homeless (in the rain, crossing the freeways), Viramontes interjects flashbacks to how Tranquilina's parents met. Her mother had a difficult labor and pregnancy in East Los Angeles, but if God saved her child, she bequeathed it to Him as if it were a sacrificial lamb. The father, who is a pastor, spreads the word of his Church. He repeats the verse, "Somos ovejas en el valle de los lobos," (86), which translates as "We are sheep in the valley of the wolves." Undoubtedly, he is aware of the vulnerable state in which people may find themselves. Yet, Viramontes critiques the father's blindness to his daughter's precarious situation when she is sexually assaulted, making violence on women's bodies a major concern. Furthermore, Viramontes calls attention to the blind followers in faith, symbolized by the sheep, and the corruption and greed of wolves, another allusion to those of power in an organized Protestant religion introduced by Anglo-Americans. Of the three main female characters, Tranquilina is also the one who appears the most innocent, like a sheep. When she observes some children playing, she reflects on the importance of returning to Los Angeles. She says,

> Against the concrete graffiti walls, sunlight broke and the shadow of the tree canopy eclipsed the old man's face. A group of kids appeared in the distance and began a stickball game in a schoolyard. The chatter of a home run shattered the monotony. The old soldier smiled. When she had finished the prayer, Tranquilina stroked his liver-spotted hand. She commented on the shouting accusations of a foul ball. They were *angels*, these kids. Tranquilina now understood why Mama wanted to return to the Eastside. This is why their ministry returned. The *angels* were never lacking here, and thus explained the name of the city. (37, emphasis mine)

Tranquilina tends to see the good nature and angelic side in humans, especially the youth, and she associates this feeling with the Spanish name of the city, Los Angeles, translated as "The Angels," a place the family must also return to because it is their home. The name of the city is also symbolic of angels living in a kind of heaven, but one located on urban streets, facing quotidian challenges, in East Los Angeles. This is a positive aspect that she has taken from her parents' religious influence. But then she has a heart-wrenching violent experience that affects her outlook on life.

In the character of Tranquilina, Viramontes addresses how gender and religion are negotiated in the novel. When mother and daughter are working in the fields in Texas, the teenager Tranquilina is sexually assaulted by the son-in-law of a rancher who owns the property in Cuero, Texas, where her family was preaching (208). Rather than think of herself as a victim of this brutal attack, she can only think of finding her underwear so as not to disappoint her parents in being a perfect, virginal daughter (214–215). In this case, Viramontes critiques institutional religion to delineate how gender plays a factor in determining a woman's fate.[15] As she grows older, Tranquilina gradually has a change in outlook regarding the ministry of her parents (97). She no longer believes in the ministry's faith to serve people, but rather in that of individuals such as the youth or "angels" who live in Los Angeles to take control of their destiny. Viramontes exposes the hypocrisy of organized religion and the blindness of the older generation because she prefers to believe in the personal spirituality of individuals, a form of agency that enables women as well as men to move forward with their lives rather than rely blindly on others waiting to help them. This is not to say that Viramontes rejects religion altogether, because it does unite the community to some extent in moments of celebration as well as crisis, but rather she alerts women to raise their consciousness and to take control of their actions to avoid victimization. She also urges individuals to be more critical within their belief system to improve their lives in the present, to move beyond the past into the future, especially in a city such as Los Angeles. Historically, according to George Sánchez, "Religion, one might say, became ethnically stratified in Los Angeles as a result of the unmet spiritual needs of the Mexican immigrant population" (167). One might note that gender further added to the social hierarchy of religion, where women were rarely given the chance to voice their concerns or defend themselves.

Viramontes portrays the friendship between Tranquilina and Ana Brady as a form of sisterhood because both young women must care for other individuals, be they family or not. While Tranquilina helps her mother care for the homeless through their Church, Ana must take care of her mentally disturbed brother, Ben Brady, who suffered a terrible accident in his childhood and who feels guilty about the death of a little boy, knowing that he was not trying to save him, as the media reported (110–114). Abused and victimized by his Anglo father during his childhood, Ben also suffers social problems because he does not always fit in at school because his peers view him as a sell-out due to his lack of a Spanish surname, Brady, symbolic of his mestizo background, blending his Mexican American and Anglo heritages. He also has mixed feelings about where his ideological loyalties lie, about whether or not to join "the planned student walkout at Garfield High School" in the 1960s. All these experiences result in confusion and neurological disorders throughout his life to the extent that he is hospitalized. What is interesting about this situation is that Ana must undertake the roles of sister, mother, and guardian while she, herself, is only an adolescent. She functions as a caretaker, a kind of *curandera* (healer), and the backbone, who must hold her brother and herself together in the absence of their parents.[16] She is also the sibling who must work to support herself and her brother. Since the absent parents disrupt the traditional family unit, Ana and Ben must rely on themselves to support one another and survive during moments of chaos in their community in the 1960s.

Even though each female protagonist leads a life independent of the others in the novel, Viramontes gives the narrative a cohesive unity at the end where their lives intersect. Although the circumstances result in tragedy in the senseless beatings of youth such as Nacho, in the conclusion of the novel, the women for the most part survive and affirm their stand against police brutality. Ermila, Ana, and Tranquilina take the initiative to search for a man at the Greyhound Bus station to protect him from violence. Ermila wishes to warn her cousin Nacho to run away from her jealous boyfriend, Alfonso, who will beat him with the aid of the McBride Boys gang, including Turtle, though she is unaware of her actions, as she is overdosed on drugs. In the meantime, Ana and Tranquilina are looking for Ben, who was in his apartment before he went missing and may hurt himself or others since he has neurological disorders. The consequences of these searches are urgent not only because the young men are beaten but also because the police once again interfere and threaten to shoot Chicana/o youth. In the end, Nacho and Turtle die. Yet, at this moment, Tranquilina has an epiphany as she represents a voice of empowerment for young Chicanas/os in the community. As she tries to heal one of the boys' heads, she screams at the officers, "*We'rrrre not dogggs!* Tranquilina roared in the direction of the shooters. Stop shooting, we are not dogs!" (324). While these youngsters must die physically, Viramontes is careful to suggest that a spiritual death may also be detrimental to the youth, especially if they do not have a sense of belonging to any community, as their lives have been fragmented by families and freeways, literally and symbolically. Rather than remain silent and obedient to patriarchal authorities, women like Ermila, Tranquilina, and Ana step to the forefront to defend their community by overcoming obstacles in their personal lives and thus resisting (or decolonizing) the legacy of the Anglo-American "invasion" of their neighborhood and homes.

Because *Their Dogs Came with Them* has the potential to become a narrative of social determinism, where humans fall prey to extenuating circumstances in their environment, Viramontes brings that fatalistic view to a halt and turns the reader's eyes to the inequalities caused by the institutions that should uphold the law, as she has done in previous works that take place in the city. She redefines criminality and gender in an urban context by shifting the blame from the victims to that of the hegemonic forces of power such as the law, the police force, and urban development. She not only illustrates the significant and unacknowledged role that the women in the East Los Angeles community play but also provides a feminist lens to judge the underlying causes and effects that lead to violence against bodies, minds, and souls of Chicanas and the youth. Critic Dionne Espinoza further notes that "a gendering of Chicana/o youth culture in Eastside from 1960 to 1970 deepens our understanding of these years" (101). By the 1960s, Chicanos and Mexican immigrants refused to be pacified by Anglo-Americans as they began to affirm their identity in the urban Chicano movement, especially in East Los Angeles. By writing about this community, Viramontes has said that it is her form of prayer or requiem.[17] She not only advocates a process of healing the mind as well as the body but also engages in what Kenyan author Ngũgĩ wa Thiong'o has called "decolonizing" the mind to liberate the spirit of a colonized people.[18] For example, even though Chicanos/Mexican Americans may be "free citizens" with equal access to education and other public services according to the American constitution, they are not treated as such as a group of people when it comes to interaction with the dominant Anglo-American culture. In *Their Dogs Came with Them*, Viramontes suggests that it is just as crucial to liberate the mind and spirit as one's geographical space or neighborhood to find a sense of home and community. Only then will the decolonial process truly begin for both men and women, in the city and beyond.

Although she took more than twenty years to write this novel, Viramontes has left her urban legacy in *Their Dogs Came with Them* in the American literary tradition.[19] With this novel, Viramontes joins a literary chorus of other Latina/o writers who feel strongly about representing Latinos/as' experiences of gender and the city. These urban narratives serve as fine examples of the literary and ideological connection between Chicano/US Latino authors and other modern writers who are dialoguing across cultures on the urban transformations as a consequence of globalization and transnational migrations. Thus, *Their Dogs Came with Them* is a milestone in representing gender and the city in multiethnic American urban literature.

Notes

1. In "Requiem for the Poor," her first short fiction for which she won a prize from California State University, Los Angeles, Viramontes begins to represent the concerns of Chicanas/os in East Los Angeles. Similar to *Their Dogs Came with Them*, this story is a structurally fragmented piece that illustrates the obstacles (i.e., patriarchy, poverty, discrimination) that several characters must endure in a city context. This short narrative may also be considered foundational in the development of her urban concerns in literature. Interestingly enough, "Requiem for the Poor" was highly influenced by Mexican author Juan Rulfo's novel *Pedro Páramo* (1959), which addresses the social inequalities in small towns in Mexico after the Mexican Revolution. Viramontes has stated that Rulfo was an important influence on the form of "Requiem for the Poor" aesthetically ("East of Downtown and Beyond," 171). She has also been involved in various aspects of the literary process that have shaped her urban perspectives in writing. For example, she was a founding editor of *XhismeArte* (also known as *ChismeArte*) (1978–1981), a Latino literary magazine formed

in Los Angeles for which she contributed to a special issue on the bicenten-
nial anniversary of the city, "Homenaje a la Ciudad de Los Angeles 1781–1981"
(Los Angeles Latino Writers Association). She also helped initiate the Latina/o
Writers Association, a writing workshop run by Latino artists and writers in Los
Angeles that began in the 1970s. Evidently, Viramontes has developed an urban
sensibility in her literary endeavors over a thirty-year period (1976–2007).

   · 2. Scholars such as Alarcón, Castillo, Harlow, Rodríguez, Saldívar, and
Saldívar-Hull have written mainly about the two short stories "The Moths"
and "The Cariboo Café," both of which form part of the collection *The Moths
and Other Stories* (1985) by Viramontes. These short stories address initial questions about the urban experience that are further developed in *Their Dogs Came
with Them*.

    3. "Urban restructuring" is a term used by scholars of urban studies such as
Soja ("Los Angeles"), who refers to the dislocation and relocation of residents,
voluntary or not, owing to urban development.

    4. Among contemporary Latina/o authors who engage urban experiences
in their novels in the twenty-first century, consider works such as Sandra Cisneros's *Caramelo*, Junot Díaz's *The Brief Wondrous Life of Oscar Wao*, Angie
Cruz's *Soledad*, Achy Obejas's *Days of Awe*, Ernesto Quiñónez's *Chango's Fire*,
and Héctor Tobar's *The Barbarian Nurseries*.

    5. In chapter twelve, "The Rise of the Second Generation" in *Becoming
Mexican American*, Sánchez discusses how Mexican American children are living out their parents' dreams by "making the best of opportunities provided
by the United States" (263). This Mexican American generation is also the one
that begins to outnumber that of the Mexican immigrant one.

    6. Rocco provides testimonies given by East Los Angeles residents and
workers who claim their right to live and work in the city that they have made
their home in response to the geographical changes of metropolitan Los Angeles. Also, in *Racism on Trial*, Haney López exposes the institutional racism
that has plagued two important historical events involving Mexican Americans
and the legal system in Los Angeles: the Sleepy Lagoon case in the 1940s and
the arrest of thirteen youths during the walkouts in the Chicano movement in
the 1960s.

    7. In "Los Angeles and the Future of Urban Cultures," Villa and Sánchez
discuss the effects of globalization on Chicano and other ethnic communities in
Los Angeles, which they argue is a new form of colonization.

    8. In *East Los Angeles*, Romo chronicles the settlement of Los Angeles by
Spaniards since 1781 and then Mexicans when they were the majority with political and cultural currency until the American conquest in 1848. Due to industri-
alization and urban growth in the late nineteenth and early twentieth centuries,
however, Mexicans in Los Angeles were slowly selling their land to groups of
European American migrants making the westward journey from the east and
Midwest, and thus they lost much political and social clout in the process. By
demonstrating that Los Angeles has always been a home to Mexicans and their

Mexican American descendants, Romo questions why they should be regarded as outsiders or "foreigners."

9. José Saldívar claims that in the short fiction "The Cariboo Café" "for Viramontes the postmodern as it is in Los Angeles is a fully planned strategy, the social and psychic effects of which are historical dislocation and cultural relocation" (102).

10. See Soja's chapter on "Taking Los Angeles Apart" to understand how "an urban cartography of power and political praxis" can shape the urban geography and influence the fragmentation of the city (235). In addition, the social and physical intervention of the Quarantine Authority with helicopters and choppers in *Their Dogs Came with Them* is reminiscent of the section "Site for New Housing" in Viramontes's short fiction "Requiem for the Poor."

11. East Los Angeles used to have many more cemeteries, but with the freeway construction in the twentieth century, some were destroyed. Viramontes is at work on a new novel, *The Cemetery Boys*, set in 1945, that captures the period before urban restructuring (Shea, 42).

12. In the critically acclaimed independent film *Real Women Have Curves* (2002), director Patricia Cardoso portrays the disparity between different generations of Mexican and Chicana women who work in a sewing factory in East Los Angeles in more contemporary times. Only one Latina character works in an upwardly mobile job as the manager of a corporation that oversees the sewing factory. However, one does not see collaborative efforts between Chicana, Latina, and Mexican women of different social classes. Also, the younger Chicana daughter must commute long-distance to her high school in Beverly Hills from East Los Angeles, which implies that the educational school system in her own neighborhood is not competitive enough to enable her to enter a university of her choice.

13. In *Their Dogs Came with Them*, Viramontes dialogues with a host of historians and urban studies scholars regarding the evolving representation of East Los Angeles in the twentieth century. If León-Portilla's *Broken Spears* refers to the indigenous heritage of Chicanos/Mexicans, Viramontes draws comparisons between the colonial period of Aztec/Spanish hostility and Chicano/Anglo police brutality in a rapidly transforming East Los Angeles. She is also in conversation with historian Romo, who observes that cities like Los Angeles in California were initially settled by Spaniards who colonized the indigenous population, first physically and then spiritually via conversion, as they settled missions in Los Angeles in the 1700s. In *City of Quartz*, Davis traces the displacement of the Mexican community in Los Angeles by Anglo-American migrations from the Midwest and East in the late 1800s (i.e., Charles Lummis and the *Los Angeles Times*), which resulted in the containment and marginalization of Chicano and other ethnic neighborhoods due to Anglo-American control of the economy and real estate to accommodate the growing Anglo-American suburban residents regardless of the growing Chicano/Mexican American population. Similarly, Viramontes critiques the consequences of

freeway construction and real estate on the Chicano community. George Sánchez's *Becoming Mexican American* examines the transformation of East Los Angeles from a primarily Mexican immigrant settlement after the Mexican Revolution of 1910 to that of Mexican Americana in the 1930s and 1940s period, when the Mexican American children outgrew their parents' generation and began to make civic demands for improved education, employment, health issues, and housing that culminated in the Chicano movement of the 1960s. In *Chicano! History of the Mexican American Civil Rights Movement*, Rosales chronicles the history of the student protest movement in East Los Angeles in the 1960s to capture quite dramatically an event that serves as a backdrop to Viramontes's ideological vision in *Their Dogs Came with Them*. In East Los Angeles in the 1960s, Chicano high school students participated in walkouts (or blowouts) to protest the quality of education and lack of curricular efforts on the part of an indifferent administration. The walkouts were the first significant urban struggle of the Chicano movement because they focused their attention on the Chicano youth living and working in the city who were no longer going to endure second-class treatment. Viramontes lived and witnessed many of these activities as a student at Garfield High School in East Los Angeles in the 1960s. Rather than glorify the Chicano movement, though, Viramontes shows the other side of the triumphs—displacement, containment, and discrimination of Chicana/o youth, especially the women in East Los Angeles—to understand the social reality of urban survival.

14. In *500 Years of Chicana History*, Martínez illustrates how young Chicanas participated in numerous social and political movements, from grassroots to institutional organizations in city spaces, to show their fight for gender and civic rights.

15. The independent film *Quinceañera*, directed by Richard Glatzer and Wash Westmoreland, also critiques the role of organized religion in controlling women's bodies and knowledge of sexuality. For instance, the father figure, also a pastor in the Protestant faith, blames rather than comforts his only daughter in a critical moment when she becomes pregnant unexpectedly, in defense of his religion.

16. Viramontes has portrayed the role of the *curandera* (healer), a recurring character, throughout her fiction. In "The Moths," the grandmother functions as the caretaker who looks after the rebellious granddaughter and heals her physical and emotional scars. Likewise, in *Under the Feet of Jesus*, the character of the mother Petra is the one who cares for those in need, regardless of whether they are her own biological children or not.

17. In the interview "Praying for Knowledge," Viramontes says, "If I did not have writing, I don't know what I would have done. It has really, really given me my prayer to the world" (154). Once again, the idea of a "requiem" may be connected to her first short fiction, "Requiem for the Poor," a kind of prayer for the struggling Chicanas/os in the city.

18. Thiong'o first develops his ideas on decolonization in his well-known book *Decolonising the Mind*, in the context of the postcolonial Kenyan period when the citizens are trying to liberate themselves from British control.

19. In Shea's "New Frontiers in Fiction," Viramontes explains why she took time to write *Their Dogs Came with Them*. She also discusses the difference of opinion she had with Pulitzer Prize–winning author Junot Díaz, with whom she shared an earlier draft of the novel upon her arrival at Cornell University where he was a graduate student in the MFA program in creative writing. In spite of his advice, Viramontes decided to keep the characters of the gang members (i.e., Turtle, Luis, and their friends) in her novel because, regardless of stereotypes in the media, they are part of the community. It should be noted that Díaz is one of the endorsers of her novel.

Works Cited

Alarcón, Norma. "Making 'Familia' from Scratch: Split Subjectivities in the Works of Helena María Viramontes and Cherríe Moraga." In *Chicana Creativity and Criticism: New Frontiers in American Literature*, edited by María Herrera-Sobek and Helena María Viramontes, 220–232. Albuquerque: University of New Mexico Press, 1996 [1987].

Castillo, Debra. "Helena María Viramontes (1954–)." In *Latino and Latina Writers, I: Introductory Essays, Chicano and Chicana Authors; II: Cuban and Cuban American Authors, Dominican and Other Authors, Puerto Rican Authors*, edited by Alan West-Durán, María Herrera-Sobek, and César A. Salgado, 549–568. New York: Scribner's, 2004.

Cisneros, Sandra. *Caramelo, o, Puro Cuento*. New York: Alfred Knopf, 2002.

Cruz, Angie. *Soledad*. New York: Simon and Schuster, 2001.

Davis, Mike. *City of Quartz: Excavating the Future in Los Angeles*. London: Verso, 1990.

Díaz, Junot. *The Brief Wondrous Life of Oscar Wao*. New York: Riverhead Hardcover, 2007.

Espinoza, Dionne. "'*Tanto Tiempo Disfrutamos . . .*': Revisiting the Gender and Sexual Politics of Chicana/o Youth Culture in East Los Angeles in the 1960s." In *Velvet Barrios: Popular Culture and Chicana/o Sexualities*, edited by Alicia Gaspar de Alba, 89–106. New York: Palgrave Macmillan, 2003.

Haney López, Ian F. *Racism on Trial: The Chicano Fight for Justice*. Cambridge, MA: Belknap Press of Harvard University Press, 2004.

Harlow, Barbara. "Sites of Struggle: Immigration, Deportation, Prison, and Exile." In *Criticism in the Borderlands: Studies in Chicano Literature, Culture and Ideology*, edited by Héctor Calderón and José David Saldívar, 149–163. Durham, NC: Duke University Press, 1991.

León-Portilla, Miguel. *The Broken Spears: The Aztec Account of the Conquest of Mexico*. Boston: Beacon Press, 2006.

Los Angeles Latino Writers Association, eds. "Homenaje a la Ciudad de Los Angeles 1781–1981: The Latino Experience of L.A." Special issue, *Revista XhismeArte*. Los Angeles, CA: XhismeArte/Popular Graphic, 1981.

Martínez, Elizabeth. *500 Years of Chicana History*. New Brunswick, NJ: Rutgers University Press, 2009.

Obejas, Achy. *Days of Awe*. New York: Ballantine Books, 2002.

Quinceañera. DVD. Directed by Richard Glatzer and Wash Westmoreland. Culver City, CA: Sony Pictures Classics, 2006.

Quiñónez, Ernesto. *Chango's Fire*. New York: Rayo Press, 2004.

Real Women Have Curves. DVD. Directed by Patricia Cardoso. United States: HBO Video, 2002.

Rocco, Raymond A. "Citizenship, Civil Society and the Latina/o City: Claiming Subaltern Spaces, Reframing the Public Sphere." In *Transnational Latina/o Communities: Politics, Processes and Cultures*, edited by Carlos G. Vélez-Ibáñez and Anna Sampaio, 273–292. New York: Rowman and Littlefield, 2002.

Rodríguez, Ana Patricia. "Refugees of the South: Central Americans in the U.S. Latino Imaginary." *American Literature* 73, no. 2 (June 2001): 387–412.

Romo, Ricardo. *East Los Angeles: History of a Barrio*. Austin: University of Texas Press, 1983.

Rosales, Arturo. *Chicano! The History of the Mexican American Civil Rights Movement*. Houston, TX: Arte Público Press, 1996.

Rulfo, Juan. *Pedro Páramo*. Translated by Lysander Kempe. New York: Grove Press, 1959.

Saldívar, José David. *Border Matters: Remapping American Cultural Studies*. Berkeley: University of California Press, 1997.

Saldívar-Hull, Sonia. *Feminism on the Border: Chicana Gender Politics and Literature*. Berkeley: University of California Press, 2000.

Sánchez, George. *Becoming Mexican American: Ethnicity, Culture and Identity in Chicano Los Angeles, 1900–1945*. Oxford: Oxford University Press, 1993.

Shea, Renee H. "New Frontiers in Fiction: A Profile of Helena María Viramontes." *Poets and Writers* (May/June 2007): 36–42.

Soja, Edward W. "Taking Los Angeles Apart: Towards a Postmodern Geography." In *Postmodern Geographies: The Reassertion of Space in Critical Social Theory*, edited by Edward W. Soja, 222–248. New York: Verso Press, 1989.

———. "Los Angeles, 1965–1992: From Crisis-Generated Restructuring to Restructuring Generated Crisis." In *The City: Los Angeles and Urban Theory at the End of the Twentieth Century*, edited by Scott J. Allen and Ed Soja, 426–462. Berkeley: University of California Press, 1996.

Thiong'o, Ngũgĩ wa. *Decolonising the Mind: The Politics of Language in African Literature*. London: J. Currey, 1986.

Tobar, Héctor. *The Barbarian Nurseries*. New York: Farrar, Straus & Giroux, 2011.

Villa, Raúl Homero. *Barrio-Logos: Space and Place in Urban Chicano Literature and Culture*. Austin: University of Texas Press, 2000.

Villa, Raúl, and George Sánchez, eds. "Los Angeles and the Future of Urban Cultures." Special issue, *American Quarterly*. Baltimore: John Hopkins University Press, 2005.

Viramontes, Helena María. "Requiem for the Poor." *Statement Magazine*. Los Angeles: California State University, 1976.

———. "The Cariboo Café." In *The Moths and Other Stories*, 65–82. Houston, TX: Arte Público Press, 1985.

———. "The Moths." In *The Moths and Other Stories*, 27–32. Houston, TX: Arte Público Press, 1985.

———. *The Moths and Other Stories*. Houston, TX: Arte Público Press, 1985.

———. "East of Downtown and Beyond: Interview with Helena María Viramontes." By Juanita Heredia and Sylvia Pellarolo. *Mester* 22–23 (1993–1994): 165–180.

———. *Under the Feet of Jesus*. New York: Dutton, 1995.

———. "Praying for Knowledge: Interview with Helena María Viramontes." In *Latina Self-Portraits: Interviews with Contemporary Women Writers*, edited by Bridget Kevane and Juanita Heredia, 141–154. Albuquerque: University of New Mexico Press, 2000.

———. *Their Dogs Came with Them*. New York: Atria, 2007.

5

Tapestries of Space-Time

Urban and Institutional Spaces in Helena María Viramontes's Short Fiction

MARGARITA T. BARCELÓ

TOWARD THE BEGINNING of her *testimonio*, "'Nopalitos': The Making of Fiction," Helena María Viramontes carefully notes her origins as a writer, to be sure, but also as a geographically and historically situated Chicana subject: "I was born and raised in the US, East LA, Califas, to be more exact, on First Street not too far from Whittier Blvd., close enough to enable me to see the smoke from the Chicano Moratorium riots" (33). This emphasis on the importance of time and space is characteristic of her long and short fiction and interviews, as well as the above-quoted testimonio. In literary texts by Viramontes, spaces are represented and theorized as dynamic social sites where discourses of race, class, gender, and sexuality intersect and collide—sometimes violently, but always actively. Contemporaries of Viramontes—such as Lorna Dee Cervantes, Cherríe L. Moraga, Sandra Cisneros, Gina Valdés, and Norma Elia Cantú—share this nuanced understanding of social space. Or as Mary Pat

Brady convincingly argues in *Extinct Lands, Temporal Geographies: Chicana Literature and the Urgency of Space*, literature produced by Mexican-origin writers "offers an important theoretics of space" (6).

In this chapter, I will provide an in-depth examination of urban and institutional spaces in three stories: "Miss Clairol" and, from *The Moths and Other Stories*, "The Long Reconciliation," and "Birthday." Space-time is an indispensable analytic tool for reading Viramontes's fiction generally, and these texts in particular. In addition to space-time configurations, I will also explore the importance of intertextuality and characterization in these "women's stories that need to be told and heard" (Yarbro-Bejarano, 19). Allow me to ground my reading of these texts by first discussing the notion of space-time, urban and institutional sites as social spaces, and the importance of intertextuality in contemporary Chicana literature.

In *Space, Place, and Gender*, Doreen Massey continues the work of social geographers who conceptualize space as a dynamic, socially constituted, and constituting, site of struggle. Gender, and not just class, she argues, is important when formulating "concepts of space and place in terms of social relations" (2). Massey, cognizant of the many ways in which time and space—or history and geography—are sometimes conceived as opposing forces, argues for a conjoining of the two. Or, in her words, "space must be conceptualized integrally with time; indeed . . . the aim should be to think always in terms of space-time" (2). The literal conjunction of the two terms reinforces the way in which history and geography are "inextricably interwoven" (261).

Like the social relations that constitute it, space is complex. Differential relations of power, discipline, and repression are all enacted spatially. Or, as Massey argues in "Politics and Space/Time," "space is by its very nature full of power and symbolism, a complex web of relations of domination and subordination, of solidarity and co-operation. This aspect of space has been referred to elsewhere as a kind of power-geometry" (265). Social relations within a variety of locations are marked by dynamics of subordination and domination, "of solidarity and co-operation." But as the stories by Viramontes demonstrate, such power-geometries are often practiced—and perhaps most profoundly felt—in urban and institutional spaces. With notions such as the heterotopia, theorists like Michel Foucault have given us provocative ways to examine the power-geometry of urban locations. In my analysis, I will pay particularly close attention to the dynamics of discipline and surveillance within a given narrative's space-time.

One way of describing the nuanced representations and theorizations of space-time in Viramontes's short fiction is through the use of figurative language, specifically metaphor. In the first part of my title, I am using the word "tapestries" metaphorically, as a way of alluding to the complexities of social space in her *obra*. Viramontes, indeed, constructs intricate tapestries of space-time in her fiction. "Tapestries" also has three other references. The word recalls, first of all, the "rebozos de palabras" of this reader's title. Second, my title echoes that of Bettina Aptheker's collection of women's writing, *Tapestries of Life: Women's Work, Women's Consciousness, and the Meaning of Daily Experience.* "In the course of a day, a week," she observes, "women carry the threads of many tasks in their hands at the same time." Poet Deena Metzger once wrote: "Each day is a tapestry, threads of broccoli, promotion, couches, children, politics, shopping, building, planting, thinking interweave in intimate connection with insistent cycles of birth, existence, and death" (39). Female writers and artists must "carry the threads of many tasks in their hands" simultaneously because women are "continually interrupted." Aptheker's and Metzger's notion of continual interruption and the resulting tapestry resonates well with the portion of Viramontes's testimonio that examines the often-interrupted, underappreciated work of "la mujer."

Third, and perhaps most significantly, I use "tapestries" as a way of acknowledging the pathbreaking work on Viramontes by *frontera* feminist scholar Sonia Saldívar-Hull. In *Feminism on the Border: Chicana Gender Politics and Literature,* Saldívar-Hull argues that with "The Cariboo Café," Viramontes's work emulates that of the "arpilleras" of Chile. The Chilean women use cloth figures superimposed on burlap to tell the story of *los desaparecidos,* or "disappeared" loved ones. Utilizing "powerful words and imagery as her cloth and thread," Viramontes constructs from "three narrative scraps" a tapestry that narrates "the unspeakable horrors that are the history of the undocumented worker and political refugee in the United States" (145). Saldívar-Hull goes on to remark how the

writer's commitment to an internationalist politics positions Viramontes as a Chicana border feminist.

The intricacy of tapestries like "The Cariboo Café" or "Miss Clairol" are best appreciated and understood in relation to one another,
and in relation to literary texts by other Chicana writers. In other
words, what follows are intertextual readings of "Miss Clairol,"
"The Long Reconciliation," and "Birthday." In their respective
analyses of *Woman Hollering Creek and Other Stories*, both Katherine Ríos and Mary Pat Brady insist on reading Sandra Cisneros's
sketches and tales intertextually. In "And you know what I have to
say isn't always pleasant': Translating the Unspoken Word in Cisneros's *Woman Hollering Creek*," Ríos presents a particularly compelling case for intertextuality. She reads "Never Marry a Mexican"
with and against the grain of other stories in the collection, most
notably the title story. She also examines Cisneros in light of poetry
by Ana Castillo and Alma Villanueva. Similarly, I will argue that an
intertextual reading of a text like "Miss Clairol" is not just a useful
strategy, but a necessary one.

"Time to remember or to forget"— "Miss Clairol"

In "Miss Clairol," Viramontes focuses her narrative lens on an alienated factory worker and her young daughter. The story, first published in *Chicana Creativity and Criticism*, is from the manuscript
"Paris Rats in L.A." As Sonia Saldívar-Hull observes in *Feminism on
the Border*, the stories in this collection are set in City Terrace, in the
Terrace Flats housing project. The narratives examine, among other
characters, Arlene, a single mother who works in a Los Angeles sewing factory. Gregorio, the eldest of her two children, is known to
his local homeboys as "Spider." Her daughter Ofelia, nicknamed
"Champ," functions as a main character and keen observer of the family's surroundings. Champ also demystifies for the reader the masks
these urban inhabitants must wear. Indeed, in her perceptive reading of two other narratives in the manuscript, the title story and
"Tears on My Pillow," Saldívar-Hull carefully notes how Viramontes humanizes these characters on the periphery of Los Angeles, and

the United States as a whole. Saldívar-Hull also argues that "City Terrace is no Aztlán, the mythical homeland of the Aztec natives and the utopian dreamland of the Chicano nationalists of the 1960s and 1970s." Female characters in "Paris Rats in L.A." are "blamed and beaten by their kinsmen and exploited by postmodern capitalism" (159). Using details from popular culture throughout the narrative, Viramontes sets "Miss Clairol" in the late 1960s and early 1970s—at the very height of Chicano nationalism and its invocation of Aztlán. In this particular story, Viramontes offers sardonic commentary on an industry that profits from and perpetuates beauty myths. She also places at the narrative forefront an "alienated, oppressed barrio woman," a factory worker and single mother (Herrera-Sobek and Viramontes, 31–32).

When the story opens, Arlene and ten-year-old Champ are strolling down the cosmetics aisle at the local Kmart. They look for hair coloring, nail polish, and eye shadow to match a borrowed dress for a special Saturday evening. In fact, the entire narrative revolves around Arlene's elaborate preparation for her big date—an early afternoon bath, makeup, her *comadre*'s dress, and "Love Cries" perfume. But "Arlene the mirror," Viramontes tells us, "is not Arlene the face who has worn too many relationships, gotten too little sleep" (104). While her mother applies the requisite makeup and squeezes into the borrowed dress, Champ watches Jackie Gleason and the June Taylor Dancers, keeps vigil for her brother's return home, and warms up a can of soup for dinner. In Arlene's pre-date reverie, she imagines "spinning herself into Miss Clairol, and stopping only when it is time to return to the sewing factory, time to wait out the next date, time to change hair color. Time to remember or to forget" (105). As Arlene leaves for her date, Champ yells goodbye. Her mother, however, "is too busy cranking up the window to hear her daughter."

The direct reference to Miss Clairol in the above quotation, the story's initial paragraph, and the title are not isolated incidents. Indeed, Viramontes carefully lists several brand names: Aqua Net hairspray, the Maybelline "rack of make-up" in the store, Jean Naté bath crystals, and the Calgon commercials that Arlene's afternoon bath mimics. By providing such a detailed list, Viramontes parodies the relentless target marketing schemes of the cosmetics industry.

Viramontes also underscores the main character's subproletarian class position. As Wendy Chapkis observes in *Beauty Secrets: Women and the Politics of Appearance*, consumers like Arlene purchase what marketing executives call the "General Motors Line" of cosmetics available at stores like Kmart (92). As their moniker implies, such products are less expensive than the Cadillac and Chevrolet lines. Nevertheless, these "discount" commodities remain profitable to the corporations because they are costly to the working-class consumer. Champ, on whom nothing is lost, "never remembers her mother paying" (102).

Between her shoplifting in front of Champ at Kmart and the "benign neglect" of her children, it is easy to dismiss Arlene as a character (Saldívar-Hull, 159). In her interview "East of Downtown and Beyond" with Juanita Heredia and Silvia Pellarolo, Viramontes confronts the question of Arlene and the politics of representation: "It is interesting because I received a lot of flack especially from the outer circles. '*Ay!* Look at the way you are portraying a Chicana! Look, she's stealing lipstick in front of her kids!'" (176). I would argue that precisely because of the complex politics of representation, reading "Miss Clairol" requires a Chicana feminist hermeneutic attentive to the nuances of both intertextuality and space-time. Examining "Tears on My Pillow" alongside "Miss Clairol" is not just a useful reading strategy, but a necessary one. And particularly helpful for understanding the space-time configuration of Viramontes's challenging literary texts are the final chapters of Edward Soja's *Postmodern Geographies: The Reassertion of Space in Critical Social Theory*.

The final essays in *Postmodern Geographies* critically examine Viramontes's setting, that is, the post-1960s socio-spatial configuration of greater Los Angeles. Soja looks at many spatial practices in "postmodern Los Angeles," but one particularly germane to "Miss Clairol" and "Tears on My Pillow" is restructuring. This socio-spatial practice, Soja argues, has led to the following conditions in the city: selective deindustrialization and therefore closure of automobile assembly plants, tire manufacturing, and steel milling; large-scale deunionization in the remaining factories, plants, and steel mills; and "remarkable industrial expansion" in the high-technology and garment industries (204). This heterogeneous combination of urban growth and decay leads Soja to suggest that "sweatshops which provoke images of nineteenth-century London have thus become as much a part of the restructured landscape of Los Angeles as the abandoned factory site and the new printed circuit plant" (207–208). Given the heterogeneity and "uneven development" of the area, Soja aptly describes LA as "a constellation of Foucauldian heterotopias" (240). In this case, "heterotopias" designate spaces that obscure the labor, surveillance, and discipline so vital to the larger city's maintenance. The shopping malls, gated communities, and other "attractively packaged places" ingeniously hide "the buzzing workstations and labour processes which help keep it together" (246). The neo-sweatshops and factories so vital to the restructured city produce alienated subjects like Arlene.

   "Tears on My Pillow" offers the reader a brief but powerful foray into one segment of the booming garment industry alluded to at the end of "Miss Clairol." The experimental narrative, written in Champ's voice, leaves no doubt as to the conditions under which Arlene labors. In "Tears on My Pillow," Champ sees a "big room with pipe guts for ceilings and no windows. All these sewing machines buzzing, buzzing, eating up big balls of string about big as my head spinning dizzy and so much dust flying 'round, makes it hard to breathe where Arlene works. Even I sneeze to no God bless yous" (114). Her memory of the noise and dust of the neo-sweatshop contributes to Champ's understanding of her mother's exhaustion at the end of any given workday: "I know it takes a long time for the buzzing of the machines in your head to stop." Thanks to an overheard conversation between Arlene and her comadre Pancha, Champ also learns an early lesson in workplace surveillance and discipline. Factory employees are afraid to use the restroom, for fear of being replaced by another worker (114). Arlene and her exclusively female co-workers comprise a pool of cheap, expendable labor, and thanks to the deunionization of restructured Los Angeles, are treated as such in the neo-sweatshop where they toil.

   In the interview "East of Downtown and Beyond," Viramontes underscores the labor-intensive, low-paying nature of Arlene's job (176). Even the "General Motors" line of cosmetics is out of her reach. But if she lacks the resources, why does Arlene put herself and her family at risk by shoplifting these expensive commodities of seemingly questionable value? One answer lies in the analysis of the beauty industry by Chapkis in *Beauty Secrets*. The "pursuit of beauty," Chapkis convincingly argues, is "one of the few avenues to success over which a woman has some measure of personal control. You can mold your body much more easily than you can force access to the old-boy networks or get the job you want, the promotion you deserve, the salary you need, the recognition you are owed. And implicit in the effort is the belief that after beauty follows the job, the money, the love" (95). Chapkis goes on to remark that "attractive" women garner attention normally not granted to female subjects in a misogynist culture. The industry "trades on this reality and the fantasy of escape" (95). Arlene's appearance is one of very few arenas where she can exert some measure of control. But given the tremendous responsibility of single parenthood, her fantasy of "spinning herself into Miss Clairol" permanently remains just that, a fantasy.

Reading "Tears on My Pillow" alongside "Miss Clairol" not only details the conditions in the sewing factory but also helps the reader appreciate the extent of Arlene's social isolation. Lil Mary G, Arlene's friend since junior high, is beaten and ultimately killed by her husband. Champ attributes the screaming they hear at night to La Llorona, but the "wailing woman of Greater Mexican folklore" is really Mary G. Mama María, Arlene's mother and Champ's grandmother, who suddenly disappears one day: "Just they never say hello and they never say goodbye. Mama María never said goodbye, she just left and that's that" (115). "Tears on My Pillow" also elaborates on the fate of Arlene's father, "Grandpa Ham." His mental collapse is briefly alluded to in "Miss Clairol." In "Tears on My Pillow," we find out that he was committed to a hospital. Before his death, Grandpa Ham attempted to run away (110). Outside of her children, the only other character remaining in Arlene's *vida dura*/hard life is her childhood friend and comadre, Pancha.

The most salient attribute of Viramontes's main character is her "estrangement from reality" (Herrera-Sobek and Viramontes, 32). Arlene is estranged from many realities in the narrative, including single parenthood. Significantly, it is Champ, and not Arlene, who "goes over to the window, checks the houses, the streets, corners" in search of Gregorio's whereabouts (104). Arlene's alienation is so thorough that she opts for romance over reality where her daughter's emergent sexuality is concerned. When Champ begins puberty, her mother is prepared to lie about her own sexual initiation. Note the semantic opposition between "the first time she made love" on the one hand and "her first fuck" on the other:

> Arlene is romantic. When Champ begins her period, she will tell her things that only women can know. She will tell her about the first time she made love with a boy, her awkwardness and shyness forcing them to go under the house, where the cool, refined soil made a soft mattress. How she closed her eyes and wondered what to expect, or how the penis was the softest skin she had ever felt against her, how it tickled her, searched for a place to connect. She was eleven and his name was Harry.
>
> She will not tell Champ that her first fuck was a guy named Puppet who ejaculated prematurely, at the sight of her apricot vagina, so plump and fuzzy.—Pendejo—she said—you got it all over me.—She rubbed the gooey substance off her legs, her belly in disgust. Ran home to tell Rat and Pancha, her mouth open with laughter. (104)

"Arlene the romantic" stands in the way of Arlene the single parent, trying to raise two children in the Terrace Flats housing project.

The protagonist is completely alienated from the conditions of her existence, not just as a mother but as a female subject in general. Indeed, Arlene's disconnection from her body is reminiscent of what film critic and theorist Rosa-Linda Fregoso, in another context, refers to as "corporal estrangement" (Fregoso, *meXicana Encounters*, 69). When trying on her comadre's dress, for instance, Arlene relies on the unexpected sense of hearing and not on sight and/or touch: "Her plump arms squeeze through, her hips breathe in and hold their breath, the seams do all they can to keep the body contained. But Arlene doesn't care as long as it sounds right" (102). There is the final scene of the story, when Arlene fails to hear Champ's rather loud goodbye. But the most striking example of her corporal estrangement is connected to an incident from her past. In the midst of Arlene's elaborate preparations, the towel covering her body "slips, reveals one nipple blind from a cigarette burn, a date to forget. She rewraps the towel, likes her reflection, turns to her profile for additional inspection. She feels good, turns up the radio" (103). Arlene's estrangement ultimately manifests itself in the form of amnesia. Or as Viramontes lyrically phrases it in the narrative's penultimate paragraph, "Time to remember or to forget" (105).

Given the sexual abuse from her past, it is possible to interpret Arlene's will-to-forget as a will-to-survive. In other words, her corporal estrangement and "forgetting" could be read as symptoms of post-traumatic stress disorder (PTSD). As Christine A. Courtois notes in a chapter from *Recollections of Sexual Abuse*, common symptoms in the "numbing phase" of PTSD include "traumatic amnesia," disturbed sleeping patterns, and "a general detachment" from people and events (80). Citing the work of other traumatic memory scholars, Courtois acknowledges "the contradictory but . . . important need to 'forget' unpleasant events in order for life to be bearable" (90). Most likely not wishing to share her father's fate, Arlene's will-to-forget can be thought of as a will-to-survive outside of the asylum. There is, after all, little opportunity for Arlene to escape the grinding monotony of her daily life; the surveillance, discipline, and sensory overload of the workplace; or the violence of the Terrace Flats housing project. Perhaps "traumatic amnesia" ultimately ensures her sanity, and her family's survival, in the heterotopic landscape of postmodern Los Angeles.

The urban terrain of "Miss Clairol" is very familiar territory for readers of Viramontes's short fiction. Her 1985 collection *The Moths and Other Stories* contains several haunting tales of life and death in the urban core. In the aforementioned interview with Heredia and Pellarolo, Viramontes comments on the power of her narrative, "The Cariboo Café." Set in 1980s Los Angeles, the fifth story in *The Moths and Other Stories* thematizes the historical and geographical displacement of both Mexican (im)migrants and Central American, specifically Salvadoran, refugees. In "Sites of Struggle: Immigration, Deportation, Prison, and Exile," Barbara Harlow argues that borders in Viramontes's story "become bonds among peoples, rather than the articulation of national difference and the basis for exclusion enforced by the collaboration of the United States and Salvadoran regimes" (152). Indeed, the text challenges and interpellates us, its readers, because, according to Roberta Fernández, we "must decide where we wish to position ourselves in relationship to the fight against injustice suffered by women (and the poor) in Third World nations as well as in our own backyard" (83). In a chapter from his study *Border Matters: Remapping American Cultural Studies*, José David Saldívar examines liminality and border crossing in Viramontes's experimental, "disjunctive narrative" (99). Saldívar holds that "from the very beginning, liminality is thematized not as a temporary condition of the displaced but as a permanent social reality" (104). And in *Feminism on the Border*, Sonia Saldívar-Hull argues that with "The Cariboo Café," Viramontes "makes that final leap from filiation to affiliation, from ties to men and women of her own blood to political ties with peoples across national borders who enter the United States in search of political liberation" (145).

"The Moths" and "Neighbors," tales that open and close the collection, have also enjoyed nuanced critical readings. Both narratives are set in the author's home geography, what Rosa-Linda Fregoso calls the "urban East-bank" (*The Bronze Screen*, 131). And in both "The Moths" and "Neighbors," elderly characters such as Abuelita (grandmother), doña Aura Rodríguez, and don Macario Fierro play central roles. Viramontes's representations venture beyond sentimentalized Chicano movement–era portraits of supernaturally inclined, indefatigable elders. The three main characters of these Eastside stories, for instance, live alone, in aggrieved conditions. The grandmother in the collection's title story is a survivor of domestic abuse. In her reading of "The Moths," Saldívar-Hull perceptively asks, "Is this why the abuela tried to save her nieta, why she offered sanctuary for this granddaughter with bull hands?" (136). For Raúl Villa in his study *Barrio-Logos: Space and Place in Urban Chicano Literature and Culture*, Viramontes's story "Neighbors" is another example of an astute "historical geographic critique" of urban California by a Chicana cultural worker (117). The final narrative of Viramontes's collection, he eloquently argues, demonstrates how socio-spatial processes such as deindustrialization and freeway construction are fundamentally implicated in the destruction of Aura and Fierro's Eastside neighborhood. "Neighbors" stands as a particularly compelling eulogy for and analysis of her "home geography," East Los Angeles.

"The decision was ultimately hers and hers alone"—"The Long Reconciliation" and "Birthday"

The urban barrio of "Neighbors" is just one of several socio-spatial constructs in Viramontes's short fiction in particular, and Chicana/o literature in general. Other popular spatial constructs include the border and, as illustrated in Viramontes's 1995 novel *Under the Feet of Jesus*, the migrant trail. Family or domestic space is also salient in her texts. But in the remainder of this paper, I want to examine the Catholic Church, a key institutional space in "The Long Reconciliation" and "Birthday." The Church functions as a common thread uniting these otherwise quite disparate tapestries of space-time. Like scores of other Chicana/o literary and cultural texts, "The Long Reconciliation" and "Birthday" suggest that religious discourse plays a crucial role in the formation of subjectivity. Viramontes's texts also demonstrate how organized religion can function as a coercive force in the imaginary lives of her female protagonists. In the case of these lesser-known stories that thematize abortion, Amanda Márquez and Alice Johnson engage in what Ellen McCracken calls "a critical hermeneutic process of decoding patriarchal attempts to control women's sexuality and reproductive functions" (177). Although the quote "The decision was ultimately hers and hers alone" is from "Birthday," both protagonists struggle with their decision in isolation from their immediate families. This relative isolation is a marked contrast to the somewhat suffocating—but ultimately loving and supportive—mother and daughter characters in Alma Villanueva's short story, "Her Choice." After all, the "something. A flesh, a membrane, a growth" that initially divides Vida and Tania ultimately reunites them at the end of "Her Choice" (338). In turning to Viramontes's characters, let us begin with Amanda Márquez. She is a Mexicana from "a very different historical period" than Tania, Alice, or the reader (McCracken, 178).

The main characters of "The Long Reconciliation" meet in an impoverished village sometime during the early twentieth-century Mexican Revolution/Civil War. The title's "long reconciliation" alludes to the fifty-eight-year separation between Amanda and her estranged husband. The protagonist is just fourteen years old when she meets and marries Chato Márquez, "a stranger nearly twice her age" (82). She enjoys sex with her husband until she becomes pregnant with a child they are unable to "feed or care for" (84). With the aid of a *curandero*, don Serafín, Amanda successfully aborts the fetus. Understandably troubled by the entire experience, Amanda turns to the confessional. It is apparent that the priest—and later Chato—cannot understand Amanda's pain. In response to her husband's conjugal rejection, Amanda has an affair with the village's despised landowner, don Joaquín. In the name of honor, Chato stabs don Joaquín. The couple does not "reconcile" until fifty-eight years later, in a hospital in the United States, where a terminally ill Chato finally "casts the stone" of his withheld forgiveness and empathy (89).

In this story, Viramontes explores the Catholic Church as a coercive force in the lives of both Amanda and Chato. In his theory of the relationship between the State and ideology, Louis Althusser identifies "the system of different Churches" as the religious Ideological State Apparatus (ISA) (143). The religious ISA, like schools, the family, and other ISAs, functions "both by repression and by ideology" (149). Indeed, in "Religion and the Left," philosopher and theologian Cornel West argues that from a Marxist perspective, "religion at its worst serves as an ideological means of preserving and perpetuating prevailing social and historical realities" of inequality (199). In the confines of the confessional, Amanda confronts the Church's hypocrisy and readily identifies its role in "preserving and perpetuating" the poverty that impelled her decision to abort the pregnancy:

> But Father, wasn't He supposed to take care of us, his poor? When you lie together, it is for creating children, *said the priest*, you have sinned, pray. Sex is the only free pleasure we have. It makes us feel like clouds for the minutes that not even you can prevent. You ask us not to lie together, but we are not made of you, we are not gods. You God, eating and drinking as you like, you, there, not feeling the sweat or pests that feed on the skin, you sitting with a kingly lust for comfort, tell us that we will be paid later on in death. (85)

Amanda rejects fatalism and also recognizes how the clergy, themselves indulging in their "kingly lust for comfort," expects the laity to renounce an earthly pleasure like sex. In other words, Viramontes's protagonist rejects the Church's ideology and reveals as transparent its role as an Ideological State Apparatus.

The village priest, acting as a supervisory agent in his parishioners' lives, gives Chato bad advice as well. Outside of the confessional, the clergyman advises Chato to "save every penny. Land is valuable and you can at least hope to grow a livelihood for you and your family; it is a hope, Chato remembers the priest saying. And he did save every penny except for the gifts he bought Amanda" (80). But the land Chato purchases is desert—far from "valuable" without costly irrigation—and owned by the Machiavellian don Joaquín. Indeed, it's quite possible that the priest actively works in collusion with the landowner. The only hope at that point in the story is a revolution led by Emiliano Zapata (or, as he is known in "The Long Reconciliation," "some indio") with a plan to divide land among the people. Chato escapes his village in part because of the revolution, but also to avoid being charged with don Joaquín's murder by the federal troops.

By weaving "woman concerns" like abortion into a story set during the Mexican Civil War, Viramontes anticipated the way in which Sandra Cisneros thematizes the sexual double standard, marriage, and motherhood in "Eyes of Zapata." These texts, with their focus on gender, do not simply bring so-called women's issues like abortion, marriage, and parenting to the fore of discursive space. First, the texts call into question the socially constructed masculine imperatives that drive the main male characters, Chato and a fictionalized Emiliano Zapata. Although he is so "tired of always having to be *el gran general*," the revolutionary leader must maintain the masculine veneer of stoicism (86). Inés, a clairvoyant *nagual* (or witch) and one of his many common-law wives, sees through the mask that a formerly jovial Zapata must wear: "Everything bothers you these days. Any noise, any light, even the sun. You say nothing for hours, and then when you do speak, it's an outburst, a fury. Everyone afraid of you, even your men. You hide yourself in the dark. You go days without sleep. You don't laugh anymore" (86). Amanda also renders transparent—indeed, she deconstructs—the "honor" that Chato invokes as his justification for murdering don Joaquín: "You killed because something said 'you must kill to remain a man'—and not for this honor. For me, things are as different as our bodies. I killed, as you say, because it would have been unbearable to watch a child slowly rot. But you couldn't understand that, because something said 'you must have sons to remain a man'" (79). Although that "something" remains unnamed by Amanda, the narrative asserts the notion of masculinity as a socially constructed ideological discourse.

Second, these and other texts by Viramontes and Cisneros also ask us to interrogate the post–Chicano movement nostalgia that often obfuscates our historical memory of this bloody epoch in Mexican history. In "Eyes of Zapata," Cisneros issues an all-out visual assault that shocks the reader out of that nostalgia. Inés's recollection of "these nine years of *aguantando*—enduring" (87) is a somber meditation on war and the inevitable devaluation of existing human life: "At first we couldn't bear to look at the bodies hanging in the trees. But after many months, you get used to them, curling and drying into leather in the sun day after day, dangling like earrings, so that they no longer terrify, they no longer mean anything. Perhaps that is worst of all" (95). In her novel *Caramelo, o, Puro Cuento*, Cisneros continues her critical meditation on the human costs of Mexico's Civil War. One character's recollection of Bertold Brecht's Mother Courage with chilling accuracy and another character's vivid memories of hunger ("During the war they'd eaten nothing but beans, atole, and tortillas") coexist with descriptions of the Reyes family's penchant for "rococo embroidery" and the assertion of "healthy lies" (135, 163). Again anticipating Cisneros, Viramontes undercuts nostalgia for the revolutionary period by using hunger as a trope in her story. The characters, the fetus, and even the "dry, cold flatlands" are "thin with hunger" (83). Indeed, the sterility of the land symbolizes the desolation of the village, and perhaps the futility of hope for immediate social change, in "The Long Reconciliation."

In this text, as elsewhere in the collection, Viramontes employs a complex narrative technique that complements her compelling female characters. In her introduction to *The Moths and Other Stories*, Yvonne Yarbro-Bejarano notes how "'The Broken Web' and 'The Long Reconciliation' make the severest demands on readers' ability to reconstruct the temporal sequence of events" (19). Amanda, like the unnamed narrator of "The Moths" and Tomás's wife in "The Broken Web," actively displays rage with her oppressive and frustrating situation. In "The Broken Web," for instance, Tomás's wife shoots and kills her husband in the middle of his drunken, verbally abusive tirade. The young unnamed narrator of "The Moths" describes how, armed with her *abuelita*'s *molcajete* in her "bull hand," she cathartically crushes roasted chile, tomato, and garlic. In her nuanced reading of this story, Sonia Saldívar-Hull discusses the traditional mortar and pestle as an important image: "To Chicanas the image of the molcajete evokes not only a rough stone grinding away at women's spirits, but a rough stone pulverizing traditions that destroy women's lives" (135).

"Crazy with hate," Amanda demonstrates her rage by tearing open don Joaquín's freshly sutured wound, then filling it with maggots (81–82). To be sure, Amanda enacts "a savage revenge on her ex-lover for telling her husband" about the affair (Yarbro-Bejarano, 13). But by ripping open the stitches and stuffing the wound with maggots, she also displaces her anger and frustration with Chato and the Church onto her former lover. After all, neither her husband nor the village priest can see past directives to "be fruitful and multiply." Amanda, on the other hand, imagines the horror of carrying the pregnancy to term, only to watch her offspring "slowly rot" from malnutrition or disease (79). In addition to her anger, Viramontes also describes Amanda's skill as an embroiderer. This character who crafts "beautiful handkerchiefs, pillow cases, scarves" is an important literary predecessor to the aged seamstress—and literary *tocaya*—in Roberta Fernández's *Intaglio: A Novel in Six Stories* (87). Images and metaphors related to Amanda Márquez's embroidery deftly tie Viramontes's complex narrative together.

Deploying a vastly different time-space than "The Long Reconciliation," "Birthday" is another story in *The Moths and Other Stories* that thematizes abortion. Alice Johnson, a college student living in the United States after the passage of *Roe v. Wade*, is older than Amanda Márquez when the former is surprised by an unplanned pregnancy. Initially, Alice is hesitant to even say or hear others—such as her best friend Terry or boyfriend Mike—utter the word "abortion," let alone consider it as a possible course of action. Only after Terry discloses that she, too, had to wrestle with this difficult decision does Alice follow through with the procedure. Terry tells her fearful younger friend, "We both know you can't have a child.

You're young and dreamy. That won't help you or your child any" (44). Terminating the unplanned pregnancy becomes "recoded" as Alice's birthday, an agonistic rite of passage necessary in her transition to maturity and adulthood (McCracken, 177).

The paucity of critical commentary on this story intrigues me. Perhaps one of the reasons is that even for Chicanas who self-identify as feminists, abortion is a complex issue. After all, safely terminating an unplanned pregnancy is only one side of the political coin. The historical practice of forced or non-consensual sterilization on poor and/or ethno-racial women complicates the discourse of reproductive rights for Chicanas, Latinas, other women of color, and working-class Euro-American women. Or as Anna Nieto-Gomez notes in one of many essays addressing the issue in *Chicana Feminist Thought*, "When a Chicana talks about birth control and abortion she does so in the context of understanding the cultural genocidal acts of this country" (91). In "¿A Que Hora Venderemos Todo?" vanguard Chicana poet Bernice Zamora adopts the voice of a poor Mexican-origin woman. Although the poem does not thematize forced sterilization, it does bring to the discursive foreground underlying issues of coercion and the perceived ignorance of poor, fertile women.

> . . . . You take me aside
> To your corner and whisper
> A-B-O-R-T-I-O-N
> As though I do not
> Recognize the end. (17)

Instead of kowtowing to authority, the speaking subject in Zamora's poem mocks her inquisitor-interlocutor, as well as his assumptions about her.

Unlike Zamora's speaking subject, the protagonist of "Birthday," Alice Johnson, is not bilingual. Beginning with her name and following through the rest of the narrative, she is not readily identifiable as a Mexican-origin character. This may be another reason for the critical silence surrounding "Birthday." Alice could be Euro-American, but she could also be a mixed-race Chicana or Latina. On the question of her protagonist's race, Viramontes leaves the narrative open to interpretation. What she does not leave ambiguous is the way in which Alice's religious, specifically Roman Catholic, training sharply conflicts with the abortion she ultimately chooses. The internal dialogue of this experimental narrative is riddled with images of destruction and sin. Once in the office where the procedure will be done, for instance, she notes how the room is "clean and white with silver objects that reflect my face in distortion. (Oh God, my God, forgive me for I have sinned.)" (46).

In addition to confronting the issue of abortion, "Birthday" is also notable for its humor. Guilt-ridden throughout the narrative, Alice has not been in the waiting room of the clinic long before she spots "a single picture of snow and church" (41). The serenity of the winter scene proves a stark contrast to her inner turmoil, and perhaps a reminder of her conflicted Catholicism. She giggles at another patient's oily hair, and when her name is called, Alice confides, "I nod my head and smile. I think I'm going to win" (43). Such levity is a much-needed counterpoint to the story's serious theme, but it also captures the bittersweet quality of this painful step on Alice's journey to adulthood.

In spite of their common theme, the time-space configurations of "Birthday" and "The Long Reconciliation" differ greatly. Viramontes reworks her representations of the Church's disciplining and supervising of female subjects accordingly. In "The Long Reconciliation," for instance, the confessional becomes a key microspace of power, discipline, and surveillance. As Foucault argues in the first volume of *The History of Sexuality*,

> The confession is a ritual of discourse in which the speaking subject is also the subject of the statement; it is also a ritual that unfolds within a power relationship, for one does not confess without the presence (or virtual presence) of a partner who is not simply the interlocutor but the authority who requires the confession, prescribes and appreciates it, and intervenes in order to judge, punish, forgive, console and reconcile; a ritual in which the truth is corroborated by the obstacles and resistances it has had to surmount in order to be formulated; and finally, a ritual in which the expression alone, independently of its external consequences, produces intrinsic modifications in

the person who articulates it: it exonerates, redeems, and puri-
fies him; it unburdens him of his wrongs, liberates him, and
promises him salvation. (61–62)

A repentant Amanda is supposed to submit to the Church's teachings after the village priest tells her, "You have sinned, pray" (85).

For Chato's young wife, surveillance of her body and its fertility
extends beyond the confines of the confessional. Amanda correctly
suspects that one of the women "cackling on the front steps of the
church" heard part of her confession. The women are right about her
visit to don Serafin, but incorrectly guess at the cause (84). Amanda
is not the only subject of their hypocritical exchange: they also gossip
about another woman in the village. In the context of the story, the
women are products and embodiments of a community that closely
supervises its female subjects. Or, as Gillian Rose phrases it in *Feminism and Geography: The Limits of Geographical Knowledge*, Amanda's experience in a public space such as the church steps involves
"women watching themselves being watched and judged" (145).

The confessional so important to the distinctly Mexican, rural,
early twentieth-century narrative world of "The Long Reconciliation" disappears in the post–*Roe v. Wade* universe of "Birthday." Alice
has so thoroughly internalized the Catholic Church's anti-abortion
ideology that she has no need of the physical structure, let alone the
actual practice, of confession. She is, paraphrasing Foucault's observations on surveillance as a system, her very own overseer, exercising
"surveillance over, and against, [her]self" ("The Eye of Power," 155):

> My God, what am I doing here? Alone and cold. And afraid.
> Damn, dammit. I should have stayed a virgin. STUPID, stu-
> pid! Virgins have babies, too. Enough Alice. Keep warm, Alice.
> No sex, Alice. Punishing me. For loving, God? Fucking, Alice.
> Fucking Alice. Stop it, Alice. Grow up, not out.
> Alice.
>   God isn't pregnant. (43)

Alice follows through with the procedure, but her internal dialogue
registers apprehension, guilt, and self-hatred until the final two lines
of the narrative.

Viramontes's complex representations of abortion are replete with
historically specific details of not just disciplinary practices but the
abortifacients as well. Amanda describes don Serafín's prescription:
teas made of corn silk and dried orange peels. Indeed, his remedy
is reminiscent of "the cure" described by Ana Castillo in her essay
"Extraordinarily Woman" (77). In both cases, the abortionist and
his or her herbal teas are reassuringly familiar to the patient. With
"Birthday," however, Viramontes shows the reader a very different
procedure. What Alice undergoes resembles the "medicinal ritual"
described by Marie-Elise Wheatwind in her poem "Abortion."

> Now we have this
> medicinal ritual:
> noisy machines and
> antiseptic instruments
> probing the uterine walls. (135)

Although the office staff and doctor are friendly to Alice, in the final
paragraphs she notes their "*[c]old hands*" (46). The clinic, which
was once a house, is also described as cold throughout the narrative. Although resolutely feminist in its pro-choice ideology, "Birthday" renders complex the medicinal ritual of late twentieth-century
legalized abortion in the United States.

It is just like Viramontes to take a vexed issue like abortion and
give it a complex narrative spin. In " 'Nopalitos': The Making of Fiction," she states, "As Chicanas, we must continue to have the courage to examine our lives" (37). To be sure, courage is not lacking
in either the content or form of stories like "The Long Reconciliation" and "Birthday." Sonia Saldívar-Hull argues that several stories
in *The Moths and Other Stories* are powerful "feminist statements
on the status of women within la familia in Chicana/o communities" (126). And Raúl Villa notes how the stories from that collection "describe the multiple and intersecting constraints of race- and
class-based oppression that threaten the cultural cohesion, physical safety, and psychological integrity of Latino communities" on
both local and global levels (115). This paper asserts and illustrates
the importance of space-time, intertextuality, and characterization
in the short fiction of Helena María Viramontes. Indeed, intricate

tapestries of space-time such as "Miss Clairol" and "Tears on My Pillow" place into bold relief the otherwise hidden "workstations and labour processes" (Soja, 246) that are so vital to the production of urban space. Her work, however, also challenges readers to imagine and continue constructing new spaces. Or, as Viramontes herself notes in the penultimate paragraph of " 'Nopalitos,' " "Our destiny is not embedded in cement. We can determine its destination. Some use the soapbox, others, weapons. I choose to write" (38).

Works Cited

Althusser, Louis. "Ideology and Ideological State Apparatuses (Notes Towards an Investigation)." In *Lenin and Philosophy and Other Essays*, 127–173. Translated by Ben Brewster. New York: Monthly Review Press, 1971.

Aptheker, Bettina. *Tapestries of Life: Women's Work, Women's Consciousness, and the Meaning of Daily Experience*. Amherst: University of Massachusetts Press, 1989.

Brady, Mary Pat. *Extinct Lands, Temporal Geographies: Chicana Literature and the Urgency of Space*. Durham, NC: Duke University Press, 2002.

Castillo, Ana. "Extraordinarily Woman." In *Goddess of the Americas: Writings on the Virgin of Guadalupe*, edited by Ana Castillo, 72–78. New York: Riverhead, 1996.

Chapkis, Wendy. *Beauty Secrets: Women and the Politics of Appearance*. Boston: South End, 1986.

Cisneros, Sandra. "Eyes of Zapata." In *Woman Hollering Creek and Other Stories*, 85–113. New York: Random, 1991.

———. *Woman Hollering Creek and Other Stories*. New York: Random, 1991.

———. *Caramelo, o, Puro Cuento*. New York: Alfred Knopf, 2002.

Courtois, Christine A. *Recollections of Sexual Abuse: Treatment Principles and Guidelines*. New York: Norton, 1999.

Fernández, Roberta. " 'The Cariboo Café': Helena María Viramontes Discourses with Her Social and Cultural Contexts." In *Across Cultures: The Spectrum of Women's Lives*, edited by Emily K. Abel and Marjorie L. Pearson, 71–85. Studies in Gender and Culture 4. New York: Gordon, 1989.

———. *Intaglio: A Novel in Six Stories*. Houston, TX: Arte Público Press, 1990.

Foucault, Michel. "The Eye of Power." In *Power/Knowledge: Selected Interviews and Other Writings, 1972–1977*, edited by Colin Gordon, 146–165. Translated by Colin Gordon, Leo Marshall, John Mepham, and Kate Soper. New York: Pantheon, 1980.

———. *The History of Sexuality, Volume I: An Introduction*. Translated by Robert Hurley. New York: Vintage-Random, 1980.

Fregoso, Rosa-Linda. *The Bronze Screen: Chicana and Chicano Film Culture.* Minneapolis: University of Minnesota Press, 1993.

———. *meXicana Encounters: The Making of Social Identities on the Border-lands.* Berkeley: University of California Press, 2003.

Harlow, Barbara. "Sites of Struggle: Immigration, Deportation, Prison, and Exile." In *Criticism in the Borderlands: Studies in Chicano Literature, Culture, and Ideology,* edited by Héctor Calderón and José David Saldívar, 149–163. Durham, NC: Duke University Press, 1991.

Herrera-Sobek, María, and Helena María Viramontes, eds. "Chicana Creativity and Criticism: Charting New Frontiers in American Literature." Special issue, *The Americas Review.* Houston, TX: Arte Público Press, 1988.

Massey, Doreen. "Politics and Space/Time." In *Space, Place, and Gender* by Doreen Massey, 249–272. Minneapolis: University of Minnesota Press, 1994.

———. *Space, Place, and Gender.* Minneapolis: University of Minnesota Press, 1994.

McCracken, Ellen. *New Latina Narrative: The Feminine Space of Postmodern Ethnicity.* Tucson: University of Arizona Press, 1999.

Nieto-Gomez, Anna. "La Feminista." In *Chicana Feminist Thought: The Basic Historical Writings,* edited by Alma M. García, 86–91. New York: Routledge, 1997.

Ríos, Katherine. " 'And you know what I have to say isn't always pleasant': Translating the Unspoken Word in Cisneros' *Woman Hollering Creek.*" In *Chicana (W)rites on Word and Film,* edited by María Herrera-Sobek and Helena María Viramontes, 201–223. Chicana/Latina Studies. Berkeley: Third Woman Press, 1995.

Rose, Gillian. *Feminism and Geography: The Limits of Geographical Knowledge.* Minneapolis: University of Minnesota Press, 1993.

Saldívar, José David. *Border Matters: Remapping American Cultural Studies.* American Crossroads 1, edited by Earl Lewis, George Lipsitz, Peggy Pascoe, George Sánchez, and Dana Takagi. Berkeley: University of California Press, 1997.

Saldívar-Hull, Sonia. *Feminism on the Border: Chicana Gender Politics and Literature.* Berkeley: University of California Press, 2000.

Soja, Edward W. *Postmodern Geographies: The Reassertion of Space in Critical Social Theory.* London: Verso, 1989.

Villa, Raúl Homero. *Barrio-Logos: Space and Place in Urban Chicano Literature and Culture.* Center for Mexican American Studies History, Culture, and Society Series. Austin: University of Texas, 2000.

Villanueva, Alma Luz. 1993. "Her Choice." In *Divisions: An Anthology of Chicana Literature,* edited by Tey Diana Rebolledo and Eliana S. Rivero, 337–340. Tucson: University of Arizona Press, 1993.

Viramontes, Helena María. "Birthday." In *The Moths and Other Stories,* 45–52. Houston, TX: Arte Público Press, 1985.

Viramontes, Helena María. "The Broken Web." In *The Moths and Other Stories*, 53–64. Houston, TX: Arte Público Press, 1985.

———. "The Cariboo Café." In *The Moths and Other Stories*, 65–82. Houston, TX: Arte Público Press, 1985.

———. "The Long Reconciliation." In *The Moths and Other Stories*, 83–98. Houston, TX: Arte Público Press, 1985.

———. *The Moths and Other Stories.* Houston, TX: Arte Público Press, 1985.

———. "Neighbors." In *The Moths and Other Stories*, 109–117. Houston, TX: Arte Público Press, 1985.

———. "Miss Clairol." In *Chicana Creativity and Criticism: Charting New Frontiers in American Literature*, edited by María Herrera-Sobek and Helena María Viramontes, 101–105. Houston, TX: Arte Público Press, 1988.

———. "'Nopalitos': The Making of Fiction." In *Breaking Boundaries: Latina Writing and Critical Readings*, edited by Asunción Horno-Delgado, Eliana Ortego, Nina M. Scott, and Nancy Saporta Sternbach, 33–38. Amherst: University of Massachusetts Press, 1989.

———. "Tears on My Pillow." In *New Chicana/Chicano Writing 1*, edited by Charles M. Tatum, 110–115. Tucson: University of Arizona Press, 1992.

———. "East of Downtown and Beyond: Interview with Helena María Viramontes." By Juanita Heredia and Silvia Pellarolo. *Mester* 22–23 (1993–1994): 165–180.

———. *Under the Feet of Jesus.* New York: Dutton, 1995.

West, Cornel. "Religion and the Left." In *Churches in Struggle: Liberation Theologies and Social Change in North America*, edited by William K. Tabb, 198–206. New York: Monthly Review, 1986.

Wheatwind, Marie-Elise. "Abortion." In *Chicana Lesbians: The Girls Our Mothers Warned Us about*, edited by Carla Trujillo, 131–136. Berkeley: Third Woman Press, 1991.

Yarbro-Bejarano, Yvonne. "Introduction." In *The Moths and Other Stories* by Helena María Viramontes, 9–21. Houston, TX: Arte Público Press, 1985.

Zamora, Bernice. "¿A Que Hora Venderemos Todo." *Releasing Serpents*, 17. Tempe, AZ: Bilingual Press/Editorial Bilingüe, 1994.

III
Ethics and Aesthetics

6

Lovingly

Ethics in Viramontes's Stories

JUAN D. MAH Y BUSCH

LOVE IS BLIND, OR SO THEY SAY. The adage means that in caring for another person, a lover supposedly is undiscerning and therefore incapable of pursuing her own self-interests. In *The Moths and Other Stories*, through her fictional characters, Helena María Viramontes depicts an alternative notion of love, one that is associated with struggle and survival as well as with learning and transformation.

In order to understand Viramontes's portrayal of love, we first must understand something about the epistemological politics of its popular meaning. If it is true and love is indeed blind, it would be an unfortunate situation for the marginalized and the oppressed; most theories of agency at least partially depend on what a person "sees." The axiom therefore divorces love and compassion from forms of liberation that are grounded in social knowledge and a critical consciousness. Blind to the way another person can affect her, a loving person would have to decide between living a more liberatory life and living more lovingly. Implicitly resisting this popular notion, Viramontes's stories demonstrate something else entirely, a form of love in which epistemological value coincides with ethical value, thereby rejoining love and liberation. In order to recognize the relationships within her stories that exist between love and knowledge, we can read Viramontes's two short stories "The Moths" and "Growing" through a significant, though under-discussed, aspect of Chicana/o identity: character.

Even though both stories are framed by social politics—whether it is patriarchal demands, sibling tensions, or religious obligations—in "The Moths" and "Growing" very little actually seems to happen. The characters' transformations, indeed, the movement of the story, are more "internal," with greater attention to interiority than to social or political action. This is somewhat paradoxical for Chicana subjectivity, an ethnic identity commonly defined by (usually undefined) social politics. If politics define Chicanidad yet these popular stories do not depict explicit social action, how then do they highlight something that contributes to our understanding of this emergent and resistant subjectivity? It is the ethics of its implied epistemology, which consequently produces forms of social knowledge. That is, Viramontes's stories regard the development of *character*. My usage of the term reaches beyond a strict narratological meaning, moving somewhat fluidly between fiction and philosophy, between narrative and ethics. In literary terms, we may consider Viramontes's many memorable characters. Chicanas and Latinas, often young, struggle to understand themselves and their social situation. It is the interior lives of these protagonists that are the narrative focus, which draws attention to philosophical discussions of what it is to be a person, to fields of inquiry such as subjectivity and epistemology. In other words, through her fiction, Viramontes's characters draw our attention to issues of character.

The literary meaning of "character" is an imaginary person in a work of fiction, but even this meaning quickly unravels into a broader sense of the word. Character is constituted by those qualities that add depth to a person; in that way it is similar to the concepts of subjectivity and consciousness, and ultimately of agency. From this broader usage, we can better circumvent the current divide between the discourses of politics and ethics, a divide that parallels the conceptual divide between love and liberation, making it difficult to discuss ethics without slipping into problematic notions of moral purity. While such hierarchical purities are appropriately critiqued, it has resulted in an abandonment of moral philosophy.

In this discursive silence, *moral character* has become blurred with *character ethics.*[1] Thus, the discursive shift toward politics has almost inadvertently made ethics seem to be more closely associated with morality, an asocial change from its classical significance, thereby making it difficult to discuss character without feeling as though we have departed from any understanding of power and social contexts. Viramontes's fiction utilizes an ethics that is more similar to the classical sense of character, though she complicates it with her vigilant focus on the oppressed and resistant politics, thereby avoiding transcendental and teleological notions of love. Similar to the ethical work of Michel Foucault and feminist ethicists, if we understand ethics as practices of freedom and of self-care, we can "read" how Viramontes's characters reveal *character* in such a way that gives rise to liberation.

For the purpose of this essay, unlike the particular systems of moral obligation and judgment, ethics is a discussion of how to live. This sense of ethics extends back to Aristotle's *eudaimonia* and his focus on human flourishing, and the concept reaches forward to modernity's complicated negation of happiness in Marx's political economies and his theory of alienation. As the adjective cognate with *ethos*, ethics is a study of happiness.[2] Discussing the classical relationship between character and perception, Nancy Sherman defines it in this way: "The term ["character"] has to do with a person's enduring traits; that is, with the attitudes, sensibilities, and beliefs that affect how a person sees, acts, and indeed lives. As permanent states, these will explain not merely why someone acted this way *now*, but why they can be *counted on* to act in certain ways. In this sense, character gives a special sort of accountability and pattern to action" (1, her italics).[3] Any theory of identity, subjectivity, or agency implies some notion of character. They each describe an aspect of what it means to be a person, which is at least some sense of a coherent pattern in thought and action. This is why even poststructuralist philosophers, those central to theories of socially constructed identity, discuss ethics as self-care and as a mechanism for the development of agency.[4] Therefore, to undo a false dichotomy between the intentionality of agency and the social constructedness of postmodernized notions of identity, in order to understand Helena María Viramontes's short fiction, I believe we must revisit the language of character ethics.

A strength of Viramontes's fiction is the depth of attention she gives to her characters, a sort of writerly compassion. Through "The Moths," Viramontes attempts to portray a single emotion between a maternal figure and her child. In "Growing," the protagonist walks with her sister, resenting the younger sibling's role as a patriarchal chaperone. In this essay I focus on Viramontes's fictional characters as narrative demonstrations of character ethics, those traits central to agency, especially to the production of knowledge. Simply put, I propose that Viramontes's love liberates because of its possible relationship to learning, which in turn enables a person to live on her own terms.[5]

The Moths as Love

In "The Moths," an unnamed retrospective speaker describes the first time her grandmother asks her for help. Throughout her life, the grandmother had helped the speaker, and now, as the grandmother approaches death, she needs the speaker's assistance. Though the story describes a memory, we readers observe a transformation in the speaker, from child to caregiver.

In the final scene, as the speaker embraces her grandmother's dead body, she describes the moment: "The bathroom was filled with moths, and for the first time in a long time I cried, rocking us, crying for her, for me, for Amá, the sobs emerging from the depths of anguish, the misery of feeling half born, sobbing until finally the sobs rippled into circles and circles of sadness and relief. There, there, I said to Abuelita, rocking us gently, there, there" (28).[6] Although Viramontes as author resists a definitive answer to the often-asked question *what do the moths mean?* she hints at some of what the image may signify for her. In an interview, she explains that the story is a result of her reflection on a single image:

> The emotion comes from a very famous black and white *Life Magazine* photo of a Japanese woman bathing her deformed child. I was overpowered by the love I saw between this mother and her child. While the child looks into space, the mother shows such love and compassion in bathing the child. I felt the

strength of bonding, love and trust between the two. I wanted
to capture this feeling in the relationship between the grandmother and her grandchild in "The Moths." ("East of Downtown and Beyond," 172)

Even though she shifts the artistic form, from photography to fiction, Viramontes portrays a similar love. However, her short story
form has advantages. It adds explicit depth to a character and dwells
on a particular standpoint, the speaker's. The narrative's focus draws
attention to the child; the grandmother's love is represented only in
how it is felt by her granddaughter.

Moving away from popular sayings, how has love been theorized?
Drawing on Erich Fromm's work, M. Scott Peck defines *love* as "the
will to extend one's self for the purpose of nurturing one's own or
another's spiritual growth" (4).[7] Since Viramontes's speaker nur-
tures her grandmother, this meaning seems to coincide nicely with
"The Moths."

In "The Moths," recognizing the speaker's language is more ver-
nacular than philosophical, her phrasing suggests that love is both
an emotion and a value; that is, it is presently felt, and it designates
a person's desire for a good that indexes the agent's future action.[8]
In *All about Love*, one of the few treatments of love that tends to a
racialized social identity,[9] bell hooks points out that before infants
learn language or even before they have an independent identity,
they learn to recognize the vibration of affection and compassion.
While I am not convinced that there is a "before language," there
does seem to be something less strictly linguistic about love, even if
it is thoroughly about language. The example of the child highlights
the significantly embodied aspect of love, especially when we discuss
it in terms of character ethics. People want to feel love. In this sensation, it is at once felt and desired, an emotion as well as a value, an
autotelic sort of value.

There is, however, critical slippage in the term "value." In the story's
opening, the speaker describes Abuelita's request for help as "only
fair" because of the care her grandmother had given her. Even when
she describes love as the story's emotional starting point, Viramontes introduces a significant second term, "trust." Aligning love with
interpersonal trust, the nature of this love narrows. While this love

is certainly felt, the speaker discusses love's value in terms of debt, a sense of exchange-value that seems to have little to do with how we think about love. The presence of trust, a form of reliance, complicates the story's depiction of love. Therefore, the attention to a child also reveals a necessary distinction within how we discuss love's value: an infant does not seem capable of love. If an infant's dependence is not love, then debt would also seem to be something else. In *All about Love*, hooks explains that there is a difference between love and cathexis, or what she calls a "process of investment wherein a loved one becomes important to us" (5). She elaborates: "We all know how often individuals feeling connected to someone through the process of cathecting insist that they love the other person even if they are hurting or neglecting them. Since their feeling is that of cathexis, they insist that what they feel is love" (5–6). We must ask, then, if love is desirable but not an investment, or debt, is Viramontes's unnamed speaker experiencing love or cathexis when she says, "It seemed only fair" (23)? Does she choose to love or does she invest some other self-interested emotion into her grandmother's presence? Or, more fundamental, how does self-interest differ from self-care? I propose that Helena María Viramontes reveals a self-care that opens up to (selected and safe aspects of) the social world. As a result, her sense of loving self-care is also, for those on the margins, in their self-interest.

In order to explore the photo's sentiment, Viramontes narrows the narrative focus to one of the photo's two subjects: the child's perspective. While as a mature woman the grandmother can feel a love for the child that may have nothing to do with a need for trust, in "The Moths" we see that the child is different. This narrowed focus enables us readers to observe more clearly certain qualities about a love given by a vulnerable subject, such as the socially marginalized. In other words, in order to create the story's sensibility, Viramontes reflects on the love represented in the photo. Although love is the predominant object of study, Viramontes draws our attention to a similar quality, trust. The child, like Viramontes's speaker, is protected by the maternal love. In "The Moths," Viramontes provides a more complex, multidimensional view of the photo. Trust is not a neutral, asocial abstraction. It represents one person's sense that a person or space is relatively safe. Trust involves a person's social vulnerability as well as her sense of safety in a particular place.

In "The Moths," love-filled trust may be the most evident senti-ment. The association between love and trust suggests the existence of various qualities in love as well as how this association relates to a person's ability to *see*. For example, since the development of self is associated with trust, self-care encourages the subject to find safety for her personal development. The person is invested in seeing hos-tile and dangerous qualities in her social context. As the speaker pushes away from discomfort, the grandmother's garden provides the speaker with this space. The speaker's self-care involves repulsion from that which feels oppressive and an attraction toward safety and comfort, security and happiness. Within this ethical-emotional push and pull, the speaker has developed methods for negotiating the demands of her immediate family with her own desires and interests:

> That [I do not go to church] was one of Apá's biggest com-plaints. He would pound his hands on the table, rocking the sugar dish or spilling a cup of coffee and scream that if I didn't go to mass every Sunday to save my god-damn soul, then I had no reason to go out of the house, period. Punto final. He would grab my arm and dig his nails into me to make sure I understood the importance of catechism. Did he make himself clear? Then he strategically directed his anger at Amá for her lousy ways of bringing up daughters, being disrespectful and unbelieving, and my older sisters would pull me aside and tell me if I didn't get to mass right this minute, they were all going to kick the holy shit out of me. Why am I so selfish? Can't you see what it's doing to Amá, you idiot? So I would wash my feet and stuff them in my black Easter shoes that shone with Vase-line, grab a missal and veil, and wave goodbye to Amá.
>
> I would walk slowly down Lorena to First to Evergreen, counting the cracks on the cement. On Evergreen I would turn left and walk to Abuelita's. I liked her porch because it was shielded by the vines of the chayotes and I could get a good look at the people and car traffic on Evergreen without them knowing. (25)

The two paragraphs signal an emotional shift: as the speaker leaves her home and goes to her *abuela*'s house, she leaves patriarchal

hostilities and enters a more comfortable space, a place covered by
well-cultivated chayote vines that function like a vibrant wall within
which the young Chicana feels better.[10] She feels loved. The question remains, though, does she love? The speaker's struggle to
flourish, a struggle animated by her desire to feel love, is based on
emotional reflection. In the passage we see the speaker sift through
several emotions. She seems to entirely reject her father's command
that she go to church, even though it is enforced by physical abuse.
She also seems dismissive of her sisters' threats of an ass kicking.

The speaker only responds to her sisters when they direct her
attention to their mother's suffering. The speaker considers this
unfair placement of blame worthy of her attention. The sisters'
appeal is effective because they utilize the speaker's sense of guilt,
but the guilt can only be imposed because the speaker feels some
connection to her mother, as well as a connection to her mother's
suffering. It is irrelevant at this point in the story whether this emotional relation is due to nothing more than gendered convention,
or whether it is a genuine love for the mother, or whether it is some
form of solidarity among the women in the family. What matters
is that the speaker feels the guilt. We know that she is aware of her
feelings. The speaker seems to respond only when the sisters point
to their mother's suffering (which also seems to imply a mother-
daughter relation that is more complicated than the mere moments
of disciplining that the reader has observed up to this point in the
narrative). This connectedness with her mother inspires sensitivity.
In turn, socially entwined sensitivity inspires a renegotiation of the
speaker's response.

As she negotiates her disinterest for attending mass with her
mother's suffering, she creates a third option: rather than succumb
to frustration and the patriarch's interests, she relieves her mother's
suffering by appearing to attend mass, then she satisfies her own
wants by going to a safer place. The impulse to disobey is only a
response to circumstance. The belief that underwrites this impulse
is the speaker's need for a safer place. The impulse to disobey, a
disobedience that is not self-destructive, reveals creativity; the commitment to that impulse reveals the degree of commitment to her
sense of self. In the renegotiation of her choices, we can see the
speaker's savvy. Her decision about how to deal with competing

emotional interests reveals a degree of perceptiveness and knowledge. Although she feels the guilt, she does not mistake this guilt as some latent feeling of betrayal toward God or toward her father. The speaker's sense of self encourages her to go to Abuelita's house. The grandmother's love supports the speaker's sense of self that inspires spontaneous evaluation and creative resolution. In the above passage, we also see that, prior to the story's opening, the independent-minded, likable speaker already had become somewhat adept at negotiating her emotions within her patriarchal, Catholic family. Several references to the ongoing nature of similar events make it clear to the reader that the speaker's ability to negotiate competing interests is not just an inborn quality but one she has fostered through a well-trained, empirical process of learning from experience. Her desire-based epistemic standpoint inevitably restructures her family's conventional patriarchal "knowledge."

In addition to epistemological advantages, it is also ethically significant that her compassionate self-care does not conform. Her inchoate love is creative and spontaneous. The result of her moral learning is the speaker's nonchalant, albeit emotionally knotted, habit-like way in which she gathers her missal, veil, and church shoes . . . and, instead of going to church, goes to her grandmother's house. The speaker's trust of Abuelita seems to allow for the development of love that animates this process of ongoing reflection and progressive learning. The speaker is clear that she has not fully dealt with the earlier guilt. She says later that while she worked at Abuelita's house she "scraped hard to destroy the guilt" (26), a sensation now possibly enhanced by deceit. She explains that she has sought a space in which she can further evaluate, illuminate, and transform this guilt.

For hooks, love is beyond cathexis and abuse; indeed, it almost seems beyond human. Such a conceptualization reveals a notion of personhood that, I believe, inadvertently disables our ability to connect love to practical matters of survival within a hostile social context. In her theory of love, hooks implicitly describes an almost Kantian pure moral agent. While hooks idealizes love, Viramontes does not. In "The Moths," the speaker transforms from a child-like debt and trust to a caregiver who loves without reciprocation or notice, nurturing Abuelita's spirit. The speaker's love is about struggle and maturation, caregiving, and ongoing transformation of social relations. In "The Moths," Viramontes associates a Chicana self with sensitivity, an exploratory openness, which is why love feels vulnerable and seeks a trustworthy place. Love's sensitivity heightens and refines the character's ability to see her social context. That is, with a resistant and self-interested desire to feel love, she sees herself as well as her situation. As a result, the speaker's ethic of self-care implies the potential formation of "objective" knowledge.[11] These qualities of a love-filled care of self mark love as a narrative's guiding value and allow us to recognize the development of love in other stories in which it may be less obvious. But this guiding value is not debt related, merely helping Abuelita. At this point in the story, love's value is in how it inspires the speaker to care for herself. It is a loving self-care.

As hooks points out, love is indeed a verb, a practice that evolves, changes, and transforms. It is in this active and open-ended sense of love, a distinctly non-teleological concept, that Viramontes's love does not blind; rather, it binds the body's sensation of a desire with the desire for a sensation, the emotion with the value. Its openendedness is a departure from Aristotelian and Marxist ethics. Moreover, Viramontes's portrayal of love further complicates hooks's (and Peck's) definition. Love is not merely an *extension of the self* for "the purpose of nurturing one's own *or* another's spiritual growth" (5). Love does not extend the subject, nor in "The Moths" is it a choice between the self's or other's nourishment, as Peck's language suggests. Peck's language for love would return the concept of love to the problem with which I opened: the oppressed would lose subjectivity precisely at the moment she struggles to achieve it. For Viramontes, love involves struggle, the struggle to survive and to care for oneself. Throughout the story, the speaker strives to exist lovingly, and that love evolves with the development of her own liberation.

Growing as Learning

In Viramontes, love does not force a person to choose between herself and the care for a loved one. Rather than extend or replace care for the self, Viramontes's portrayal seems to suggest that love merges love's subject with its object. Love gives rise to a shared identity.[12] It is in this moment that the moth imagery in Viramontes's story becomes both messy and beautiful. It is a loving moment shared by the two Chicana women of different generations. In "Growing," Viramontes depicts a similar portrayal of love. Adding to "The Moths" image of a love as sensitivity, a perceptive self-care, in "Growing" we readers can observe not only an interplay between love and social knowledge but also a knowledge-producing dialectic. Unlike "The Moths" safe trust, in "Growing" the unjustified patriarchal distrust threatens to preclude Naomi's loving attitude. Since she must contend with a seemingly loveless moment, we can better observe why her love encourages her to seek knowledge, and consequently why it provides a sort of safety.

In "Growing," fourteen-year-old Naomi walks to Jorge's house, "hand in reluctant hand" (35) with her younger sister Lucía, who accompanies Naomi as a chaperone—as "commanded" by her father. Jorge is never present in the story, though; he is little more than an aside that provides a demonstration of Naomi's hostile patriarchal context. What is significant is how Naomi's self-care propels her to the story's last line, itself a complete paragraph further signifying her emotional shift: " 'Tomorrow,' [Naomi] whispered lovingly to her sister, as she entered the yard, 'tomorrow I'll buy you all the ice creams you want' " (38).[13] Naomi utters a promise. But it is not what Naomi does that is of primary importance. Even if the story let the reader observe the promise's fulfillment, which it does not, Lucía does not seem to hear it, nor does she need the ice cream. What is important is how Naomi relates to Lucía: in the place of reluctance, Naomi whispers *lovingly*. The narrative content of "Growing" responds to a single question: what is the moral-epistemological process that bridges the emotional space between Naomi's initial reluctance, a reluctance filled with undirected disdain, to lovingly whispering an offer of unlimited ice cream to her younger sister, who is an unwitting agent of Naomi's oppression?

In "Growing," in other words, through the course of the story, Naomi's love and liberation connect, even though we readers only observe interior "activity." Love and vision are not just simultaneous, parallel processes: they are entwined with one another. Heightened understanding increases Naomi's ability to love—her attitude becomes more loving.

Significantly, Naomi's love and acquisition of knowledge occur in spite of intense distrust. This distrust is caused by the patriarchal culture, but more importantly, the distrust individuates the story's two characters in a competitive relationship with one another. The story opens with describing Naomi's frustration and Lucía's childish lack of awareness. The patriarch imposes a structure on the two sisters that exacerbates natural and psychological differences due to age, and it thereby creates a relationship of disconnection between the two siblings. The imposed structure makes interpersonal love difficult and diminishes the ease for a loving self-care. The story ends, however, with Naomi in a different emotional state, as I mention above. This shift reveals Naomi's love as a strength because her increased ease and self-love occur despite an unchanged social context.

In contrast to its closing passage, in the opening passage of "Growing," notice Naomi's resistant sentiments toward Lucía:

> The two walked down First Street hand in reluctant hand. The smaller one wore a thick, red sweater which had a desperately loose button that swung like a pendulum. She carried her crayons, humming "Jesus loves little boys and girls" to the speeding echo of the Saturday morning traffic, and was totally oblivious to her older sister's wrath.
>
> "My eye!" Naomi ground out the words from between her teeth. She turned to her youngest sister who seemed unconcerned and quite delighted at the prospect of another adventure. "Chaperone," she said with great disdain. "My EYE!" Lucía was chosen by Apá to be Naomi's chaperone. Infuriated, Naomi dragged her along impatiently, pulling and jerking at almost every step. She was 14, almost 15, the idea of having to be watched by a young snot like Lucía was insulting to her maturity. She flicked her hair over her shoulder. "Goddammit," she murmured, making sure that the words were soft enough so that both God and Lucía could not hear them. (31)

Reluctant, infuriated, and disdainful, Naomi impatiently drags her sister. Both sisters are oblivious to the other's standpoint. The passage introduces Naomi as the narrative focus while the reader immediately observes a seemingly out-of-control frustration. In the second paragraph, Naomi observes her sister as "unconcerned," as if Naomi expects Lucía to be concerned about exactly the same things that Naomi is or to be otherwise guilty of insult. Naomi eagerly wants to be considered older than she is currently treated, and her contained murmur's quiet restraint demonstrates that she unadmittedly fears the patriarchal context of which she is becoming increasingly aware.

Yet, despite these knotted feelings of anger, fear, and anticipation, "Growing" ends with a lucid description of Naomi's situation as well as of her different emotional state:

> Naomi felt like a victor. She had helped once again. Delighted, she giggled, laughed, laughed harder, suppressed her laughter into chuckles, then laughed again. Lucía sat quietly, to her surprise, and her eyes were heavy with sleep. She wiped them, looked at Naomi. "Vamos," Naomi said, offering her hand. . . . Jorge's gate hung on a hinge and she was almost afraid it would fall off when she opened it. She felt Lucía's warm, deep breath on her neck and it tickled her.
>
> "Tomorrow," she whispered lovingly to her sister, as she entered the yard, "tomorrow I'll buy you all the ice creams you want." (38)

Feeling like a victor, Naomi laughs and giggles as she physically carries the young, tired Lucía. The development of Naomi's character, how she sees herself, results in greater degrees of love. Naomi fondly reflects on Lucía's age and the gap between Lucía's degree of awareness and Naomi's growth of consciousness, thus the story's title "Growing," which refers not only to a common human process of socialization but also to Naomi's specific transitions regarding her interpersonal relations and sibling politics. Initially a reader is tempted to identify fatherly distrust as the primary component of the narrative content, that which animates the story.[14] This reading, however, is premature, and consequently becomes a critical misreading. Although patriarchal distrust of a postmenarcheal daughter circumscribes the story and frustrates Naomi, "Growing" regards Naomi's ability to mature emotionally—and by extension, to mature in the depth of her human and social knowledge—and consequently she is able to (re)connect with Lucía. Love connects. And in the story, this connectedness signifies love, a strengthened love. As a result, Naomi seems pleased.

The story requires that the reader see both the sexist distrust and Naomi's defiant ability to grow despite her sexist circumstance. Since the reader never directly observes Naomi's father, the person who embodies distrust is left unchallenged in the story. The narrative content consists of Naomi's shifts in disposition, in her transformed character. There are four explicit stages in Naomi's treatment of Lucía: general reluctance, sympathy, irritation with her tattling, and love. Each stage signals Naomi's ongoing critical reflection and analysis of her situation. In the first passage above, we observe Naomi's initial frustration and her reluctance to associate with Lucía. This outright anger toward Lucía becomes "sympathy" as Naomi begins to identify her father and cultural "custom" as the actual agents of the distrust that frustrates her (32). Naomi recognizes that Lucía unwittingly embodies these customs; that is, Lucía is being used. "TÚ ERES MUJER" exclaims Naomi's father. "He said those words not as a truth, but as a verdict" (36)—and, as if to reveal her own childishness as well as an embodied connection to Lucía, Naomi tugs on the arm of her unknowing younger sister. As Naomi insightfully refines her understanding of circumstance, she analyzes the words as well as the tone of her father's utterance, the cultural force behind the ethical presupposition that as a postmenarcheal woman Naomi is not considered trustworthy.

Out loud and to herself, Naomi responds significantly with, "So what's wrong with being a mujer" (32). The narrator tells us that Naomi asks, or exclaims, *out loud* and *to herself;* Naomi openly criticizes her father's sexism, but does so guardedly within the safety of her solitude (and her unaware younger sister). We readers recognize Naomi's consciousness as somewhat defiant even if she remains fearful. In order to continue to love herself and to strengthen the self-care, Naomi becomes conscious of the incorrect moral judgment as well as her vulnerability as a disempowered member of the family. Naomi realizes that her father's verdict is only justified by his mistaken belief about gender. After all, Naomi is a woman, and she realizes that this has little to do with her moral character. The discord between her own moral (self-)knowledge and her father's belief allows her to distinguish the truth of the utterance from her father's mistaken cultural verdict that biology represents some "natural," negative ethical implication about Naomi's character. With an ethics defined by resistant self-care, her lovingly self-interested perception refines her knowledge. It is significant that the strengthening of love is associated with safety and solitude, which we observe in Naomi's guardedness, similar to the speaker in "The Moths." Love is not blind to danger; in fact, it is highly sensitive to it. Such a love of self tends to the relevant details in order to maintain the self. Moreover, since Lucía does not change, we learn that love has little to do with the person being loved.

Meanwhile, in the middle of the narrative, as Naomi's reflections occur unbeknownst to Lucía, the narrator shows us that Naomi's frustration again overflows physically onto her sister as Naomi tugs in order to reprimandedly hurry the young, short-legged Lucía. However, Naomi is now more precise with her assignment of responsibility: "If it wasn't for Lucía's willingness to tattle, [Naomi] would not have been grounded for three months" (32). Naomi is angry with Lucía for Lucía's eagerness to comply with Apá's request for information. Only the passing-by male motorist who sexistly belittles Naomi enables her to forget "for a moment that Lucía told everything to Apá" (33). In that moment, sexism brings the two sisters together rather than divides them. This sexist social interaction coalesces solidarity between the sisters and mitigates the atomizing effects of the father's distrust. This contradiction reveals the space within which Naomi can choose a more strategically connected, liberatory relation with Lucía. Or, for the purpose of self-defense (narrowly defined), Naomi can be complicit with patriarchy by maintaining the individualist disconnect. Naomi's reflections then waver and wander regarding her situation until the two sisters come upon a neighborhood baseball game. It is the baseball game that allows Naomi to further reflect on her own growth of character.

As with Lucía in the story's opening passage, Naomi initially distinguishes herself from the playful children, a playfulness quite distinct from the sexual playfulness described in Naomi's reflection about her boyfriend Joe. But her condescending distinction quickly turns into an admiration: "She enjoyed the abandonment with which

they played" (34). The children's playfulness is not as significant as
the abandonment with which they played, for it is with this recognition that Naomi becomes aware of degrees of consciousness.
Unrestrained, the children surrender to their impulses: the children
play with abandon because they are unaware. Since they do not
understand, they cannot perceive the significance of social circumstance; thus, relatively speaking, they cannot choose, in a rational
or reflective sense. Such choice requires awareness of alternatives.
They only respond and care for their impulses. Even if Lucía tattles
in order to win favor from the patriarch, she does so without awareness. Naomi's problem with Lucía is not due to Lucía's distrustful
actions—trust has something to do with predictability, and Naomi
seems to know exactly how Lucía will act. The problem is due to
Lucía's lack of understanding. Since she does not perceive the significance of her actions, she is unaware. Naomi's knowledge allows
her to ease; she watches her young friends play playfully. Eventually,
"no longer concerned with her age, her menstruations, her breasts
that bounced with every jump" (37), Naomi participates—not just
in the game but in the game's abandon.

Naomi's relationship to her father is the context of her situation, but Naomi's relationship with Lucía forms the narrative. From
reluctantly and angrily to understandingly and lovingly, Naomi
learns not to distrust Lucía; rather, she learns that Lucía's childish lack of understanding of social implications requires Naomi's
careful treatment of Lucía. Naomi connects with and opens up to
Lucía. She opens up not by telling everything about herself but by
being sensitive to Lucía's perspective. Naomi begins to see her own
circumstances and social relations more accurately and more justly.
Thus, Naomi's sisterly relationship with Lucía demonstrates Naomi's achievement of a more loving state of being. Significantly, this
state of being is the direct result of clearer understanding. Naomi
recognizes that social verdicts are not necessarily personal truths. She
realizes that there is a difference between the social consequences of
Lucía's actions and Lucía's intentions; that is, recognizing Lucía's
state of consciousness is necessary to evaluate her character ethics.

Naomi recognizes various degrees of consciousness, which allows
her to recognize various forms of consciousness: while the children are

playful and in the immediate present because of a lack of fuller social understanding, Naomi accesses her own uninhibited playfulness as a moment of calm amidst greater social burden. She pursues her own playful impulses. Naomi's decision to enjoy the moment's abandon, by contrast, reveals her more general decision to sift through social circumstance in order to refine her understanding. Through this playfulness, Naomi eases, she separates from her father's verdict, and she better accepts herself. Her ability to love herself has to do with her capacity to be at ease in the moment. Thus, as we saw in "The Moths," loving self-care requires a degree of safety and an ability to be in the moment. It is with this knowledge of her own character and her circumstances that she relates lovingly to Lucía. By rejecting as unjustified the impulse to distrust Lucía, a distrust that is more directly attributed to the patriarch, Naomi enables another impulse, to love and to learn.

Conclusion

In "The Moths," we learn about love, about how a person who loves herself struggles to care for herself. Viramontes also depicts a love that opens up and sensitizes a person's perception. The speaker ends the story at the moment in which she begins to share a loving identity with her grandmother. In "Growing," we see a love-knowledge dialectic as Naomi is able to care for herself and her sister as she learns about herself and her social situation. Viramontes's seemingly simple stories have some philosophically significant implications. Those concerned with theories of agency and critical knowledge would do well to return to questions fundamental to character ethics. For instance, if an ethics of self-care, one grounded in and guided by love, undoes some of the political borders of subjectivity, such as the self-other divide, without undoing the need to protect and to resist, what does this do to our notion of struggle and solidarity? What does this do to how we conceive of critical knowledge and the politics of the ethical? In "The Moths" and "Growing," Helena María Viramontes seems to suggest that the liberatory standpoint is the one in which the oppressed person exists lovingly.

Notes

1. The former often regards evaluation of rules and obligations; it is one person's judgment of another person's moral constitution, an assessment of her integrity and honor. Such a concept is as suspect as a blinding love for those who are disempowered by such moral discourses, discourses that often are little more than a system of ideological euphemisms for "civilizing the barbaric."

2. For this understanding of the term, see Terence Irwin's translation of Aristotle's *Nicomachean Ethics*. For a discussion of Aristotelian ethics in Marx's thought, see McCarthy's *Marx and Aristotle*.

3. From Sherman's *The Fabric of Character: Aristotle's Theory of Virtue*. I depart from certain aspects of this definition; Sherman adheres to Aristotle's notion of character as a person's "permanent states" since she focuses on *good* character. Even without this notion of a timeless and transcendent moral good, the concept of character remains within the realm of ethics. Nor does character diminish its force in establishing patterns of action, which is its more sociopolitical manifestation.

4. Michel Foucault's later work is rife with discussion of the ethical, and Emmanuel Levinas's influence on Jacques Derrida's deconstruction has been well documented. For example, see Foucault's interview, "The Ethics of Concern for Self as a Practice of Freedom," and see Simon Critchley's *The Ethics of Deconstruction: Levinas and Derrida*.

5. When I discuss *character*, I am doing so from the standpoint of the agent. I am uninterested in the interpersonal, judgmental use of the term. Also, character's focus on interiority and moral psychology need not compete with attention to the social and political context, as is commonly assumed. This is a misunderstanding caused by discursive divisions between ethics and politics and "exterior" and "interior," as if the skin on a person's body is some sort of morally significant border, as individualism would have us believe, in the same way that it is a political boundary.

6. All citations of "The Moths" come from *The Moths and Other Stories*.

7. Quoted by bell hooks in *All about Love*.

8. While this essay is not the place for a discussion of the various debates regarding *love*, I realize that some philosophers would not call love an emotion or a value. For instance, see O. H. Green's "Is Love an Emotion?" For that matter, "emotion" and "value" are contested terms. For the purposes of this essay, I use emotion broadly to include any range of felt experiences.

9. To bell hooks's treatment of love and social identity, I would add María Lugones's essay, "Playfulness, 'World'-Traveling, and Loving Perception." However, whereas hooks addresses identity while she primarily discusses love, Lugones discusses love in the context of her concerns with identity and perception. While I agree with the critique of hooks that her recent work draws too uncritically on "self-help" literature, her work also remains one of the few

treatments outside of Euro-American feminisms that tends to the social location of the subject.

10. While I propose that this emotional push and pull enables the development of social knowledge, this does not commit me to the idea that every development is an improvement. The idea that there is a potential relationship between an oppressed person's happiness and social knowledge does not compete with notions of epistemological error.

11. My use of "objective" follows feminist philosopher Sandra Harding's notion of a socially embedded "stronger objectivity." See her book, *Whose Science? Whose Knowledge?*

12. In a different context in which he discusses romantic love, Robert Solomon uses the language of "merge" and "shared identities." See his *About Love*, especially the end of chapter one.

13. I should note that although I refer to the story's conclusion as it appears in *The Moths and Other Stories*, the version that appears in *Cuentos*, edited by Alma Gómez, Cherríe Moraga, and Mariana Romo-Carmona, does not change the character's sentiment in a way that alters the significance of the sisters' relationship. Although "lovingly" is not explicitly cited, the *Cuentos* version ends with a distinctly different relationship than that with which it opens, one that is more explicitly about gendered Chicana solidarity. It is similar, even if less explicit, to the story's later version.

14. For instance, in the introduction to *The Moths and Other Stories*, Yvonne Yarbro-Bejarano focuses on how the stories represent Viramontes's "social consciousness" (18). She is correct to identify as significant the social consciousness weaved throughout the collection. My departure from her reading regards its emphasis rather than its content. She seems to consider the primary narrative focus to be the social. With an emphasis on the social, she focuses on the female-male relationships. Admittedly, Yarbro-Bejarano's reading is intended to serve as a brief introductory remark, but I believe this reading represents a more general problem. Even though her reading is correct, the introductory brevity of her description allows Yarbro-Bejarano to privilege social location over the development of agency.

Works Cited

Aristotle. *Nicomachean Ethics*. Translated, with introduction, by Terence Irwin. Indianapolis, IN: Hackett, 1985.

Critchley, Simon. *The Ethics of Deconstruction: Levinas and Derrida*. West Lafayette, IN: Purdue University Press, 1999.

Foucault, Michel. "The Ethics of Concern for Self as a Practice of Freedom." In *Ethics: Subjectivity and Truth*, edited by Paul Rabinow, 281–302. New York: The New Press, 1994.

Green, O. H. "Is Love an Emotion?" In *Love Analyzed*, edited by Roger E. Lamb, 209–224. Boulder, CO: Westview Press, 1997.

Harding, Sandra. *Whose Science? Whose Knowledge?: Thinking from Women's Lives*. Ithaca, NY: Cornell University Press, 1991.

hooks, bell. *All about Love: New Visions*. New York: HarperCollins, 2000.

Lugones, María. "Playfulness, 'World'-Travelling, and Loving Perception." In *Making Face, Making Soul/Haciendo Caras: Creative and Critical Perspectives by Feminists of Color*, edited by Gloria Anzaldúa, 390–402. San Francisco: Aunt Lute Foundation Books, 1990.

McCarthy, George E., ed. *Marx and Aristotle: Nineteenth-Century German Social Theory and Classical Antiquity*. Savage, MD: Rowman & Littlefield, 1992.

Sherman, Nancy. *The Fabric of Character: Aristotle's Theory of Virtue*. Oxford: Clarendon, 1989.

Solomon, Robert C. *About Love: Reinventing Romance for Our Times*. Lanham, MD: Rowman & Littlefield, 1994.

Viramontes, Helena María. "Growing." In *Cuentos: Stories by Latinas*, edited by Alma Gómez, Cherríe Moraga, and Mariana Romo-Carmona, 65–73. New York: Kitchen Table Press, 1983.

———. "The Moths." In *The Moths and Other Stories*, 27–32. Houston, TX: Arte Público Press, 1985.

———. *The Moths and Other Stories*. Houston, TX: Arte Público Press, 1985.

———. "East of Downtown and Beyond: Interview with Helena María Viramontes." By Juanita Heredia and Silvia Pellarolo. *Mester: Chicana/o Discourse* 22–23 (1993–1994): 165–180.

Yarbro-Bejarano, Yvonne. "Introduction." In *The Moths and Other Stories* by Helena María Viramontes, 9–21. Houston, TX: Arte Público Press, 1985.

7

Metaphors to Love By

Toward a Chicana Aesthetics in *Their Dogs Came with Them*

MARY PAT BRADY

AT THE HEART OF RAMÓN SALDÍVAR'S foundational text, *Chicano Narrative*, is a claim about scale: *Chicano* rather than, for example, *Tejano* is the scale at which a particular set of texts may be suitably analyzed; their relationships may be properly scrutinized *within* that scale. *Chicano Narrative* is also a critique of the practices of scaling—that is to say, of the scaling of US literature within the American imperial imaginary that scales *out* Chicana/o authors. In 2006, Saldívar published *The Borderlands of Culture: Américo Paredes and the Transnational Imaginary*.[1] The title signals a crucial shift in scale: on the one hand, it echoes or implicitly repeats an argument Sonia Saldívar-Hull had made nearly a decade earlier, that Chicana intellectuals, rather than focusing on the US national project, were suturing together a transnational imaginary that highlighted the inter-relatedness of struggles for cultural and communal viability.[2] Nevertheless, *Borderlands of Culture* does here suggest a rescaling of literary analysis from one centered on Chicana narrative (and implicitly the United States and the scale of the nation-state) to one that entails a broadly world-systems sense of the transnational.

This move does not mean an evisceration of "Chicano" as an analytical rubric, but rather suggests a broadening of the terrain in which the reach of Américo Paredes may be appreciated.

This shift in the field imaginary that Saldívar invokes also parallels the shift in the locus of analysis that leading American Studies scholars have sought to encourage.[3] These challenges to how scholars scale analyses that start first as challenges to the organizing power of the nation-state ask also that we reconsider history—since it is a shared historicity that drives Saldívar's rubric, or that could be said to justify or support his choice of rubrics. And it is the particularities of history that the scale of "Chicano" makes visible or, some might say, meaningful. That is to say, such challenges to the scale of the nation-state as the crucial metric enable scholars to consider the networks and traffic that nation-state–centered analyses eschew, scale out, or fail to articulate. Similarly, a number of other scholars, such as José Quiroga and Debra Castillo, have marked the shift from "Chicano" to "Latino" as a shift toward a trans-American imaginary that opens away from state-centric thinking and the logics of governmentality; in this sense they applaud the jump in scale from Chicano or Cubano to Latina or the transnational.[4]

Certainly scale jumping has a long history in US politics; to get a sense of its political import, it is worth looking at an argument about scale that might, at first glance, seem very far afield. Speaking in 1819 while the United States debated whether or not to admit Missouri as a slave state, De Witt Clinton, then governor of New York and the man who propelled the Erie Canal into existence, linked the construction of the canal to the preservation of a union among states:

> A dissolution of the union may therefore be considered the natural death of our free government. And to avert this awful calamity, all local prejudices and geographical distinctions should be discarded, the people should be habituated to frequent intercourse and beneficial inter-communication, and the whole republic ought to be bound together by the golden ties of commerce and the adamantine chains of interest. When the Western Canal is finished and a communication is formed between Lake Michigan and the Illinois River, or between the Ohio and the waters of lake Erie, the greater part of the United

States will form one vast island, susceptible of circumnavigation
to the extent of many thousand miles. The most distant parts of
the confederacy will then be in a state of approximation, and the
distinctions of eastern and western, of southern and northern
interests, will be entirely prostrated. To be instrumental in pro-
ducing so much good, by increasing the stock of human happiness, by establishing the perpetuity of free government, and by
extending the empire of improvement, of knowledge, of refine-
ment and of religion, is an ambition worthy of a free people.[5]

Clinton advocates the creation of a "people" at a national scale,
a group that identifies with the national and that emerges out
of its production.[6] What I would like to highlight here, however,
is Clinton's sense of urgency over the production of this national
scale. Perceptively suggesting that for the United States in 1819 the
national will emerge not through common culture, language, or
heritage but through technology, transportation, and communica-
tions systems and that these will structure the formation of a "people," he calls for shifting the significance of regional scales, thereby
defeating the South's challenge to Northern supremacy. Clinton's
language reinforces the nested hierarchies of scale helping to structure capitalism even as he predicts that the regional would, indeed
must, learn, over the course of the nineteenth century, to prostrate
before the national. Furthermore, his comments neatly anticipate
how important the national scale would become to industrial expansion just as his deployment of the rhetoric of national union, of sub-
mission to national good, anticipates the secessionist conflict. While
Clinton also suggests that a national "people" may already be in
place—one that can be defined through a reference to the discursive
(knowledge, manners, religion)—he also implies that the empire of
improvement (infrastructure) in the hands of capital would go much
further to produce such a "free people." Government-supported
capital investment would create the conditions of freedom—a claim
long resonant with efforts at intertwining capitalism with nationalism and democracy. And here, in the meshing of the concept of
nation with that of people, in the connection between constructing
a nation and constructing "a people," thereby creating a category
of people comparable to the scale of the national—a project that

preoccupied the nineteenth-century intellectual elite across the Americas and that girded the declarations of governors and capitalists such as De Witt Clinton—one can see the significance of scale to narratives of nation and identity and, importantly for my purposes here, the antecedents to the problematics of the formation of the category, "Latino," and the rescaling of cultural analysis in terms of the "transnational." Clinton here argues for the usefulness of scale for managing and mitigating dissent even while he might be puzzled by his sought-after national scale's failure to adequately define and structure a homogenized people. What scaling does, Clinton tells us, is to establish relations between scales, but also, crucially here, scaling entails the consolidation of power and the establishment of affiliations within the order of the scale itself.

Clinton's use of scale to construct affiliation is not dissimilar to the work of scholars who wish to deconstruct "the nation" as the crucial metric of scholarly reach or as the central problematic for understanding the terms through which such complex processes as citizenship and sexuality may be formed. Perhaps not coincidentally, in the same period as Americanists have challenged the field paradigm and worked against the dominance of the national scale that De Witt Clinton labored to produce, geographers have developed a rich and complex theory of scale itself. Traditionally, geographers have understood scale as a term for describing spatial registers within a vertical metric from the local, to the regional, to the national, to the global; scale is also understood as the size of something.[7] Scale works then as a register of extension (horizontality) and level (verticality). Scale theory has tended to focus on analyzing at what scale crucial decisions are successfully made or unmade. Geographers, for example, study the ways in which cities and states, in the current round of globalization, are "reterritorialized to produce 'glocal scalar fixes' "[8]—to organize capital in ways that can effectively maneuver around regional or national regulations. Such scalar configurations (global, local, national) are not, geographers argue, ends in themselves, but rather the "outcomes of sociospatial processes that regulate and organize power relations."[9] In this sense, scale is a representational trope, a narrative that structures and partially determines content.[10] Similarly, political geographers have utilized an analysis of scale to consider how activists reap benefits from taking local issues and jumping scale with them—turning them into regional or national or transnational questions—leveraging what appears to be a local issue (say the construction of an incinerator or prison) with a claim to its regional or national significance as a question of justice. For many, the crucial contribution of scale theory is that it puts spaces into (frequently dialectical) relationship with other spaces and suggests the interanimating (and shifting) value of those relationships. Additionally, geographers have adeptly shown the extent to which scalar processes are crucial structures of capitalism. Understanding how various actors seek to control scalar forces at moments of seminal political and economic change enables scholars to predict their impact and consequences.

Some very innovative geographers, however, have begun to cast enormous doubts on the usefulness of scale. Drawing on the work of Mexican philosopher and artist Manuel de Landa, among others, Sallie Marston and her colleagues have suggested a set of concerns about scale that have relevance for those considering how best to locate our literary/cultural analyses. First, they note the way in which studies of scale have tended to prioritize large-scale structures. Not surprisingly, "globe talk" implicitly renders as parochial the quotidian practices of social reproduction, "thereby eviscerating agency at one end of the hierarchy in favor of such terms as 'global capitalism.'"[11] Such scale talk creates what Henri Lefebvre called "phallic verticality" privileging a "small-large imaginary" and "preconfigured accounts of social life that hierarchize spaces of economy and culture, structure and agency."[12] One can easily see this sensibility in operation given the privileging of global and hemispheric comparisons over the seemingly regional and local:

> Hierarchical scale (de)limits practical agency as a necessary outcome of its organization. For once hierarchies are assumed, agency and its "others"—whether the structural imperatives of accumulation theory or the more dynamic and open ended sets of relations associated with transnationalism and globalization— are assigned a spatial register in the scaffold imaginary. Invariably, social practice takes a lower rung on the hierarchy, while "broader forces" such as the juggernaut of globalization, are assigned a greater degree of social and territorial significance.[13]

The result, Marston and her collaborators suggest, is a tendency to direct "critical gazes toward an 'outside over there' that, in turn, hails a 'higher' spatial category."[14] In other words, structuralist and Marxist legacies have taught the field to depend on "prior, static conceptual categories" as a priori explanations in which form determines content. They call for an effort to "overcome the limits of globalizing ontologies," but admit that doing so will require " 'sustained attention to the intimate and divergent relations between bodies, objects, orders and spaces'—that is, to the processes by which assemblages are formed."[15]

The rich critique of scale offered here compels us to take the processes of scaling itself seriously, to understand how sites and events morph and how they exist only through interactive practices and through the processes by which conditions of possibility for some are the conditions of constraint for others. In this sense I have tried to suggest, in using "Chicano" and "Latina"—terms traditionally used as ethno-racial signifiers—as scalar terms, that these ethnoracial categories also function as a form of scale entailing affiliation and power consolidation and inevitably signaling inter-relations between scales, as well as a phallic verticality or a scaffold imaginary that may not be attuned to the political work of Chicana feminist studies.[16] In this sense, I wish to turn to a text whose critique of the scaffold imaginary challenges the "Newtonian worldview" that lends the scaffold its commanding primacy.

One can read Helena María Viramontes's novel *Their Dogs Came with Them* (2007) as a disturbingly curious sequel to María Amparo Ruiz de Burton's *The Squatter and the Don* (1885),[17] which describes the process by which the southern route for a transcontinental railway was settled and mapped by Callis Huntington and others. And further, one can read both novels as critiques of Clinton's celebration of the need to make the regional "prostrate" before the national. In his celebratory call to rescale states into the nation, Clinton gives little thought to the costs of such a scalar fix. Ruiz de Burton, on the other hand, in describing how the incorporation of regions necessitated the decorporation of peoples and cultures, makes it clear that Clinton's vision entails a refined and hypocritical narrative of race and space. More especially, in *The Squatter and the Don*, she shows that the expansion of the nation and the creation of a new national scaffold imaginary made possible through the building of railroads entailed corruption, misinformation, and demagoguery. Ruiz de Burton details the incredible land speculation involved in this process and the economic devastation that rent San Diego when Los Angeles emerged as the railway's terminus. In this sense, her novel sets the stage for understanding Viramontes's own dystopian story of transit gone awry.

After Callis Huntington completed his transcontinental empire, his nephew, Henry Huntington, went to work developing Los Angeles.[18] He purchased vast quantities of land across the Los Angeles basin and built streetcars and a rail system that largely emanated from the central railroad terminus in downtown LA.[19] In this way, he developed new communities such as Long Beach, Santa Monica, and Glendale by creating and extending an interurban housing system that dovetailed with the rail lines. While his mass transit system lost money, he made millions through the real estate speculation that solidified the philosophy that if you build it they will come. Yet in a well-told story, his Pacific Electric light rail system dominated Los Angeles for just a few decades. By mid-century, the city and the nation had committed themselves to an auto-centric organization of space. Crucial to this process was a cultural and economic shift from a celebration of the collectivity enshrined in mass transit to the elevation of the individual's car as the central method of transportation. If the rail system subsequently became the pattern for the Los Angeles freeway system, it also helped create and solidify the hyper-segregation that bedeviled post-WWII Los Angeles, because the success of Huntington's new developments depended on restrictive covenants and redlining practices to keep his new suburbs "white" and to ensnare black and Latino communities in the residential areas closest to downtown. In following the course of the Pacific Electric light rail systems, the new interstate freeway system in Los Angeles further strangled these communities because their residents were not only cemented into place but also now utterly dependent on cars and a shaky bus system for mobility across the area.

Los Angeles freeway construction began officially in the mid-1940s with the Arroyo Seco freeway from downtown Los Angeles to suburban Pasadena. But before an inch of concrete could be laid down, freeway boosters spent thirty years radically altering the region's scalar imaginary to create a Los Angeles metropolitan area that reduced neighborhoods and towns from Boyle Heights to Long Beach to Pasadena to mere nodules on a vertical and greatly expanded scaffold imaginary where the region claimed larger and overriding significance. Once that rescaled regional imaginary had been established, the freeways could then be celebrated as the logical means to circumnavigate the region. The state and auto and oil industries, as well as many others, promoted freeways as the best way to give individuals and businesses broad access to the LA basin— in effect enlarging the scale of movement for individuals and thus liberating them from a regional mass transit system that seemingly governed and limited their access. Businesses could circulate their products over a grander scale and enhance their profits. Individuals could search for work across a broader region because, as David Brodsley explains, "the area of land within a thirty-five minute drive from the civic center [in downtown Los Angeles] rose from 261 square miles in 1953 to 705 square miles by 1962, an increase of 175 percent" (61).

By the time *Their Dogs Came with Them* opens in 1960, freeway construction was fully underway. Indeed, the region of East Los Angeles and Boyle Heights, where the novel takes place, quickly became home to "the stack"—the euphemism for the major interchange between no less than *four* freeway systems. Altogether, six freeways moving the half-million vehicles that course through East Los Angeles daily. Not surprisingly, the language of "blight" subtended this choice of a location for the stack and the six massive freeways, even though the freeways plowed through and disappeared thriving black and Chicana/o neighborhoods; the freeway authorities celebrated their projects' beautifying attributes by claiming to slice through "thoroughly blighted" areas identified by housing authorities as "slums" and in this sense continued enacting a Los Angeles vision of itself as the "horizontal city of the future."[20]

In the US spatial imaginary, the "blighted areas" disappeared by freeway construction have their roots in the tenements of late nineteenth-century New York. As Priscilla Wald astutely shows, tenements were both "repository and mirror" for anxieties about the spread of disease.[21] The seeming capacity of tenements and slums to breed and grow diseases fostered a crisis narrative demanding that such spaces be sealed off and their diseases spatially contained. As reformers and novels of the period pointed out, however, tenements and slums were anything but "effective spaces of quarantine."[22] Nevertheless, by the turn of the twentieth century, tenements and contagion were fully intermeshed in the US spatial imaginary. Tenements, slums, and "blighted areas" are structured as public health hazards and are thus the site of pervasive regulation. "Next to the police and tax assessors," Nayan Shah notes, "municipal public health administrators assumed the most sweeping authority to survey and monitor the city and its inhabitants."[23] The metaphorization of tenements and slums as spatialized loci for disease, as large-scale petri dishes, justified the intensified policing and regulation powers that health administrators assumed. Blight discourse works "as a spatial form of racial project linking images of targeted neighborhoods and bodies to validate massive infusions of state intervention and capital."[24]

So if *Squatter* ends with Huntington's choice to "settle" Los Angeles and to suture together a new kind of Erie Canal—one in which, in a well-known formulation, Los Angeles could be described as the port of Iowa,[25] *Dogs* begins with Los Angeles's effort to evict the rail system and suture together a new sense of itself as an multi-urban metropole whose future is seemingly hinged by freeway construction. But rather than celebrate the effort to elevate Los Angeles, rather than rhapsodize over the rescaled city or signal the "liberation" from the mass transit system's many limitations, *Their Dogs Came with Them* offers a profound critique not simply of the effects of the freeway construction but also of the scaffold imaginary whose celebration of a phallic verticality entails not just the belittling and devastation of a Chicano community but also a failure to understand the social systems and affiliations that function alongside and apart from that imaginary. In this sense, the novel radically critiques the Enlightenment philosophy that erected the scaffold imaginary in the first place. More especially, *Their Dogs Came with Them* endows its critique with an analysis of the temporal ideology animating the scaffold imaginary and in doing so amplifies that scaffold's weaknesses and viciousness.

The novel opens with an epigraph from Miguel León-Portilla's *The Broken Spears: The Aztec Account of the Conquest of Mexico*, which describes the arrival of the Spanish *conquistadores* and notes: "Their

dogs came with them, running ahead of the column. They raised
their muzzles high; they lifted their muzzles to the wind. They
raced on before with saliva dripping from their jaws." This epigraph
clearly ties the freeway story to the history of colonialism and links
the rescaling of Los Angeles to the very coloniality of power that
ensared the *Américas* in a global capital vision. The bulldozers are
the new dogs: "The earthmovers, Grandmother Zumaya had called
them; the bulldozers had started from very far away and slowly
arrived on First Street, their muzzles like sharpened metal teeth
making way for the freeway" (6). Similarly, the dozers, "their bellies
petroleum readied," slowly and methodically "bite" into neighborhoods (12, 146), creating "condemned, windspooked houses" (134)
and "whole abandoned blocks to get lost in" (303), thereby con-
suming not just houses but also memories and legacies. Through
the metaphor of the bulldozers as dogs, the freeway construction
is likened to Spain's genocidal practices; the freeways and construction vehicles are part and parcel of another wave of community
destruction.[26]

   Unlike other novels that center on the Los Angeles freeways such
as Thomas Pynchon's *The Crying of Lot 49* or Joan Didion's *Play
It as It Lays*, *Dogs* considers not the effects of driving the freeways,
not the sense of "communion" Didion celebrated, but rather those
disappeared by the freeways. And ironically, the novel focuses not
on the liberating effects of driving a car on the Los Angeles freeway system (as described by Chester Himes in *If He Hollers Let
Him Go* or as celebrated by Jean Baudrillard in *America*) but rather
on the enclosing effects for those who are car-less: the pedestrians
and bus passengers who must navigate around the freeways.[27] The
novel follows the actual footsteps of a set of pedestrians: Ermila, a
young teenager, who "trotted the four neighborhood blocks netted
together by thick overhead wires, which dipped and lobbed from
telephone pole to pole to house to pole in an endless cat's cradle
until she arrived on the living side of First Street" (59); Tranquilina, an impoverished street preacher, who, along with her mother,
learns the freeway overpasses and narrow alleys while walking East
Los Angeles in search of food for their ministry; Turtle, an AWOL
member of the McBride Boys who runs from hideout to hideout;
and Ben, a troubled survivor of a horrific accident, and an unnamed

homeless women, both of whom walk up and down the streets of the city seemingly without connection to much that is near to them. If these pedestrians and bus riders consider the freeways as largely obstacles and destructive forces rather than the providers of opportunity and liberation, the novel itself utilizes the freeways in an ingenious way. Much like the four-freeway stack that destroyed Ermila and Turtle's neighborhood, the characters' lives touch and intersect but never precisely connect—they move around and past each other, seeing each other, but not really knowing much about each others' points of origin or crises and trajectories for the present. And in order to assimilate the plot of the novel, a reader must be willing to pay attention to the entire freeway map, as it were, that is, all of the characters' trajectories, as the narrative structure recursively unspools in an intermittent series of revelations, meditations, and mergers.

By refusing to fetishize the freeways' seemingly liberatory effects, *Dogs* underscores the incredible, unaccounted loss that their construction entailed:

> She looked out at her own house and all the other houses on Grandfather's side of First Street; the houses on the saved side were bright and ornamental like the big Easter eggs on display at the Segunda store counter. Some of the houses had cluttered porches with hanging plants or yards with makeshift gardens; others had parked cars on their front lawns. Some built wrought-iron gate fences while others had drowsy curtains swaying in wide-open windows. In a few weeks Chavela's side of the neighborhood, the dead side of the street, would disappear forever. The earthmovers had anchored, their tarps whipping like banging sails . . . In a few weeks the blue houses and all the other houses would vanish just like Chavela and all the other neighbors. (12)

Ermila's sense of being is structured by these disappearances—the vibrancy of one half of the street continually utters the lost names of the other half. The young child can only think of Chavela, an elderly woman herself displaced at least once before by a massive Mexico City earthquake, who had provided a refuge for a then-five-year-old

Ermila escaping her tense and sorrow-filled house. The construction equipment, like Cortez's ships, sails into the neighborhood to wipe out and leave for dead any in its way.

In order for scalar processes to work, space must be rationalized. All spatial differences have to be eradicated and all spaces treated as the same on a theoretical scalar plane. Such rationalization necessarily refuses to understand space as radically dissimilar or particular and refuses any sense of individual spaces as sacred or transcendent, or indeed locally meaningful and distinct. Ermila's inventory here could be said to refute that theory of space. Within Ermila's view are homes with vibrantly distinct personalities: the yards and homes express different affinities and desires. This particular place is not simply a location on a map but also, the novel suggests, something meaningful and creative. Ermila refutes spatial rationalization; *Their Dogs Came with Them* militates against it. In giving us one dense portrait of East Los Angeles after another, Viramontes argues against the inhumanity and reductive aggression of the spatial rationalization inherent to the scaffold imagination. Spatial rationality works as a kind of crime.

In other words, it is not just people who have been displaced by the demands of a rescaled Los Angeles—it is the vast networks of affiliations and place-linked memories that have been ripped away. The disorientation fueled by the abrupt erection of the freeways underscores this loss for Tranquilina and Mama:

> The two women struggled through the rain in a maze of unfamiliar streets. Whole residential blocks had been gutted since their departure and they soon discovered that Kern Street abruptly dead-ended, forcing them to retrace their trail. The streets Mama remembered had once connected to other arteries of the city, rolling up and down hills and in and out of neighborhoods where neighbors of different nationalities intersected with one another. But now the freeways amputated the streets into stumped dead ends, and the lives of the neighbors itched like phantom limbs in Mama's memory. (32–33)

The deep texture of a place and its relationship to one's sense of connection and belonging are eviscerated by the anonymous mountains of concrete haphazardly claimed by taggers. The text highlights the argument that the freeways destroyed vitality, but the palpable quality of that long-gone vitality pains with a haunting and forceful memory; their spatial relations have been altered and their memories are confounded. Such discombobulation, caused by what one can reasonably call a new enclosure movement, leaves the East Los Angeles residents, such as Ermila's grandmother, struggling to find some measure of interior stability:

> If she paced up and down the hallway, the repetitious groans from the loose floorboard reminded her she was entrapped. If she looked out the window, the freeway construction bit endless trenches into the earth that resembled a moat, fortifying their safety from all that furious violence outside. No sooner would her sense of consolation override any panic than she realized the construction of the freeway was ridding the neighborhood of everything that was familiar to her. The memory of who lived where, who buried their children's umbilical cords or grew lemons the size of apples, done away. Grandmother thought about how carnivorous life was, how indifferent machinery teeth could be, and all these murky thoughts swirled the dust and tar and heat into a speeding meteor gathering strength. (146)

As Grandmother's survey of loss suggests, the destruction of the neighborhood shatters her relationship to her past as well as to the present. The freeways leave her marooned and bereft of groundedness. She experiences the loss of the neighborhood less like death than like the disappearance of her own daughter many years before. As the narrator notes, "Death is finite but disappearance is not and so you see her face everywhere" (147). It is this sense of the ever-present quality of the lost neighborhood that *Dogs* captures—the kind of infinite quality that makes the loss felt intricately as an aching, absent presence outside of a linear temporal structure and beyond the scale of the daily. Disappearance is infinite, the narrator tells us; it haunts us, leaving us unsure if we might be surprised or disappointed, continually unsettled in our expectations and confidence. *Dogs* further suggests the tangible quality of disappearance through

the story of Renata Valenzuela. The name of the abducted child is
repeatedly invoked by parents as a warning to girls who stray. But
she also functions as a kind of allegory of the lost neighborhoods,
as a signal of the fragility of human connections, given "how carnivorous life was, how indifferent machinery teeth could be" (146).

While the freeways strangled memories and set them loose like
phantom limbs, they have also further impoverished people, by shrink-
ing the scale of circulation for laborers and indeed making movement more onerous rather than less. Buses are slower than the rail
lines; their routes are not as extensive, nor their travel as frequent.
Ermila, who must take buses to get anywhere she cannot walk to,
meditates daily on the centrality of the bus to her working neigh-
bor's lives:

> Four freeways crossing and interchanging, looping and stack-
> ing in the Eastside, but if you didn't own a car, you were
> fucked. Many were, and this is something Ermila always said in
> her head: You're fucked. Though this morning she said, We're
> fucked, as the men passed her window to gather on the corner
> for the Rapid Transit 26 bus where the women already waited,
> all ready. Each morning Ermila saw them from her window:
> several women in several sizes and ages who carried with them
> the weight of a family or two or three, their backs slumped
> over as they sat on the bus bench, their sweaters draped over
> their shoulders for protection against the morning chill. They
> toted their history of muted desires packed tightly in the bags
> under their eyes, and carried with that the poker face of their
> responsibility, a grimace left over from their splash of cold
> water on their cheeks each morning. The five-thirty bus took
> the first set of female passengers to the Westside where, *if* they
> spoke English, they worked as nannies for hire (and did the
> ironing) or, if they didn't speak the language, they worked as
> housekeepers (ditto with the ironing) . . . all of them jour-
> neyed out of the neighborhood and outward into the massive
> unknown to become a part of the city's working migration. It
> might have strained lesser believers, might have broken their
> profound belief in hard work, were these women not made
> of gut and grist and a gleam of determination as blinding as a

California sun. They sat on the bus bench, canvas bags beside them, filled with the day's essentials: fearlessness scrambled with huevos con chorizo and wrapped in a tortilla as thin as the documents they carried to prove legality. Why bother looking at the bounce of purposeful step, their bus timetables tucked inside wallets, these men and women who hastened to their destinations feeling a sense of commitment, compelled to believe they held the world together with the glue of their endless sweat? They carried everything needed to assist them in holding up the operations of commerce, and carried it all onto the bus except laziness. (176–177)

In this exquisite meditation, a kind of praise-song for laboring Chicana/os, Ermila emphasizes the costs the freeways impose on the car-less. What Ermila asks us to admire is the steady determination of her neighbors to work despite the infrastructure built to undermine their futures. It is as if the freeway stack itself rubs their class-status in and forces those who ride inefficient, packed buses to greet their labors with ever more determination. In dwelling on the residents' "sense of commitment" and their "muted desires," Viramontes also takes up another aspect of the scalar masquerade of spatial rationalization. On the one hand, in order for Los Angeles to rescale itself, it had to embrace the logic of spatial rationalization by treating space as the same. Yet oddly enough, it could not fully achieve that desired scalar leap without rationalizing the choice of freeway routes through the discourse of blight. One kind of rationalization entailed another kind. Such inherent contradiction meant that Los Angeles could suggest that for the purposes of achieving new capital efficiencies, all space was the same. But in order, precisely, to make that claim, it had to argue that some spaces were less deserving (i.e., more blighted) than others. Viramontes pushes back against that spatial rendering with a reverent portrait of the barrios' inhabitants as they wait for buses to take them to work. She insists that we understand East Los Angeles not as "blighted," but as home to brave and determined people caring for other people.

The alienating effects of the freeways are further underscored by an exceptional series of observations Ben makes after he watches a homeless woman struggle across a pedestrian bridge spanning the

Hollywood Freeway. Ben muses on how little drivers zooming beneath her on the freeway might care about her disheveled state, or think of her fragility. Terrifically scarred and fragile himself, Ben projects onto the woman his own sense of how others might perceive him as he seeks to understand the workings of empathy: "One would have to be close enough to look into her eyes, jump into the trunk of her heart, lift the stage curtains to see behind her props. It was one thing to assume, another to conjure, and yet another *to feel for her. One would need metaphor to love her*" (125). In a novel that steadily considers harsh and violent situations, this quiet meta-comment on the significance of imaginative labor disrupts the text's almost cantankerous attention to the coloniality of power.[28] Ben senses the bridging function of metaphors, their capacity to transport or carry concepts, and so grasps how metaphor enables the work of love particularly within and amidst the omnipresence of violence. Just as *Dogs* uses the freeway stack as a model for narrative structure, it also uses the image of a woman alone on a pedestrian overpass above thousands of disinterested, moving cars as an image of the freeway system's isolating and alienating effects—and yet it envelops that sense of alienation within the folds of vividly sculptural language, suggesting a detour around that very alienation. Ben's insights also argue that the scalar processes that are so much a part of the working of coloniality can indeed be circumvented through literature and the imagination. The strategies behind the scaffold imaginary can be made clear and less potent. Metaphor does the work of love, and it is the hard streets of a post-stack East Los Angeles that also require that translational act of labor that the novel attempts to provide.

The freeway construction grounds the novel historically. That historical modality is twice signaled for readers before the novel even opens—first with the epigraph from Miguel León-Portilla, which both explains the novel's title and signals its ongoing engagement with coloniality, and second with the bold print "1960–1970," which seems to suggest the facticity of the novel itself. Overlaid onto the story of the freeways' arrival is a post-surrealist account of the Quarantine Authority—the QA—whose mission, we are told, is to rid the barrio of rabid dogs. The QA is the counterhistorical aspect of the novel; it's the story of the enforcement of deranged power.[29]

If the bulldozers are the new dogs in 1960 when the novel opens, the helicopters are the new bulldozers by 1970. The QA establishes a set of checkpoints and a curfew and demands that residents prove their right to enter the QA zone—a zone patrolled by police and guns where documents structure spatial belonging. At night, squadrons of QA helicopters fly over the quarantined area shooting stray dogs as they roam the streets. Characterizing the arrival of the QA as a subsequent invasion within a history of invasion and conquest, the novel insists on this framework:

> Ten years later the child becomes a young woman who will recognize the invading engines of the Quarantine Authority helicopters because their whir of blades above the roof of her home, their earth-rattling explosive motors, will surpass in volume the combustion of engines driving the bulldozer tractors, slowly, methodically unspooling the six freeways. She will be a young woman peering from between the palm tree drapes of her grandparents' living room, a woman watching the QA helicopters burst out of the midnight sky to shoot dogs not chained up by curfew. Qué locura, she thinks. The world is going crazy. The chopper blades raise the roof shingles of the neighborhood houses and topple TV antennas in swirls of suction on the living side of First Street. (12)

It is certainly almost crazy to imagine even the LAPD claiming it could eliminate a rabies epidemic by shooting dogs from helicopters.[30] The surreal quality of the plotline is hard to swallow unless one considers Ben's ode to metaphor. The QA plotline doesn't just tie the novel to the Vietnam War or to the long history of imperial conquest, it also underscores the effects of scalar processes. To reduce East Los Angeles to a blighted area entailed a further reduction and dehumanization of its inhabitants. The QA reinforces that account. The freeway construction that the novel memorializes worked to perform a scalar fix that enabled a new round of capital accumulation by rescaling capital relations from a series of small-scale relations to a larger, regional scale and simultaneously rescaling the barrio, enabling (1) its reduction in importance in terms of capital flow and (2) enhancing by enclosing its policeability. In giving us

the ludicrous story of the QA, Viramontes pulls from the shadows
the operative legacy of coloniality. She asks us to think about the
ways different scales frame realities differently, and in juxtaposing
the real scalar fix of the freeways with the surreal scalar fix of the
QA, she is showing us how particular scalar fixes are only, in Neil
Smith's words, "temporary spatializations of certain social assumptions." The story of the QA makes those social assumptions visible. Viramontes hones our attention and hones our capacity to pay
attention to those segments of spatial processes where the narrative
about a place (as blighted, for example) instantiates the practices
that do indeed incapacitate them. In other words, the discourse of
contagion produces the space supposedly contaminated.

The QA reinforces the scalar structure of the entire region by
further strangling East Los Angeles. If the freeways created one set
of enclosures and rescaled the barrio within a rescaled Los Angeles,
the QA further solidifies these enclosures and indeed reduces the
scale of movement for the residents even further. As the narrator
dispassionately recounts:

> The girlfriends lived within the shaded boundaries of the map
> printed in English only and distributed by the city. From First
> Street to Boyle to Whittier and back to Pacific Boulevard, the
> roadblocks enforced a quarantine to contain a potential out-
> break of rabies. *Let's work together to keep our families and our
> city safe*, the end of the message urged.
>
> Yea, Mousie added. You know some culero will be, like,
> "you got your ID or INS or SS card wit you?"
>
> For sure, like, "Hey, let me see your IUD?" Lollie joked,
> opening her knees wide and then saying, "Yea, wanna check
> it out?"
>
> Except for troublemakers, the neighborhood people bit into
> their quarantine without questions. Ermila's own grandparents
> were convinced that the curfew and the shooting and the QA
> all *contained the rabies epidemic*. (54–55)

Viramontes draws together two racializing forms here. The narrative notes the official discourse of scale, the map with its boundaries
demarcating the barrio's place in the broader bounded region of the

city. Placed into a flattened relationship here is the cutting phrase "printed in English only"—the narrator's reversal of the more colloquially common "printed only in English" signals the anti-immigrant rhetoric that has served as a neoliberal version of Jim Crow segregation across the country and clearly indicates how the QA functions as a racializing mechanism. The girls' jokes challenge the policing mechanism that supports the scaling processes that would contain them and turn those mechanisms into a means to signal their own desires to resist that containment by taking control of their bodies and their reproductive capacities. The narrator then continues the joking by noting that the barrio "bit" into the quarantine. Viramontes here brilliantly puns further on "contained" as if to suggest that the actions of the QA have both stopped the rabies epidemic and actually possessed it, i.e., spread rabies (in a writerly deconstructive move—the quarantine performs what it claims to prevent). This reinforces the narrator's suggestion that the rabies epidemic is not real at all. Finally, the term challenges us to consider what and who is contained by the curfew, signalling the state's desire to contain and to penalize, to create penal endpoints for peoples of color. The narrator's implicit critique of the barrio's passive acquiescence, however, is framed by examples of the girls' own critique. For, as Ermila later complains, "She wondered if she was the only person to doubt this peculiar situation or had found it as confusing and crazy as she" (62).

The surreal quality of the QA is further reinforced by Ermila's strange encounter with a dog. One evening, lying in the interstices between sleep and wakefulness, Ermila vaguely hears "the freeway bumble" as well as "the sporadic spray of bullets" and the "drone of engines," and then she sleepily spots "a small curled-up dog" who is "ludicrous on its sausage legs" (75). Ermila is at first convinced that her grandmother had placed the dog in her room to guard and restrict her movements and then she is terrified when the dog suddenly "gnashed its fangs" and strikes her (75). The next morning, with a throbbing wound, Ermila asks her grandparents about the dog, but despite her bandaged hand, no one evinces any belief that such a dog might exist or even be allowed in the house in the first place (179–183). Is the dog an apparition? Ermila's blood can only tell her that it is not. But how then could the dog appear only to her and yet still bite her? The dog is both phantom and figural motif, a signal of the ongoing violence of imperial structures whether they be freeway stacks or rabbies quarantines or rigged ships. The dog continually threatens Ermila over the course of two days and opens another aspect of Viramontes's critique of the scaffold imaginary.

The problem with phallic verticality and scale production is that in fixing capital by narrating and rationalizing space, scale also fixes time, locks it down into a linear structure. Woven into the scaffold imaginary is the Enlightenment's temporal narrative of history as a record of linear progress.[31] The corollary to this account is the assumption that the further along one moves on the spatial scale, from village to metropole, the further along one moves temporally from the past into contemporaneity via the track of modern future movement. De Witt Clinton grasped this structure when he argued so persuasively that building the Erie Canal was not simply a means to transform the scale of US industrial production but also a way to construct the future. The regional, the local, the parochial are not merely spatial structures: they are temporal coordinates. In the scaffold imaginary they are inevitably left behind, left back, left outside not just the "horizontal city of the future" but also relegated to the past to serve as contemporary ancestors.

And it's that exchange, that slipping a certain temporal logic into scale production that partly accounts for the power of scales and scale jumping in the first place.[32] In the scaffold imaginary, one scale is always left behind, set back in time in a linear, temporal logic of progression. That is what Viramontes points to in *Their Dogs Came with Them* as Ermila contends with the dog that materializes seemingly out of nowhere and bites her viciously. The dog's haunting materialization is of course a reference to coloniality, an allegory of sorts, but it's a rupture that also asks us to think about the way haunting troubles linear time and thereby bites into the phallic verticality of scalar thinking.

Haunting refutes linear temporality; it mocks it. If linear temporality suggests "there is no going back," haunting suggests the effervescence of a denser "now" that is endowed with a more complex temporal structure of flows, swirls, and connections. The dog bites Ermila for realizing the "locura" that surrounds her, for not biting into the phallic verticality that renders East Los Angeles obsolete, primordial, and heavily policed. But the novel rebukes linear temporality not just in its deployment of the haunting dog but also through its narrative structure. Because it weaves through and around the plot's basic events (which take about forty-eight hours) by moving in and out of the decade of the sixties and back and forth within the decade so that the reader is constantly unsettled by the temporal shifts, it suggests our desire for linear temporality and highlights the extent to which we have been trained to think through it. In this manner, it further debunks Newtonian logics of time and space and their deployment through scalar politics.

The massive outlay of public money to fund the Los Angeles freeway construction and to keep it operating despite its environmentally devastating effects requires a great love of phallic verticality and a naturalized faith in the utility of the scaffold imaginary. *Their Dogs Came with Them* refutes this logic and argues that phallic verticality—the love of the large with its entrenched faith in a scaffold imaginary in which the transnational, the hemispheric, and the global are seen as more vital than the local, the barrio—depends on a bankrupt philosophy of temporal linearity and spatial rationality. It suggests that like the snarling and gnashing dog, the philosophy bites us, but no one knows who did it or how it happened; we simply find ourselves bleeding. *Their Dogs Came with Them* reveals the scaffold imaginary's willingness to wound and draw blood in order to keep its spatial/temporal cover.

Acknowledgments

I would like to thank those who have helped me work out the ideas in this essay: Ariana Vigil, Belinda Rincón, Omar Figueredo, John Alba Cutler, Armando Garcia, Yolanda Padilla, and the students in my First Year Writing Seminar (Paul Bennetch, Hanna Groback, Valerie Campbell, Ishani Dhaon, Michelle Eisner, Michael Hebusch, Sofia Lopez, Chidnma Okafor, and Allison Pinterpe). I also want to thank Gabriella Gutiérrez y Muhs for her infinite patience and generous encouragement. Finally, my deepest gratitude to Helena María Viramontes, whose friendship and collegiality I treasure intensely.

Notes

1. Saldívar, *Chicano Narrative* and *The Borderlands of Culture.*
2. See her "Feminism on the Border."

3. See Levander and Levine's influential volume, *Hemispheric American Studies*.

4. Quiroga, *Tropics of Desire*; Castillo, *Redreaming America*. For a critique of the neoliberal employment of the term "Latino," see the crucial work of Arlene M. Dávila.

5. Clinton, "Opening Speech to Forty Second Session of New York State Legislature, January 1819."

6. For an important discussion, see Rivera, *The Emergence of Mexican America*.

7. The literature on scale is long and vexed. For one of the most thorough and current bibliographies on scale, see Marston, Jones, and Woodward, "Human Geography without Scale." For attempts to think about scale and race, see my *Extinct Lands, Temporal Geographies* and Clement Lai's "The Racial Triangulation of Space."

8. Marston et al., 418.

9. Marston et al., 418.

10. Marston et al., 420.

11. Marston et al., 421.

12. Marston et al., 422.

13. Marston et al., 427

14. Marston et al., 425.

15. Escobar, "The 'Ontological Turn' in Social Theory," 109.

16. I am further suggesting that we think about how racializing processes produce scales that are not necessarily or not apparently spatial, but that can be seen to emerge in part through scaling and spatializing processes. In this sense I am suggesting that scaling may be one of the most crucial producers and stabilizers of racialization and that the attempt to jettison these ethno-racial categories runs the risk of leaving a racializing logic in place and undeterred.

17. Viramontes, *Their Dogs Came with Them*; Ruiz de Burton, *The Squatter and the Don*.

18. According to David Brodsley, "Henry Huntington retained control of a consolidated inner-city streetcar system, the Los Angeles Railway Company. Operating over 1,110 miles of track and providing about 700 miles of service by 1925, the Pacific Electric gave the Los Angeles metropolitan area the largest electric interurban railway in the world. . . . Of the 42 cities incorporated in the area by the mid-thirties, 39 owed their early growth to the electric railway" (69).

19. For exceptionally thoughtful histories of the Los Angeles freeway system, see Avila, *Popular Culture in the Age of White Flight* and Hutchinson, *Imagining Transit*.

20. A phrase apparently coined by a Los Angeles city planner, Gordon Whitnall, in 1924. See Foster, *From Streetcar to Superhighway*, 71.

21. Wald, 114.

22. Wald, 114.

23. Shah, 3.

24. Clement Lai, draft of " 'Totally Oriental': Redevelopment, Postwar Orientalism, and the Imagineering of Japantown." Unpublished.

25. Brodsley, 71.

26. It's worth noting that Viramontes was not the first to link freeway construction to Spain's colonial projects. *California Highways and Public Works* (Sept. 9, 1950) celebrated the freeway construction initiative with a review of California's colonial history, including discussions of Junipero Serra and Juan Bautista de Anza. It also includes a discussion of the extent to which contemporary California arteries follow the paths traveled by Spanish explorers (vol. 29). See especially Eric Avila's discussion of the uses of romantic missionary discourse around freeway production.

27. But see Baudrillard, *America*; Didion, *Play It as It Lays*; and Himes, *If He Hollers Let Him Go*.

28. Cutler perceptively reads this passage as a suggestion that "literature here seeks to impel action," 166.

29. Bridget Kevane links the Quarantine Authority to a rabies panic in Los Angeles in 1955. See her *Profane & Sacred: Latino/a American Writers Reveal the Interplay of the Secular and the Religious*, 25. Neel Ahuja links the QA to the history of the Border Patrol and its practices of quarantining immigrants.

30. As an aside, my sense of this surreal quality may be generational. When I taught the book recently and asked my students whether they had been struck by the oddity of this image, one said no because it seemed "normal, something you'd see in a computer game."

31. Marx, *The Machine in the Garden*, 197.

32. As Marston and colleagues note in "Reply: Situating Flatness," "a Newtonian worldview continually haunts the calculus of mobilization and resistance. At its most basic, this resolves itself in size fetishism, where global capitalism and imperialism can only be combated by entities operating at a similar scale. This leaves those who are constrained by various 'militant particularisms' (Harvey, 1996), or who are too under-resourced or disorganized to 'scale jump' (Smith, 1992), on the bench when it comes to the zero-sum game of global resistance" (274).

Works Cited

Ahuja, Neel. "Postcolonial Critique in a Multispecies World." *PMLA* (2009): 556–563.

Avila, Eric. *Popular Culture in the Age of White Flight*. Berkeley: University of California Press, 2004.

Baudrillard, Jean. *America*. Translated by Chris Turner. London: Verso, 1989, c1988.

Brady, Mary Pat. *Extinct Lands, Temporal Geographies: Chicana Literature and the Urgency of Space*. Durham, NC: Duke University Press, 2002.

Brodsley, David. *L.A. Freeway: An Appreciative Essay.* Berkeley: University of California Press, 1981.

Castillo, Debra. *Redreaming America: Toward a Bilingual American Culture.* Albany: SUNY Press, 2005.

Clinton, De Witt. "Opening Speech to Forty Second Session of New York State Legislature, January 1819," In *Messages from the Governors,* edited by Charles Lincoln, 966–967. Albany, NY: J.B. Lyon, 1909.

Cutler, John Alba. "On Recent Chicano Literature." *Western American Literature* 44, no. 2 (2009): 159–167.

Dávila, Arlene M. *Latino Spin: Public Image and the Whitewashing of Race.* New York: New York University Press, 2008.

Didion, Joan. *Play It as It Lays.* New York: Farrar, Straus and Giroux, 1970.

Escobar, Arturo. "The 'Ontological Turn' in Social Theory. A Commentary on 'Human Geography without Scale,' by Sallie Marston, John Paul Jones II and Keith Woodward." *Transactions of the Institute of British Geographers* 32 (2007): 106–111.

Foster, Mark. *From Streetcar to Superhighway: American City Planners and Urban Transportation, 1900–1940.* Philadelphia: Temple University Press, 1981.

Harvey, David. *Justice, Nature, and the Geography of Difference.* Cambridge, MA: Blackwell Publishers, 1996.

Himes, Chester. *If He Hollers Let Him Go.* New York: Thunder's Mouth Press, 1986.

Hutchinson, Sikivu. *Imagining Transit: Race, Gender, and Transportation Politics in Los Angeles.* New York: Peter Lang, 2003.

Kevane, Bridget. *Profane & Sacred: Latino/a American Writers Reveal the Interplay of the Secular and the Religious.* Lanham, MD: Rowman and Littlefield, 2008.

Lai, Clement. "The Racial Triangulation of Space: Japanese Americans and African Americans in the Urban Renewal of the Multiracial Fillmore·District." *The Annals of the Association of American Geographers* 102, no. 1 (2012): 151–170.

León-Portilla, Miguel. *The Broken Spears: The Aztec Account of the Conquest of Mexico.* Boston: Beacon Press, 1992.

Levander, Carolyn, and Robert Levine, eds. *Hemispheric American Studies.* New Brunswick, NJ: Rutgers University Press, 2008.

Marston, Sallie A., John Paul Jones III, and Keith Woodward. "Human Geography without Scale." *Transactions of the Institute of British Geographers* 30, no. 4 (2005): 416–432.

———. "Reply: Situating Flatness." *Transactions of the Institute of British Geographers* 32, no. 2 (2007): 264–276.

Marx, Leo. *The Machine in the Garden.* Oxford: Oxford University Press, 1964.

Pynchon, Thomas. *The Crying of Lot 49.* Philadelphia: Lippincott, 1966.

Quiroga, José. *Tropics of Desire.* New York: NYU Press, 2000.

Rivera, John-Michael. *The Emergence of Mexican America.* New York: NYU Press, 2006.

Ruiz de Burton, María Amparo. *The Squatter and the Don.* San Francisco: S. Carson and Co., 1885.

Saldívar, Ramon. *Chicano Narrative: Dialectics of Difference.* Madison: University of Wisconsin Press, 1990.

———. *The Borderlands of Culture: Américo Paredes and the Transnational Imaginary.* Durham, NC: Duke University Press, 2006.

Saldívar-Hull, Sonia. "Feminism on the Border: From Gender Politics to Geopolitics." In *Criticism in the Borderlands: Studies in Chicano Literature, Culture, and Ideology,* edited by Héctor Calderón and José David Saldívar, 203–220. Durham, NC: Duke University Press, 1991.

Shah, Nayan. *Contagious Divides: Epidemics and Race in San Francisco's Chinatown.* Berkeley: University of California Press, 2001.

Smith, Neil. "Contours of a Spacialized Politics: Homeless Vehicles and the Production of Geographical Space." *Social Text* 33 (1992): 54–81.

Viramontes, Helena María. *Their Dogs Came with Them.* New York: Atria, 2007.

Wald, Priscilla. *Contagious: Cultures, Carriers, and the Outbreak Narrative.* Durham, NC: Duke University Press, 1998.

8

Crowbars, Peaches, and Sweat

Coming to Voice through Image in *Under the Feet of Jesus*

R. JOYCE Z. L. GARAY

CHICANA WRITER HELENA MARÍA VIRAMONTES'S *Under the Feet of Jesus* is a novel centered on US migrant laborers. To convey their world as a historical and contemporary reality, Viramontes relies upon imagery of the everyday, organic, and familiar to the realm of migrant labor—agricultural products, the natural world, and tools. These images of the everyday, beyond typical descriptive function and beyond dialogic utterance, emphatically speak the silences and violences that Viramontes's migrant family endures as disenfranchised, subaltern. I view Viramontes's imagery and its magnification of the fissures in dominance through which one migrant family disappears as a theoretical and poetic response to Gayatri Spivak's question about subaltern voice(lessness).

In her renowned essay, which has become a cornerstone of postcolonial theory, "Can the Subaltern Speak?: Speculations on Widow Sacrifice," Spivak focuses on the image of a Bengali woman's self-immolation upon her husband's funeral pyre.[1] Solely interpreted as tragedy reifying the colonistic and patriarchal determinations of gendered behavior appropriate upon the death of a husband, the woman's death is not understood as an act of self-representation. Not heard, not understood by those witnessing her act, the widow's subalternity retains silence as essential condition. As Spivak explains, the Bengali woman's action is a desperate substitution for speech that is unavailable to her, for speech is a dialogic process that demands both a listener and a speaker (82). Refusing to provide a resolute answer to the question posed in the title of her essay, Spivak instead emphasizes that systematic "unlearning" of privilege by those in power who are meant to hear and understand is mandatory in order for the subaltern, potentially, to be heard and understood (91). The revolutionary objective, then, is not to speak *for* (or merely interpret the actions of) the subaltern, but to revamp the script to work to provide access to (potential) subaltern voices.

Significantly, Spivak clarifies in an interview with Leon de Kock that subalternity is not merely being silenced by oppression, but is having "limited or no access to the cultural imperialism," being excluded by, erased from the dominant cultural (capitalistic) script. Further, Spivak explains that the working class is certainly disenfranchised and oppressed within the system of capitalism, but is not wholly silenced, or subaltern. Members of the working class are not outside of a hegemonic system, even as an exploited labor force, the lowest tier within that system.

While Viramontes's central characters may loosely be considered working class, I contend that they fit the subalternity that Spivak defines because of their complex positioning not only as working class laborers but also as liminal or non-citizen, as Mexican/Mexican American, as provisionally English literate, and as members of a non-normative family. Viramontes's migrant family is outside the first-world system and hegemonic discourse of the United States and is, in fact, made subaltern by its socioeconomic and cultural institutions, most dominantly market economy, health care, and education. As outside even working-class US citizenship, Viramontes's migrant family is homeless, incessantly migratory, destitute, denied any legitimate social place or privilege, uncertain daily of how basic needs will be met, and terrified. Through image, Viramontes artfully and relentlessly conveys this social reality that is otherwise unspeakable.

Through image, she does not speak *for* but speaks what creates and surrounds the silences that envelop her subaltern characters.

While the images through which Viramontes composes literary setting and those through which she constructs other characters—especially the husband and father figure, Perfecto Flores, a man of seventy-three years whose body and mind are declining after a lifetime of hard labor—are crucial to the novel, I focus in this essay on the images central to the two central female characters, Petra, the middle-aged mother of five children, and Estrella, her eldest daughter. Because gender in part both compels and complicates Petra's and Estrella's voicelessness, I see Viramontes's imagistic acumen most prominently in the development of these two characters. Thus, in the discussion that follows, I first analyze Petra, and the images that convey her character and her social position,[2] before dedicating the bulk of my discussion to the images associated with Viramontes's central character, Estrella, whose coming of age is a complicated intertwining of her migrant status and socioeconomic position, her race, and her gender. In tracing these images, I show, first, how Viramontes illustrates Petra's attempts to self-determine and, then, how Viramontes grants Estrella unique capacity to manipulate her understanding of her everyday world toward utterance she is otherwise disallowed.

Petra: Self-Mutilation and Faith

At thirty-five, Petra's life has worn her body and spirit well beyond her years. Her body fails her, as she struggles with the pain of varicose veins treated with elixirs of garlic, and confines her, as she confronts both the birth of a sixth child and the uncertain future that will welcome it. She is an immigrant, with a battered Social Security card, questionably her own, and an I.D. card (not a driver's license) she keeps fiercely guarded under the feet of Jesus upon her altar with the birth certificates of her children that represent their citizenship (166).[3] She is additionally primarily a speaker of Spanish negotiating an English-dominant US environment, a fact conveyed through her reliance upon Estrella's ability to translate for her as well as through the numerous Spanish phrases and sentences Viramontes leaves untranslated. In these ways, Petra is generationally removed/ kept from the potential Estrella and her siblings have to achieve voice and place in the United States.

In characterizing Petra through image, speaking the silence of her subaltern position—which is compounded by her status as woman, single mother, Spanish speaker, and immigrant—Viramontes combines iconic religious imagery with the images of nature associated with both *curanderismo* and the agricultural environments Petra knows most intimately. Indeed, these three realms of knowledge and experience are the lenses through which Petra perceives her world, assigns meaning, survives psychologically, and makes a place for herself and her children where no literal place exists.

Petra's substance is revealed in the psychotic break occurring when the impossibility of her position following her husband's abandonment is most clear to her and in its aftermath. With last notices piled in a shoebox, empty cupboards and starving children, no cash or employment, and not having heard from her husband in months, Petra locks herself in the bathroom, her only refuge from the despair of her family and her anonymity in a place in which she is invisible, ineffectually prays the rosary, and self-mutilates. Biting into her thumb, self-silencing, is recognition of her dire situation and futility. A language-less utterance, this act clearly evidences Petra's isolation and disenfranchisement; she is without community, without social support, and, certainly, beyond a position in which any could answer a vocalizing of need. As Petra exits the bathroom and vents her fear and frustration in screaming at her children until they cower, Estrella screams back, scolding her, and insisting her mother return to her central role as caretaker. In response to her mother's psychological deterioration, Estrella has been compelled to adopt the mother role herself, the twins even "calling her mama" (13). Simultaneously ashamed, outraged, and simply psychologically exhausted, "Petra broke, her mouth a cut jagged line. She bolted out of the apartment" (19). Significantly, the understated image of a mouth, uneven and bleeding, connotes Petra's incapacity to find in language either expression or solution. With sounds colliding in chaos around her, Petra does not know exactly where she is going or where her escape will end. On the verge of suicide or physical escape, which would leave her children orphans, Petra instead courageously makes the

decision to shoulder her responsibility and their needs. Her decision and determination are conveyed through the simplicity of six
words—"one foot up, one foot down" (20). The immediate aftermath of this scene is not textualized, though its consequences are
clearly implied: the family abandons Petra's dreams of a life apart
from the fields and the migrant cycle, and she abandons any hope
of the return of her life's love, her husband, and soon finds another
man, Perfecto Flores, with whom to align her life and to help provide for her children.

Narrated prior to but chronologically after her psychological break
in the city, the opening scene of the novel establishes the importance of both traditional religion and folk belief to Petra. Leaving
the rosary hanging from the rearview mirror, Petra looks first to her
outdoor "kitchen" space, while Perfecto plots a layout for residence
by seven individuals in the two rooms of the dilapidated bungalow.
His first concern being Petra's well-being, he immediately reserves
a corner for her *altara* (8). Also, guarding Petra from her own fear
and knowing she would see it as an omen of death, Perfecto quickly
removes a dead sparrow, commenting, significantly, that it is an
ignorant victim of the way birds "[find] their way into abandoned
houses only to bombard themselves against the walls," an image
resonant with the family's situation within the United States (8).
Petra's beliefs established enough for Perfecto to plan around, Petra
herself solidifies the depth of these beliefs when, having scraped the
grate over the fire pit clean, her next action is to draw a circle in
the dirt around the home to keep the scorpions at bay. That Petra
believes her icon of Jesucristo and her line in the dirt will keep her
children safe evidences her implementation of coping mechanisms;
her faith is the only tool she owns.

Not surprisingly, then, Petra relies upon both prayer and folk
belief to establish a sense of efficacy in protecting her family. For
example, not wanting Estrella's future children to be born with
harelips, Petra pleads with her not to join the other *piscadores* at the
corral on a night when the moon is full (69). Of course, the obvious
cause of such birth defects is exposure to pesticides and the obvious threat in Estrella's presence at the corral is the predominance of
men present and her naïvety about her ripening adolescent body, yet
Petra processes via faith, as makes sense to her. Similarly, she keeps

the key to the station wagon under her shirt, next to her skin, again, to superstitiously protect the health of the fetus, the "lima bean" growing within, though a perceptive reader also sees the action as a pragmatic mechanism preventing Perfecto from abandoning the family (72, 125).

That Petra's faith is actually less faith than a way to maintain a sense of control is perhaps most clear in a scene near the conclusion of the novel. When the family is on the verge of yet another departure, the final departure of the novel, and each, as Cecelia Lawless argues, is on the "threshold" of individual departure, Petra prays and makes an offering to Jesucristo to ask for intercession that will convince Perfecto to stay (365). Her body awkward in pregnancy, she knocks the statue to the floor: "The head of Jesucristo broke from His neck and when His eyes stared up at her like pools of dark ominous water, she felt a wave of anger swelling against her chest" (167). Yet rather than duplicating the psychological breakdown of her time in the city, Petra, without lamentation, lifts and pockets the head of Jesucristo, its size and weight "like a walnut in the palm of her hand" (167). Her faith shaken, Petra sees the stick she uses to draw her scorpion-preventing circle around the bungalow as "slight and feeble" and realizes that "all she [has]" is "papers and sticks and broken faith and Perfecto," which "[seem] as weightless against the massive darkness, as the head she [holds]" (169). Her faith is not attached to the icon, nor even truly religious, but is utilized to help her negotiate her reality, as staring out at Perfecto in the darkness she tightens her grip on the small severed head of her Savior and longs to look into Perfecto's eyes to know the true answer to her prayer (169).

This secularizing of religious faith is corroborated in Petra's conflation of the smell of good garlic, the most effective treatment in providing her relief for her "legs shackled by varicose veins" with the smell of roses that accompanies the Virgen de Guadalupe (9). It is through the worldly, the practicality of nature, that Petra finds religion applicable. In a kitschy montage that adorns the wall of the convenience store where Petra and her children shop for overpriced necessities, a "lopsided poster" of the Virgen de Guadalupe, glamorously outlined by "red and green and white twinkling Christmas lights" that Petra sees as "a sequin necklace," is sandwiched between iconic shots of Elvis Presley and of Marilyn Monroe "holding her billowing white dress down" (110). Clearly not equal in the popular imagination with the images she is framed by, and stripped of religious meaning, the Virgin of the poster is an obviously commodified image, a mechanism of advertising directed toward an exploited consumer population of which Petra is part. Yet, "[each] time the lights blinked, Petra saw herself reflected in La Virgen's glossy downcast eyes. Unlike Marilyn's white pumps which were buried under the shriveled pods of Chile Negro, La Virgen was raised, it seemed to Petra, above a heavenly mound of bulbous garlic" (110). Petra's recognition of herself in the image of the model for her selflessness aptly represents her assignment of her children's needs before her own.[4] As imperfect and human as Petra is, she consistently strives to provide for, nurture, and protect her offspring. Garlic is the one necessity she insists upon to alleviate her own suffering, a privilege she maintains even when Estrella begs for the luxury of eggs. It is an interruption to the reverie of digging to the bottom of the bin for the freshest bulbs when she meets Perfecto, who, having closely observed her, knows what she is seeking and hands her a bulb smelling of roses and, to Petra, "blessed by the Virgin" (112). The strength of his handshake, the confidence in his walk, his generosity in giving her children waiting outside scraps of ice to cool their mouths, but, most strikingly, his ability to perceive her faith, persuade Petra that she can indeed trust him, as he has requested (114). Ultimately, Petra's faith is an active idea, rather than passive trust, as she calls *faith* what she has evidence to support otherwise.

This secular faith, for example, also grounds her fundamental belief in community. When her daughter Estrella's first love, Alejo, a young man working as a *piscador* solely for the summer to earn money he will use to purchase school supplies when he returns to his home in Texas, experiences devastating pesticide exposure and is abandoned by his only family member, Gumecindo, Petra decides to take him in, against Perfecto's wishes and despite the hand-to-mouth survival of her own children. Her pact with Alejo was made when in introductory exchange for his gift of pilfered peaches Petra wordlessly reciprocates with tortillas and a small bag of pinto beans (44–45). Beyond reciprocity, her motivation for taking him in is simple: "If we don't take care of each other, who would take care of us? . . . We have to look out for our own" (96). Pragmatically, Perfecto suggests that the place for Alejo is his own home, that he is "sicker than any yerba, any prayer could cure," and that Petra, in constant pain herself, is in no condition to care for such an ill young man (96–97). Petra's receipt of his discouragement as challenge compels Perfecto to forbid her from taking Alejo in, a refusal Petra overrides, demonstrating the stubborn determination she has passed down to Estrella. Acting as a mother and, as an afterthought, "for the love of God," Petra puts faith into action, not merely believing that God will heal Alejo, but nurturing him through natural remedies and supporting Estrella's determination to get him to the clinic and then the hospital, which, to his credit, Perfecto eventually assists with (124). When the Chevy Capri is mired in the mud, and their trip to seek help for Alejo is put in jeopardy, Petra's faith in community is confirmed as a truck full of piscadores, already exhausted after a long day's work in the sun, empties and the laborers strain to release the car from the earth's grip. This faith in community and karmic reciprocity, conveyed through simple image, grounds Petra's world.

Petra's vision of the world through what is familiar to her also aids in her instinctual evaluation of situations she is otherwise barred from accessing, a capacity that resonates with Gloria Anzaldúa's definition and illustration of *la facultad*. As Anzaldúa defines it,

> *la facultad* is the capacity to see in surface phenomenon the meaning of deeper realities, to see the deep structure below the surface. It is an instant "sensing," a quick perception arrived at without conscious reasoning. It is an acute awareness mediated by the part of the psyche that does not speak, that communicates in images and symbols which are the faces of feelings, that is, behind which feelings reside/hide. . . .

> Those who are pushed out of the tribe for being different are likely to become more sensitized (when not brutalized into insensitivity). Those who do not feel psychologically or physically safe in the world are more apt to develop this sense. Those who are pounced on the most have it the strongest— the females, the homosexuals of all races, the darkskinned, the outcast, the persecuted, the marginalized, the foreign. . . . It's

a kind of survival tactic that people, caught between worlds, unknowingly cultivate. (60–61)

Petra's reality and her ability to intuitively gauge her surroundings exemplify Anzaldúa's theory of la facultad. Petra inventories what she knows and then evaluates her environment, beyond conscious thought and language in the space she occupies "between worlds," to intuit threat. Entering the clinic, a threatening space with an exterior that reveals its façade of utility—a "white trailer [sticking] out like partially buried bone in the middle of [a] vacant plot" and "an orange and white ambulance [with] rusty chassis propped up with mason bricks" and missing tires—Petra first notices a jar of "too white" cotton balls (133–134, 136). She relates the cotton balls to the cotton she has herself harvested, noting how their fluffy symmetry is so unlike the coarse raw bolls she stuffed into sacks and dragged behind her. The scale reminds her of the guilt she felt in weighting each sack with rocks in order to make enough money to feed her family (136). In these imagistic correlations, Petra correctly recognizes the falsity of the clinic, its ineffectuality, and how, like those who weighed her sacks of cotton, the nurse is entirely ignorant of their reality. The nurse's perfume nauseates Petra, and she sees through her appearance, "too white" like the cotton, and knows Alejo will receive no help from her (141). The nurse having charged them for the visit, Petra's evaluation of "y por qué?" merely echoes her more nuanced and intuitive evaluation conveyed by Viramontes through image (144).

Estrella: "Heart Strong Enough to Summon Home"

While no page of Viramontes's novel is free of rich and layered image, the image sets associated with the central character, Estrella, are most provocative. Estrella is the most liminal figure of the novel: she is between nations, between generations, between adulthood and childhood; she is androgynously gendered in responsibility and dress; and she has slipped through the cracks of educational and health care systems in ways that retain her status as disenfranchised, despite what Viramontes ultimately intends readers to see as her potential to achieve voice and locate place other than cultural and socioeconomic interstices. As liminal, Estrella occupies most centrally that precarious and potentially empowering space defined by multiple theorists: by Gloria Anzaldúa as mestiza consciousness, by Homi Bhabha as third space, by Chela Sandoval as oppositional consciousness, by Cordelia Candelaria as "wild zone," a concept she borrows from anthropologists Edwin and Shirley Ardener and builds upon in application to Chicana literary texts (248).[5,6] A benefit of recognizing the "wild zone," or the "separate political and cultural space" Chicanas occupy through the complex intertwining of race, gender, and ethnicity, is that "expression in language and other mediums of creativity is defined from *within* Chicana experience and not solely *in relation* to the dominating political hegemonies, public or private" (248, 251). Thus, the "wild zone" schema is a revision of perception that has potential to allow readers to hear/understand Estrella's subaltern silences and actions.

At thirteen, Estrella is, through the hard work, responsibility, and instability that have marked her childhood, already more woman than girl, though yet naïve and malleable about her place in the world and about her maturing body. Her perspective is betwixt the innocence and idealism of childhood and the resignation of the road stretching before her. Resentful of her stepfather, Perfecto, and confounded by Petra, her mother whom she simultaneously loves and finds ineffectual, Estrella is profoundly affected by her father's abandonment of her, her siblings, and her mother. This primary loss affects both Estrella's early realization of the false bottom of any seeming stability and the self-reliance she consequently develops.

Like her mother who, in the image of bodies like "two fingers crisscrossing for good luck," retains the memory of unity with the man who abandoned her, Estrella holds tightly to the concrete and idealistic image of her father peeling an orange: "What impressed her most was the way his thumbnail plowed the peel off the orange in one long spiral, as if her father plowed the sun, as if it meant something to him to peel the orange from stem to navel without breaking the circle" (19, 12). In her interpretation of memory, the father is omnipotent and benevolent, and the family, like the orange, whole. While the father does break the circle of the family, Estrella's defense against overwhelming grief and rage is to remember him as whole and to deflect resentment toward Petra and Perfecto.

Thus, directly following Estrella's memory of her father peeling the orange, the reader is compelled to visit the family's past before and shortly after their father's abandonment. Estrella's perspective of the family's desperation foregrounds her mother's breakdown, her own savvy perception of her father's intentions, and the burden of responsibility transferred to her when Petra's mental health slowly deteriorates and then temporarily crashes. Reversing roles in confronting her mother before Petra flees their apartment, Estrella scolds, "You, *you* stop it, Mama! Stop this now!" and Petra watches in shock as Estrella takes the only item in the cupboard (aside from a slip of spilled salt and a handful of dead cockroaches) in hand and transforms it into a kind of fulfillment for her siblings—if not food, distraction:

> Estrella grabbed the chubby pink cheeks Quaker man, the red and white and blue cylinder package and shook it violently and its music was empty. The twins started to cry, and for a moment Estrella's eyes narrowed until Petra saw her headlock the Quaker man's paperboard head like a hollow drum and the twins sniffed their runny noses. One foot up, one foot down, her dress twirling like water loose in a drain, Estrella drummed the top of his low crown hat, slapped the round puffy man's double chins, beat his wavy long hair the silky color of creamy hot oats and the boys slid out from under the boxspring. Estrella danced like a loca around the room around the bulging bags around Petra and in and out of the kitchenette and up and down the boxspring, her loud hammering tomtom beats the only noise in the room. (18–19)

Reading the Quaker Oats man as representative of US capitalism, the dominant narrative in which Estrella and her family are nonentities, subaltern, is hardly a stretch. The red, white, and blue of the canister speak of a nationalism that rings empty for this family. The "chubby pink cheeks" and "double chins" of this "round puffy" man speak of an abundance (and a white complacency) this family has never known. Eyes narrowed in battle stance, Estrella grabs, shakes violently, headlocks, drums, slaps, beats, hammers the Quaker Oats

canister for the powerlessness, the voicelessness, the world it represents compels. That the beating of this canister is the "only noise in
the room" is not only a consequence of the stunned or distracted
silence of her audience but also a complex and complicit recognition
of and participation in, if only by Petra, a revolutionary act. Estrella's appropriation of an everyday object so multivalently loaded with
what is basic to mainstream US cultural identity—wholesomeness,
full bellies, smiling goodness—speaks of her capacity to articulate
through action what she cannot articulate through language, exem-
plary of Candelaria's concept of "wild zone." Viramontes conveys
through a simple image of the everyday a reverberating critique of
Estrella's location in the US food chain.

On a more simplistic and narrative level, Estrella's usurping of
the mother role is critique of Petra's weakness. Estrella's grip on
an idealistic memory of her father is perhaps so strong because, in
juxtaposition, she is more aware of her father's intentions to abandon the family and more pragmatic in coping with the disaster that
ensues. Her intuition is conveyed through the image of new shoe-
laces her father promptly cuts to appropriate length, attentively lac-
ing his boots: "He had pinched spit on the loose ends to rethread
the laces carefully through the eyes of his shoe, then bent his chin
to his knees as one foot vanished into a thick leathered shoe then
the other" (16). As his feet disappear into his shoes, Estrella intuits
his disappearance will follow, and she begs Petra, "Mama, hide his
shoes so he won't go" (24). Hailing of her mother *as* mother for
perhaps a final time in this moment, Estrella is unprepared for her
mother's deterioration. Her acute perception is not without psychological consequence; Estrella lives in fear and constant preparation
to be abandoned yet again, as is clear in her initial appraisal of Perfecto's toolbox as sitting "like a suitcase near the door" (24). This
terror and vigilance are again apparent in her response when, having
retrieved a watermelon from the irrigation canal, and having noticed
both the absence of Perfecto's station wagon in the driveway and
Petra's anxious gaze down the road as she awaits his return from
the store, Estrella masks her own anxiety and suggests that should
he not return, the watermelon could be breakfast (41). Drawing the
protective circle in the dirt to allow Petra to rest, Estrella voices a
question, "Don't you ever get tired?" which Petra answers with a

single word, "And?" followed by a verse from a ballad that evokes the longing to hold a beloved in one's arms (42). With minimal interaction, Estrella learns from Petra lack of choice and longing, a lesson she simultaneously absorbs and ultimately refuses to repeat in her own life.

While *Under the Feet of Jesus* is characterized dominantly by a tone of despair, the thread of hope within the novel takes the form of the love story between Alejo and Estrella. Alejo sees Estrella not as an already beaten-down and trapped migrant woman but as a young woman with opportunities beneath her feet, within her grasp. He teaches Estrella how to communicate and how to imagine. Alejo's strong sense of self and place is manifest in the imagery consistently associated with him—stones, bones, the earth: "He loved stones and the history of stones because he believed himself to be a solid mass of boulder thrust out of the earth and not some particle lost in infinite and cosmic space. With a simple touch of a hand and a hungry wonder of his connection to it all, he not only became a part of the earth's history, but would exist as the boulders did, for eternity" (52). With aspirations of becoming a geologist, Alejo's sense of permanence and vision of the future is a stark contrast to Estrella's subaltern sense of self, place, and future. Alejo is a temporary piscador, with a permanent home in Texas and his sights set on higher education. That the future of Alejo, the individual who seems to have the most promise and sense of place in the United States, even his very life or death, hangs in the balance at the novel's conclusion is a dark irony that crushes the narrative thread of the love story, reemphasizing the havoc migrant labor and its realities wreak upon loving relationships.

Nevertheless, before his distressing departure from Estrella's life, Alejo initiates an opening of Estrella's mind to a world larger and with more potential than the limits of her experience as *piscadora*. Enamored with story and the "hungry wonder" at the world around him, Alejo teaches Estrella about the composition of the earth, about the process of the once-living falling to the bottom of the ocean, decomposing to become soil, then rock, then, under pressure and with time, oil, the energy at the foundation of industrialized life (86–87). Stuck within her own frame of reference, Estrella struggles to comprehend Alejo's vision: "She found it hard to imagine the cool silence of the ocean floor when her feet were itching with swelling

sweat and she could feel the constraint of her shoes as if her feet were
bound" (87). Less so by her feet than by her mind, she is bound in
a way of life with no seeming escape, and so she absorbs Alejo's
words, but without real comprehension. The distance between the
images that dominate Alejo's worldview and Estrella's speaks of the
disparate locations of their lived realities.

Central to the increase in self-awareness Estrella learns in relationship with Alejo is the slow, but steady, discovery of authentic
communication. Estrella's communicative skill evolves from their
first conversation to their last. Having met Estrella shortly after her
arrival, Alejo is immediately attracted to her and initiates conversation on their way to the fields. Making small talk, he asks her about
her name, which she says she received from her father (66). While
Alejo is well intentioned, he is oblivious to the hole of emotional
trauma he has uncovered. The conversation continues:

> —What does he call you now?
> —My papa's gone.
> —Dead?
> —Things just happen . . .
> —What about him? And he pointed to Perfecto. . . .
> —Huh?
> —What about him?
> —I can't hear you. (66)

Estrella shuts down, unable and/or unwilling to share with Alejo
her feelings of betrayal, of resentment, of anger, of fear. Feigning
inability to hear him or understand him, she evades, self-protects.
But Alejo is persistent, not knowing necessary silence:

> —What things happen? he asked.
> —I don't know. Things. She shrugged her shoulders and busied
> herself reading the faded washing instructions on the label of
> Arnulfo's T-shirt.
> —How many brothers you got? Alejo asked. She bit her bot-
> tom lip as if she was thinking. He could barely see her almond
> eyes under the shade of a hat which was beginning to unravel
> at the rim.

—That's kinda a funny question.
—You don't like questions?
—Not really. Only asking maybe.
—What's your full name?
—Talk louder.
—Last name. What's your last name?
—What's it to you, she snapped back. (67)

Having tolerated what she interprets as prying and what he means as interest, Estrella loses patience, becomes too uncomfortable to nonchalantly evade his queries. Her behavior shows discomfort and defensiveness, her hands busy with her younger brother Arnulfo's T-shirt label, her head lowered. Estrella's intial and extreme reticence to converse with Alejo is a product of her frustration in being unable to express her thoughts and emotions, the unfamiliarity of conversation not necessitated by the pragmatic demands of daily life, and exercise of silence as learned distrust of people in general. However, by the time Estrella expresses herself in their final conversation on the way to the hospital in Corazón, her frustration bears lingering remnants of not being able to give voice to *exactly* what she means, but is also tinged by impatience with Alejo for not being able to read the nuance of her words.

Her expectation that he understand her is intricately connected to the physical intimacy that has increased in parallel to Estrella's communicative growth. Alejo is the first and only individual outside of her family whose scent and touch she has come to know. He awakens her blossoming sexual self, a gendered self her responsibilities have not allowed her to realize in any form. She dons overalls and workshirts to labor alongside the men in the field. She assists Perfecto with his construction and repair jobs and runs as free as her brothers. In contrast, Petra is very aware of her daughter's age and impending sexuality:

How tall she had gotten with a matter of months. Estrella would be fourteen soon. Soon? Soon Estrella would begin menstruation, and Petra thought of blood in the glow of the fire, the amber red of molten wood, and in the absence of her own menstruation. Was she waiting as well?

. . . When it was time, it was time and not even Petra's glare at her eldest daughter was enough to halt the weather of what was to come, halt the flesh and blood pieces of Estrella's heart from falling to the ground. (120–121)

Estrella's impending womanhood is a condition to mourn with a limited range of meaning to Petra—pregnancy, heartbreak, and toil. Attempting to police her contact with and behavior around men with authoritarian directives and "glares," Petra does not speak directly and with the benefit of her own experience to Estrella about her changing body and the feelings that will unquestionably arise.

Whether Estrella herself perceives herself as woman or not, Alejo does. When Estrella sheds her clothes to fetch the renegade watermelon her family has placed in the irrigation canal to chill, Alejo does not see the pragmatic choice she makes to keep her limited supply of clothing clean and dry, but "[loses] his footing" as he watches the "bulbs of her buttocks bobbing," and "velvet waves" of water "licking" her body (40). Leaving the peaches with Petra, a gift meant to impress Estrella and to win the good graces of Petra, the love story in Alejo's perception of Estrella is palpable as he equates the English meaning of her name with the awe and respect he has for the natural world: "He saw . . . the woman who swam in the magnetic presence of the full moon, a woman named star" (46). When Estrella is jostled by the rough road in the back of the truck on their way to the fields, Alejo, aroused, notices the feel of his zipper in seeing the flesh "like flan custard" under Estrella's nondescript and androgynous attire (65). Sharing a platonic bed with Estrella as Petra works to cure him, he voices a yearning that speaks his desires beyond the physical: "I wish I could spend a whole day with you and talk about everything under the sky. I mean it" (116). Alejo opens Estrella's eyes to her worth and to possibility. Only when Estrella begins to see herself through Alejo's eyes and to feel herself through his hands does she recognize the woman-self she is on the verge of becoming.

Estrella works to process the unfamiliar feelings and intimacy with Alejo through the only images she has access to—images of travel, of the highway. Under the truck on a blistering hot day, before the worst of the symptoms attached to Alejo's pesticide exposure descend, the two young lovers explore bodies and express growing affection. Alejo seduces through words, explaining tar, oil, and the cycle of life beneath the sea, so foreign to Estrella, and she follows his lead wordlessly:

> Alejo carefully smoothed her fingers flat as if unfolding a map. His mouth pressed against the center of her palm and his lips, which felt as dry as baking soda, lingered until the heat of his air welded into the cup of her hand. Her fingers closed on his chin gently like the tentacles of a sea anemone. He then pressed his cheek against the nakedness of her palm and his bristles tickled and she smiled in her darkness, until Alejo kissed her again, but this time longer, damp and pleadingly and still. Her oiled handprint, the shape of her fingers, imprinted onto his face. And that was all he had to do.
>
> Estrella lay very still, very quiet, her eyes closed tightly, trying not to think of Exits and Entrances, of Stop signs and Yields. She fisted her hand with a grasp as tight as a heart . . . She uncrossed her ankles. (88–89)

Whether a romantic and innocent first kiss or the loss of Estrella's virginity, signified by the uncrossing of her ankles, her sense of self is transformed by intimacy of both thought and body. She longs to put her experience into language for a girlfriend, but, without this recourse, runs instead to the barn, noticing her own body anew in the mote-filled sunshine of its shelter.

As Alejo introduces Estrella to a depth of communication she has not known before and to a more profound sense of self, she also becomes increasingly aware of her status in the world around her. In both seeing the world through Alejo's lens and experiencing a deepened self-awareness, Estrella gains access to the abstract, to the ideological, as it impacts her and her family. Mary Louise Pratt's work on the concept of contact zones, the oft-quoted definition of contact zones as "social spaces where cultures meet, clash, and grapple with each other, often in contexts of highly asymmetrical relations of power," is relevant to Estrella's escalating social consciousness and echoes Candelaria's "wild zone" thesis that places Estrella's consciousness outside the dominant (584). An easy connection to Spivak's ideas about subalternity and voicelessness also lies in the concept of asymmetry; while individuals exist and (attempt to) self-define in the spaces of contact zones, still some are confined to silence. Pratt's ideas echo Estrella's initial resigned awareness of the dominant culture that surrounds her and of its falsity, and the reassignment Estrella ultimately effects.

Hard at work picking grapes under a blistering afternoon sun, Estrella recognizes the erasure of the work she does harvesting grapes in the advertisement for the final product, raisins. The iconic woman of the Sun-Maid Raisin box, an image similar to the Quaker Oats man, taunts Estrella:[7]

> Carrying the full basket to the paper was not like the picture on the red raisin boxes Estrella saw in the markets, not like the woman wearing a fluffy bonnet, holding out the grapes with her smiling, ruby lips, the sun a flat orange behind her. The sun was white and it made Estrella's eyes sting like an onion, and the baskets of grapes resisted her muscles, pulling their magnetic weight back to the earth. The woman with the red bonnet did not know this. Her knees did not sink in the hot white soil, and she did not know how to pour the baskets of grapes inside the frame gently and spread the bunches evenly on top of the newsprint paper. She did not remove the frame, straighten her creaking knees, the bend of her back, set down another sheet of newsprint paper, reset the frame, then return to the pisca again with the empty basket, row after row, sun after sun. The woman's bonnet would be as useless as Estrella's own straw hat under a white sun so mighty, it toasted the green grapes to black raisins. (50)

Framing her own experience as contrast to the Sun-Maid Raisin woman with her pristine attire and smiling demeanor, Estrella deconstructs the innocuousness of the image on the box and the hours of labor it elides. Again playing with image, Viramontes conveys Estrella's awareness of consumerist illusion. Tinged with anger, Estrella's perception of the disparity does not yet extend to revolution.

Resonant images colliding, Viramontes carries Estrella directly from grape field to baseball field. Carrying the tools of her day's work with her—"basket, jug, and knife bundled under the crook of her arm," Estrella adds exertion, but also solitude, to an already

exhausting day (58). She sees in the Little League play a recognizable scene, "the ball like a peach tossed out to hungry hands" (59).
But when the stadium lights illuminate the field, she sees instead the
headlights of *la migra*, the Border Patrol. The fence separating her
from the field becomes the fence of the border, and she becomes disoriented. "Where was home? A ball hit, a blunt instrument against
a skull. A player ran the bases for the point. A score. Destination:
home plate. Who would catch the peach, who was hungry enough
to run the field in all that light? The perfect target. The lushest peach.
The element of surprise. A stunned deer waiting for the bullet. A few
of the spectators applauded. Estrella fisted her knife and ran" (60).
Ready for self-defense, Estrella runs, the haunting question "where
is home" chasing her away from the prototypical American game
whose very object is the run for home base. Though a citizen, with
papers under the feet of Jesus on Petra's altar in their temporary
abode, Estrella knows the wire fence that keeps her outside the baseball field is a border more threatening than what it seems.

Safe at "home" and cradling Perfecto's crowbar in her lap, Estrella
is reassured by Petra, who teaches her a lesson about place: "Don't
run scared. You stay there and look them in the eye. Don't let them
make you feel you did a crime for picking the vegetables they'll be
eating for dinner. . . . Tell them que tienes una madre aqui. You are
not an orphan, and she pointed a red finger to the earth, Aqui" (63).
With years of experience beyond Estrella, Petra's bilingual negotia-
tion of her own disenfranchisement stands as a powerful example
for her daughter, and it is one of the few clear examples of Petra's
individual strength. Petra emphasizes for Estrella that the mother
Estrella has is not only Petra herself but also a relationship with the
earth of which those who consume its products are rarely mindful.

Taking this line from Petra—"Don't let them make you feel you
did a crime"—as title for her discussion of *Under the Feet of Jesus*,
Anne Shea links Viramontes's novel to farmworker testimony and
to discourses of nation and law. Asserting that Viramontes's novel
is a "narrative that articulate[s] . . . oppositional knowledge and
identity," Shea illustrates how Viramontes's characters articulate
through action an understanding of and response to the discourses
that marginalize and even criminalize them (123). Viewing Estrella
as the fulcrum of this understanding and response, Shea argues that

the events and characters in Viramontes's novel are direct reflections of social realities. While foregrounding political developments of the last decades that have significantly worsened the lives of migrant workers, such as Proposition 187,[8] and narratives of migrant workers, Shea parallels this social reality with the experiences of Estrella and her family, and emphasizes the cultural resistance embedded in witnessing, in telling the story.

Estrella does not experience a true epiphany about the injustice inherent in a society in which disparity of wealth and exploitation of labor are ugly truths and lived realities often overlooked until Alejo is near death. Dormant yet seething like the bones that turn into oil, Alejo's words click into place in Estrella's mind in the novel's climax. Having rushed Alejo to a dilapidated, barely functioning health clinic only to have the condescending nurse on duty take the $9.07 the family collectively possesses in a gesture of disingenuous generosity (a discount on the standard fee) for the diagnosis that he needs hospitalization in a city some miles distant, aptly named Corazón, Estrella recognizes that the family needs the $9.07 in order to buy fuel to make the trip. She utilizes her skill in bartering gleaned from Perfecto's example, offering every resource the family has available to them, but to no avail. The nurse shrugs off Estrella's efforts, annoyed by her persistence and believing she has fulfilled her responsibility to the family. As Shea points out, the "white nurse . . . does not see the systemic violence that bears down on the migrant family because it is rendered invisible through its normalization" (140). At her wits' end, Estrella recalls Alejo's tar pits with revelation:

> She remembered the tar pits. Energy money, the fossilized bones of energy matter. How bones made oil and oil made gasoline. The oil was made from their bones, and it was their bones that kept the nurse's car from not halting on some highway, kept her on her way to Daisyfield to pick up her boys at six. It was their bones that kept the air conditioning in the cars humming, that kept them moving on the long dotted line on the map. Their bones. Why couldn't the nurse see that? Estrella had figured it out: the nurse owed *them* as much as they owed her. (148, original emphasis)

Seeing no alternative, Estrella leaves the clinic, only to return with the crowbar to make her point, to make the nurse see. Slamming the bar down on the counter, Estrella asks for the return of their money, taking only the $9.07 when the frightened nurse relinquishes the cash box.

The deed done, Estrella feels a split within herself: "She felt like two Estrellas. One was a silent phantom who obediently marked a circle with a stick around the bungalow as the mother had requested, while the other held the crowbar and the money" (150). This inner duality represents Estrella's emergence from passivity into action. She recognizes power, but also its consequence. Speaking to Alejo as they travel to Corazón, Estrella laments the act of violence, but without apology: "She sighed with resignation. She tried to understand what happened herself. You talk and talk and talk to them and they ignore you. But you pick up a crowbar and break the pictures of their children, and all of a sudden they listen real fast" (151). Alejo reads Estrella's act of violence as a compromise of self, and as a justification for the negative stereotyping of Mexicans as violent thieves, degenerate, less than human. He warns Estrella, "Don't make it so easy for them," but, justifying her action and reversing positions with Alejo, making him see from her vantage point, she has the last word as he drifts into sleep or unconsciousness, "Can't you see they want to take your heart?" (153).

The image of the heart, an echo of Estrella's hand in the intimacy they shared in the shade under the truck at the outskirts of the field, is repeated again in the "odd" vision of a store display of bell peppers that she remembers as Alejo drifts. She

> remembered how the brilliant red and green and yellow peppers were stacked like layers of granite stone into small and solid pyramids. The colors became something so completely breathtaking that one had to stop and ask why, why would anyone want to create an incandescent mosaic out of something as nondescript as bell peppers? Estrella wanted to tell the mother, to say, *Mama, take a look at that,* but a woman walked in the store and toppled the peak by removing the top single red one, shiny as new love, and it was as easy to dismantle all that work as it was to kick a can on the road. (152–153)

An image that also recalls Petra's vision of garlic as the Virgen de Guadalupe's throne, Estrella's processing of this memory and its meaning encapsulate her revolutionary perception from her subaltern, liminal position. She realizes that the beauty is visible only to her and to others who occupy her position as invisible laborer. She realizes the reality of silence, how she is unable to say what she wants to say before what she wants to say disappears, is "dismantled," and becomes inaccessible through action of the dominant, the colonizing.

In the final scene of the novel, Estrella's body speaks her mind and self. Returning finally to the barn, the barn she agreed to help Perfecto deconstruct in service to Alejo's need and against her recognition of its parallel to workers like Perfecto and herself, Estrella conquers through the sheer strength of her body what confines her. Estrella notes the injustice of the barn's disrepair and potential destruction when Perfecto first solicits her help:

> It's not fair, Estrella said. . . . She looked up at the barn as she had done when they first arrived and tried to imagine herself with the ball of a hammer, pulling the resistant nails out of the woodsheet walls. The nails would screech and the wood would moan and she would pull the veins out and the woodsheet wall would collapse like a toothless mouth. Nothing would be left except a hole in the baked dirt so wide it would make one wonder how anything could be so empty.
>
> Is that what happens? Estrella thought, people just use you until you're all used up, then rip you into pieces when they're finished using you? (74–75)

Scenes reverberating, the idea of mindless consumption of what is living and beautiful to whom it is visible remains central. The revelation that labor and those who labor are invisible to those who consume resounds. Thus, when Estrella makes her way to the rooftop of the barn by utilizing her own "back like a shovel" against the door barring her from its confines, she makes herself visible, but not to all, only to "those who strayed," who do not register on social radar (174, 176).

Leaving Estrella standing on the verge of nothingness and every-thing, Viramontes does not speak for her or her future. Instead, and ultimately, as Estrella, existing on the periphery of US society, real-izes the injustice of the exploitative labor she and her family provide without reward, she pries wide the reader's awareness of the forceful collision of the grating of subaltern existence against US consumer-ism and privilege. Through her imagistic depiction of how her char-acters negotiate environment, Viramontes compels her readers to actively engage her text, to connect Perfecto's, Petra's, Alejo's, and Estrella's wordless clarity of action to otherwise silent subalternity and to work to hear the actions that speak louder than words.

Notes

1. I realize the contentious discussion surrounding the application of what is termed "postcolonial theory" to a novel produced in the United States and representing US realities. As a single example that foregrounds this debate, see the collection of essays by Singh and Schmidt, *Postcolonial Theory and the United States.*

2. Viramontes does not assign Petra and her children a surname, emphasizing their father's abandonment, as well as their social anonymity/invisibility.

3. The Social Security card has been "torn and mended," and Viramontes does not indicate whose name appears on the card, or by whom or why it has been abused (166). If read as false documentation and as Petra's, the card may have been torn by government officials when she applied for social aid of some kind, or even a driver's license. If read as her husband's card, it may have been torn by Petra herself in anger and disappointment. Or, battered as it is and if Petra's, perhaps Viramontes intends the card to be read as meaningless because Petra can-not utilize it or does not know she can or how to utilize it to receive any of what she is due as a citizen. A final possibility is that the card is Estrella's, her potential, and that it is solely battered through haphazard and ceaseless migration.

4. In their introduction to the chapter "Myths and Archetypes" in *Infi-nite Divisions,* Tey Diana Rebolledo and Eliana S. Rivero acknowledge that while "the Virgin of Guadalupe represents certain values considered positive: unselfish giving, intercessor between earth and spirit, and ideal qualities of motherhood . . . she is also seen by many Chicana writers, ironically, as a symbol of failure . . . the Virgin is often seen as not active enough . . . [or] as the image of the unattainable. She has failed to intercede for her people in the United States; she advocates acceptance and endurance, not action" (191). In con-necting Petra so directly to the cultural icon of the Virgen de Guadalupe and juxtaposing this epitome of motherhood with illustration of Petra's humanity

and her shortcomings, Viramontes surely means for readers to interrogate the pressures of cultural prescription regarding gender that Petra confronts.

5. To gain an abbreviated sense of Bhabha's concept of third space, see Rutherford, "The Third Space." For a more thorough understanding, see Bhabha's tome *The Location of Culture*. Note that Bhabha's theory of third-space privileges the written as means for its construction, and thus demands some extension for application to Viramontes's novel.

6. See Sandoval's "U.S. Third World Feminism: The Theory and Method of Oppositional Consciousness in the Postmodern World."

7. Viramontes likely intends Chicana/o readers of her novel to imagine not only the dominant image of the Sun-Maid Raisin box but also Ester Hernández's 1981 rendering of this image, *Sun Mad*, a critique of the use of pesticides. Under a bonneted *calavera*, desiccated grapes in skeletal hand, is the caption, "Sun Mad Raisins: Unnaturally Grown with Insecticides; Miticides; Herbicides; Fungicides." To access a reproduction, see the Art Folio section of Moraga and Anzaldúa, *This Bridge Called My Back*.

8. Passed by voters as a ballot initiative in 1994, California's Proposition 187 aimed to deny undocumented immigrants access to social services, including health care and public education. Implementation of its policies was immediately barred judicially on the state level, and in 1998, the majority of the proposition was ruled unconstitutional by the US Supreme Court. While defeated as policy, the proposition itself and the fact that voters supported its objectives conveyed a political and social climate clearly oppositional to migrant families like the family Viramontes fictionalizes in her novel.

Works Cited

Anzaldúa, Gloria. *Borderlands/La Frontera: The New Mestiza*. 2nd ed. San Francisco: Aunt Lute Books, 1999.

Bhabha, Homi. *The Location of Culture*. London: Routledge, 1994.

Candelaria, Cordelia Chávez. "The 'Wild Zone' Thesis as Gloss in Chicana Literary Study." In *Feminisms: An Anthology of Literary Theory and Criticism*, edited by Robyn R. Warhol and Diane Price Herndl, 248–256. New Brunswick, NJ: Rutgers University Press, 1997.

de Kock, Leon. "New Nation Writers Conference in South Africa." *Ariel: A Review of International English Literature* 23, no. 3 (July 1992): 29–47.

Lawless, Cecelia. "Helena María Viramontes' Homing Devices in *Under the Feet of Jesus*." In *Homemaking: Women Writers and the Politics and Poetics of Home*, edited by Catherine Wiley and Fiona R. Barnes, 361–382. New York: Garland, 1996.

Moraga, Cherríe, and Gloria Anzaldúa, eds. *This Bridge Called My Back: Writings by Radical Women of Color*. 3rd ed. Berkeley, CA: Third Woman Press, 2002.

Pratt, Mary Louise. "Arts of the Contact Zone." In *Ways of Reading*, 5th ed., edited by David Bartholomae and Anthony Petrosky, 582–596. New York: Bedford/St. Martin's, 1999.

Rebolledo, Tey Diana, and Eliana S. Rivero, eds. "Myths and Archetypes." In *Infinite Divisions: An Anthology of Chicana Literature*, edited by Tey Diana Rebolledo and Eliana S. Rivero, 189–195. Tucson: University of Arizona Press, 1993.

Rutherford, J. "The Third Space: Interview with Homi Bhabha." In *Identity, Community, Culture, Difference*, edited by J. Rutherford, 207–221. London: Lawrence and Wishart, 1990.

Sandoval, Chela. "U.S. Third World Feminism: Differential Social Movement." Part II in *Methodology of the Oppressed* by Chela Sandoval, 41–66. Minneapolis: University of Minnesota Press, 2000.

———. "U.S. Third World Feminism: The Theory and Method of Oppositional Consciousness in the Postmodern World." *Genders* 10 (1991): 1–24.

Shea, Anne. "'Don't let them make you feel you did a crime': Immigration Law, Labor Rights, and Farmworker Testimony." *MELUS* 28, no. 1 (2003): 123–144.

Singh, Amritjit, and Peter Schmidt, eds. *Postcolonial Theory and the United States: Race, Ethnicity, and Literature*. Jackson: University Press of Mississippi, 2000.

Spivak, Gayatri Chakravorty. "Can the Subaltern Speak?: Speculations on Widow Sacrifice." In *Colonial Discourse and Postcolonial Theory: A Reader*, edited by Patrick Williams and Laura Chrisman, 66–111. New York: Columbia University Press, 1994.

Viramontes, Helena María. *Under the Feet of Jesus*. New York: Dutton, 1995.

9

Our Dogs Came with Us

Viramontes Prays to Xólotl with Digna Rabia

ALDO ULISSES RESÉNDIZ RAMÍREZ

What Came to Pass

IN HELENA MARÍA VIRAMONTES'S NOVEL *Their Dogs Came with Them*, the tumultuous urban landscape of 1960s East Los Angeles resembles a vanquished Aztec[1] burial ground of unearthed corpses where the construction of the LA freeway results in the siege and ensuing dismemberment of an entire Chicano community / run-down homes "as empty as toothless mouths" are grinded to the ground / amputated streets carved into stumps, dead-end body maps are left to unrest / concrete rubble succumbs like mangled limbs strangled by dripping electric arteries and beaten, violated, graffiti-splattered walls are remnants of ancient codices waiting to be interpreted— malicious prose written on whitewashed plastered bones; nopal-fruit red warning signs for what came to pass; red- and black-inked tattoos on a tribal concrete of flesh; gang-acronymic epitaphs inscribed *por vida* on the perpetuity of the collective Chicana/o consciousness.[2]

Their Dogs Came with Them can be regarded as Helena María Viramontes's own rendering of Miguel León-Portilla's classic book

The Broken Spears: The Aztec Account of the Conquest of México.[3] Written five hundred years after the Spanish invasion of the Américas and over a hundred and fifty years after the US takeover of the American Southwest, in the twentieth-century context of a Chicano community in East LA, Viramontes's novel can be read as both a Chicano codex of ancient omens—that is, of a ruminating déjà vu of violent colonization engraved in the cultural memory of Chicanos[4]—as well as a eulogy for the barrio.

Their Dogs[5] is an account of, perhaps, the last largely visible manifestation of late colonialization and inward US expansionism on the mainland into the urban enclave of a Chicano community in the precursory and ongoing years of California's Chicano movement of the 1960s and early 1970s. Moreover, it is a celebration of Chicana/o life, an unyielding testament to the community's indomitable spirit, admirable resiliency, and continuing struggle. In *Their Dogs*, Viramontes reasserts herself not only as an urban Chicana writer but also as a *curandera*, a healer resisting the US neo-colonial and imperial project in its various forms—not least of which is urban displacement—through her activism inherent in her literary and spiritual creative process.

Similar to the work of a Chicana Renaissance muralist, Viramontes transforms *Their Dogs* into a large "dynamic canvas" where the novel's characters come to life amidst "the weight of surveillance, the destruction of the old way of life, and the already turbulent political period [of the civil rights movement, the Chicano movement, Chicano Moratoriums, and the Vietnam War]." Like a mural, the sophisticated literary mappings of *Their Dogs* are of grand proportions, yet they can be readily interpreted through the novel's vivid "image details" craftily wrapped in metaphor.[6] Although as fragmented as the community it portrays, the novel's narrative structure remains artfully braided in a spirally ruminating temporality; each section in the novel serves as an entry-point strand that precipitously conducts the reader to the dramatically shifting environment of East LA's ravaged streets.[7]

Espinosa and García (2008) state in their interpretation of Gloria Anzaldúa's spirituality in her seminal book *Borderlands/La Frontera: The New Mestiza*, "Anzaldúa's religious vision is dedicated to the healing of the wounds of the borderlands. The Chicano community is a wounded community, and she employs an array of language strategies to try and bring healing through her voices" (237). A contemporary of Anzaldúa, Viramontes is also dedicated to the healing of the Chicano community through her literary voice.

Before *Their Dogs* was published, in an interview with Gabriella Gutiérrez y Muhs, Viramontes shares her motivations for writing the novel: "I'm trying to decolonize or understand what colonization does to one's mind, one's body, one's soul" ("Interview with Helena María Viramontes," 125). In another interview, Viramontes states that she "excavated" *Their Dogs* from a space of questioning the various violent elements of Chicano colonization, both Spanish and Anglo-American, and the connection with ongoing gang violence in her native East LA. She expands, "At first I wanted to write about the colonized imagination—how we have learned to hate ourselves as a people so much that we kill one another, as in gang violence. This is the basic premise" ("Praying for Knowledge," 154).

Viramontes's *Their Dogs* is the result of both profound questioning and a plea for answers in the face of internalized oppression as reflected in mounting community violence. In her unpublished essay titled "On Writing *Their Dogs Came with Them*," Viramontes further outlines some of the questions that haunted her while writing the novel: "Why is there so much brown on brown violence in my community? What does it mean to have a colonized imagination? How do marginalized people keep their sanity in unstable times? Faith in stories? God, each other? Trust?" (as quoted in Kevane, 11). Thus, this process of inquiry is part and parcel of Viramontes's own healing project of decolonization, which birthed *Their Dogs Came with Them*.

"Dejad que los perros ladren, Sancho . . . Es señal que vamos avanzando"

Their Dogs opens up with the following epigraph, an excerpt from *The Broken Spears* from where the title was also extracted: "Their dogs came with them, running ahead of the column. They raised their muzzles high; they lifted their muzzles to the wind. They raced on before with saliva dripping from their jaws" (selection from *Their*

Dogs epigraph; also in León-Portilla, 41). This passage is a direct reference to colonization. In the aforementioned interview, she elaborates: "I felt that I had to excavate the history of colonization . . . the whole idea of dogs, how the Spaniards have brought in these dogs and trained them to rip flesh. I can unravel the violence . . . and the ambiance that perpetrates it. I can go back to the sixties. It deals with a lost community divided by freeways. It deals with fragmentation of the self and society" ("Praying for Knowledge," 154). As the title prefaces, the novel is about dogs, those that came *with them*—the Spanish colonizers who in 1519 arrived on Mexican shores and advanced into the heart of the Aztec empire, making alliances with indigenous groups subjected to Aztec rule, and finally occupying and destroying the capital city of Tenochtitlán (present-day México City) by 1521. In their quest, the Spanish murdered the local indigenous populations that opposed them, which in conjunction with the spread of diseases brought by the Europeans caused a dramatic demographic decline that left only one-third of the original population of central México alive by 1524.[8]

As narrated in *The Broken Spears*, the Spanish brought with them "wild animals on leashes," which the Aztecs described as "lions and ounces so ferocious that they ate people" (León-Portilla, 44; Bonfil Batalla, 80). What some Aztec accounts describe as fierce felines were, in reality, breeds of dogs unknown to them—ferocious greyhounds and mastiff canines (44). During the early stages of Spanish colonization, the Spaniards would unleash their war dogs, trained in the art of ripping flesh, against the indigenous populations. Urged by their masters, the Spanish canines would track, terrorize, torture, tear apart, and ultimately devour their prey, who were not only those who resisted the invasion but oftentimes simply those unfortunate enough to cross their path.[9]

Similarly, in the opening paragraphs of *Their Dogs*, the arrival of bulldozers to the streets of East LA conveys stark images of colonization in action. These "earthmovers" forecast the construction of the freeway resembling the coming of the Spanish dogs: "The bulldozers had started from very far away and slowly arrived on First Street, their muzzles like sharpened metal teeth making way for the freeway" (6). Also closely resembling the European colonizers' anchored ships, the stationed bulldozers had "tarps whipping like banging sails" that when running would bite "trenches wider than rivers," chewing up entire blocks and, in the process, "ridding the neighborhood of everything that was familiar" (12, 146, 169).

If Aztec accounts in *The Broken Spears* bear witness to the arrival of the Spaniards and *their dogs*—the Spanish translation from Nahuatl, the Aztecs' language, suggesting that the indigenous populations identified the canines, using "their" only to connote the difference in possession—it then begs the question, "What about *our dogs*, those that belonged to the indigenous peoples?"

Before the arrival of the Europeans, dogs were one of the first domesticated animals in Mesoamerica, along with the *guajolote*, or turkey. They were also a food source (Bonfil Batalla, 5, 12). Upon their arrival, the Spanish most likely encountered three breeds of dogs that archeologists have found existed in Mesoamerica and that were also used in funeral ceremonies; the most well known among them is the Mexican hairless, which to this day still preserves its Nahuatl name, Xoloitzcuintli. Mesoamerican indigenous peoples viewed dogs as guides and guardian figures since they believed that after death dogs such as the Xoloitzcuintli escorted souls to the underworld, or Mictlán (the nine-level "Land of the Dead"), where they would help them cross a river.

According to Read and González in the *Handbook of Mesoamerican Mythology*, the indigenous dog was often revered in Mesoamerican cosmology, following "three broad mythological streams: the first, concerning the creation of people; the second, food—particularly the discovery of maize . . . ; the third, the underworld, death, the evening star and Quetzalcoatl" (170).[10]

Xólotl (pronounced SHO-lo-tl) was a Nahua dog-like deity (often depicted as a dog-faced or dog-bodied god with torn ears) and was the Aztec god Quetzalcoátl's animal aspect, twin brother, and, in some ways, his antithesis. In a Nahua myth, Xólotl is chosen by his 1,600 fellow gods to accompany his twin brother Quetzalcoátl to Mictlán to shed blood on the bones of those who inhabited the previous world for their resurrection and creation of new life. This re-creation of life is reenacted every night when Xólotl (representing Venus as the Evening Star) guides the sun through the earth's body, emerging at dawn until his counterpart Quetzalcoátl (Venus as the Morning Star) takes over (Read and González, 171–172).

In another Nahua myth, the creation of the sun and moon as narrated in the *Florentine Codex* (Sahagún et al.) recounts how Xólotl
was haunted by Death during the creation of the Nahua Fifth Sun.
In this myth, Xólotl escapes Death by hiding in a maize field in
the shape of a double-headed corn plant known by the same name.
When Death found him there, he ran away again and entered a
maguey cactus field, where he shape-shifted into a two-part maguey
plant called "mexolotl." When found again, he transformed himself into the shape of a Mexican salamander ("water-dog") known
as axolotl. But there he was cornered by Death and finally killed
(Markman and Markman, 125). Hence, Xólotl's shape-shifting faculty is associated with three sacred indigenous foods, including
maize, Mesoamerica's own "human creation" and the quintessential
symbol of Mexican civilization.[11]

In *Their Dogs*, Viramontes's "hypnotic prose"[12] takes the reader
into a deep spiritual journey of wounded psyches, bodies, and hearts
through the lives of the novel's characters. Perhaps like no other Chicana writer of our time, Viramontes embodies the healer *shamana/
nahuala* described in Gloria Anzaldúa's seminal book *Borderlands/
La Frontera: The New Mestiza*. Anzaldúa noted, "The ability of the
story (prose and poetry) to transform the storyteller and the listener
into something or someone else is shamanistic. The writer, as shape
changer, is a *nahual*, a shaman" (66). In further describing the shamanistic attributes inherent in art creation, Anzaldúa maintains that
artists are modern-day shamans capable of performing ancient tasks,
including psychological healing through artistic expression.[13] Like a
nahual, the writer shape-shifts into her characters by accessing the
realms of the imagination ("Quincentennial," 252).[14] With *Their
Dogs*, Viramontes invokes an ancient prayer, a questioning of the
effects and consequences of colonization. A mestiza writer, Viramontes transforms herself into a nahuala where the creation of the
characters' identities serves as a catalyst for her own metamorphosis.
In describing this transformation, Anzaldúa wrote:

> And in descending to the depths I realize that down is up, and
> I rise up from and into the deep. And once again I recognize
> that the internal tension of oppositions can propel (if it doesn't

tear apart) the mestiza writer out of the *metate* where she is being grounded with corn and water, eject her out as *nahual*, an agent of transformation, able to modify and shape primordial energy and therefore able to change herself and others into turkey, coyote, tree, or human. (*Borderlands*, 74–75)

In *Their Dogs*, the dog is the *nagual* or animistic entity that accompanies Viramontes in her journey to excavate the history of colonization. Much like the journey of Quetzalcóatl and Xólotl, Viramontes takes the reader to an underworld called East LA where the novel's characters roam in a maze of unfamiliar streets and where the remnants of the Chicano community of Viramontes's childhood lie buried under the LA freeway.

Throughout the novel, the liminal space that both humans and animals inhabit is explored. A dialectical relationship between ambulatory characters and roaming street dogs develops in the shared urban landscape of East LA. In a nexus of transitions, both people and dogs share a precarious life, struggle for their survival in bordered territories, and, oftentimes, morph together in the frailty of their own existence. Thus, Viramontes's dogs come to life, surfacing from the *Their Dogs* epigraph and barking their way into the novel's multilayered narrative. These street dogs are more than symbols, in spite of the fact that their presence may appear seemingly coincidental for some characters; they are omens of tragedy to others. They become a discernable sign for what will come to pass.

Moreover, Viramontes's narrative takes the reader to a place full of metaphorical symbolism. In an ever-changing trajectory of perspectives, the repetition of images in the novel shifts contexts and meanings from character to character, cementing them in an urban concrete of realities and revealing their complex interiorities, personalities, and motivations. Viramontes uses rhetorical devices to move the narrative, kaleidoscopically, alternating between first- and third-person narrations and constantly shifting into settings in the present, past, and future. This form of literary nagualism constitutes a shift from a character's state of consciousness to another, instead of a literal metamorphosis from human to animal form by the characters.[15]

Una Vida de Perro o Una Perra Vida

The characters in *Their Dogs* are Viramontes's "broken spears," lying upon the roads, wandering around where gangs swarm along the dead-end, reviled streets of East LA. Using a multiplicity of voices, Viramontes re-inscribes traditionally stereotyped Chicana/o characters, especially in regards to gang subjectivity, and weaves them in a tapestry of coexisting perspectives. Four of the core protagonists in the novel are young women—Ermila Zumaya, María Antonia Gamboa aka "Turtle," Ana Brady, and Tranquilina—who interact with a number of other main characters as well as other peripheral characters. From vanquished to vanished, the characters in the novel are begotten from a violent history of neo-colonization and a current state of precarious survival. The narrative follows them as they steer over the streets and unearth their daily realities.

Their Dogs opens up by introducing the reader to the Zumaya child (five-year-old Ermila) and to seventy-seven-year-old Chavela, an evicted casualty of the freeway construction who soon vanishes along with her entire block on their side of First Street. Chavela, whose ghostly memory would later be conjured up by other characters throughout the novel, compares the evisceration of her barrio to the catastrophic earthquake of her youth, of her *país*, in which "the dogs and gente went crazy from having the earth pulled out right from under them" (7). At the beginning of the novel, Chavela admonishes the Zumaya child with these haunting words, "Pay attention . . . because displacement will always come down to two things: earthquakes and earthmovers" (8). Setting spatial and temporal displacement as the backdrop of the novel, the freeway bulldozers crack the resident's "tierra firme," sending seismic waves into the lives of the displaced and those who manage to survive in between the street-mapped fault lines. In so doing, Viramontes brings the shared experience of urban displacement to the foreground and underscores the characters' fragmentation.

Following the old war adage of divide and conquer, the freeway system eviscerated entire blocks, dismembering the neighborhood and causing the decorporation of the Chicano community's place-based culture. By fragmenting the spatial map of East LA, the freeway arteries divided communities, further alienating them and creating "a maze of unfamiliar streets," effectively erasing the old Chicano enclave from the residents' mental map (32). This Cartesian split would later allow for gangs to demark their own territory: the names of streets, landmarks, and local spaces morphed into acronymic hand signs that would serve to determine a gang member's sworn affiliation and oftentimes also their opposition to other gangs, as in the case of Turtle's McBride Boys: "Limited to a few city blocks which surrounded McBride Avenue and which provided a safety net of fences and alleys, it seemed, at least in Turtle's head, that their dominance, their ownership of those precious city blocks was now thrown into question by their rivals, the Lote M Boys. Consequently, when she walked the streets, she loomed as inviting to them as a bull's eye target" (20). In Viramontes's East LA urban aesthetics, chiseled and graffiti-sprayed posse walls become battlegrounds where cemented banners herald the arrival of "new conquerors over old ones" (217). Hence, in *Their Dogs*, hegemonic powers are at play creating a true trickle-down effect: global and national imperialist forces represented by urban renewal plans and the construction of the freeway impact the local, creating community fragmentation and ensuing gang turf in the barrio, and, in turn, encroaching into the more personal, reflected in Turtle's alienation from her family, her gang, and the larger Chicano community. Hence, as Anzaldúa stated in her essay "En rapport, In Opposition" while examining the internalization of the colonizer's oppression in our communities: "They have us doing to those within our own ranks what they have done and continue to do to us—*Othering* people. That is, isolating them, pushing them out of the herd, ostracizing them. The internalization of negative images of ourselves, our own self-hatred, poor self-esteem, makes our own people the Other" (143).

Viramontes's portrayal of gang subjectivity through Turtle as an androgynous woman, and also through her material, social, and emotional uprooting, challenges stereotypical notions of a contemporary Chicano spatial imaginary that ascribes young Chicano males the roles of *cholos*, or gang members, as intrinsically "native" to the barrio. In all irony, as Chicana critic Sonia Saldívar-Hull notes in her reading of "Neighbors," one of Viramontes's short stories in *The Moths and Other Stories*, "These 'homeboys' [using a self-identifier] exist as deterritorialized subjects of an 'America' that refuses to acknowledge Chicano and Chicana identity as indigenous to the geographic area" (152). Thus, countering imperialist notions that overlay the concrete of capitalist urban modernity over sheer human nature, Viramontes's tight inner-city gangs are searching for a vanished sense of community; they circumnavigate the streets, reterritorialize the land, travel in packs made up of their own, ferociously resist the trespass of others, and make pacts for life. In the case of the McBride Boys, "The boys all vowed to be there for each other, always and por vida, hasta la muerte, because that's what it's all about. About loyalty. About tightness. About protecting and serving" (27).

QA: Perro que ladra, no muerde or so they say . . .

Claiming "rising cases of rabies," the LA authorities put the neighborhood under siege through the Quarantine Authority (referred to as the QA), which enacts an arbitrary curfew (from 8 p.m. to 6 a.m.), sets up roadblocks in the streets, and implements a checkpoint system in a seeming war-zone East LA. The QA sets out to seal off the neighborhood and quarantine the community under the pretext of containing the dog rabies outbreak. This leads to an intensified police presence in the barrio, which maintains surveillance on the residents. Hence, the QA, as the visible force of a police state, becomes the new invader of the 1960s.

The QA checkpoints restrict people's freedom of movement and make it difficult for residents to reach places of work and study, and to visit family and friends. In the case of many of the novel's characters, the checkpoints are the source of inconveniences and delays that render it exhausting for them to carry out their daily life tasks. Moreover, although not portrayed in the novel, the QA occupation could also have other effects on East LA residents, such as preventing people from attending places of worship or even more life-threatening consequences such as those caused by the inability to access medical care or obtain other basic goods and services.

Reminiscent of Israeli military checkpoints in occupied Palestine, East LA residents are forced to show their identity cards to the QA while they lethargically wait in line to enter their neighborhoods:

> The city officials demanded paper so thin and weightless, it resisted the possibility of upholding legal import to people like herself, her cousin Nacho, her girlfriends and all the other neighbors with or without children who had the misfortune of living within the shaded designated areas . . . A neighbor's idea of validity was totally incongruent with the QA's norms or anyone else's, for that matter. Business was done differently in the East side . . . Need legal status? For those without papers, legal status became a shift in perspective, a matter of dubious demarcation, depending on who the border belonged to. (66)

Residents are forced to show the identification cards to the QA to prove their membership to the state, an entity unaware of how things are done in the barrio. Hence, residents declare their sense of state collectivity only in the abstract, as these "thin and weightless" papers can never substitute for the human aspect of one's ties to the community. As Ralph Cintron maintains, community membership "does not necessarily entail a writing act that declares a relationship between an individual and the abstraction the individual belongs to. In contrast the state cannot exist without these recorded relationships" (57).

In *Their Dogs*, the presence of the QA in East LA cannot be justified merely by the presence of rabid dogs; instead, it shows how residents are treated by the state as if they themselves had rabies. Certainly, in an encroached urban landscape, dissent is more easily managed and mitigated; people are easy to contain, round up, and, with no doubt, they become an easier target to shoot at. Hence, the patrolling of East LA portrays the reach of the US government's low-intensity warfare on the country's communities of color. Paralleled to the Vietnam War of the time, the siege of East LA shows how often the US government's more visible tactics of occupation, containment, and colonization of territories and peoples abroad are equally implemented within its own arbitrary borders. As time has shown again and again, Viramontes's East LA is much more than just a surreal environment. Indeed, the more recent implementation of SB 1070 in Arizona and similar anti-immigrant laws across the United States, particularly in the Southwest, reminds us that the apparent fictional occupation of the barrio is ever-increasingly more real than imagined.

In the fringes of the City of Angels, the novel's homeless shadows crawl onto the asphalt with the setting sun, camouflaging their socially rendered immaterialized bodies in the dark. Refugees at night, they wake up, only to find themselves strangers in their own streets, thrown away, dispossessed of their newly found urban dwellings, once again confined to the invisibility of the event of daylight heralded by the rising sun. Viramontes writes:

> The city buildings, once brightly specked with fashionable, neatly creased people, were now deserted as night fell on the streets of downtown and more people like her squeezed out of the crawl spaces and crevices of the alleys. At sundown, war was declared between the haves who abandoned their office buildings for home, and have-nots who pushed their portable cardboard homes in shopping carts to reclaim a place in the streets denied them during daylight. Dogs emerged, packs of them gathering in numbers as they roamed the streets to scavenge, to challenge the have-nots. (124)

Thus, contesting the streets, the dogs and the "have-nots" (both the homeless and gang members) scrabble for an alleyway, seeking self-preservation. Looking for tierra firme, night dogs trespass the limits of demarcated territories, roaming between private and public spaces.

Conclusion

As stated at the beginning of this essay, in *Their Dogs* Viramontes sets out to excavate the dialectics of what she calls the "colonized imagination." In one of her aforementioned interviews, she further explains internalized oppression in action as reflected in external community violence and its relation to the use of dogs by the Spaniards as military tools in colonizing indigenous peoples:

> And these dogs were trained to rip flesh, were trained to bite into and not let go, you know, like pit bulls. And I see that and I see what is [has] colonization done? What is the linkage of the way I have been feeling now with what Lorna Dee Cervantes again describes as, excuse me, pun? And the preoccupation of not feeling myself, you know what I mean? Where do those feelings come from if not through that colonization? And so I have to look at what happened five hundred years ago and how it's connected here. And my source of connection here is this idea of violence in East LA and how it's turned on us, and why it's turned on us. ("Interview with Helena María Viramontes," 135)

The Spanish colonization of the Américas was a violent encounter that left a long trail of blood in the so-called "new" world. The indigenous peoples who survived the encounter with the Spanish colonizers (and, certainly, their war dogs) soon found themselves strangers in their own homeland. In the scheme of colonial domination, the ensuing negation and delegitimization of indigenous culture were major acts of ethnocide whose consequences are still felt today, more than five hundred years after the arrival of the first European "earthmovers" to our shores.

In line with Anzaldúa's spiritual activism, in writing *Their Dogs*, Viramontes seems to answer Anzaldúa's call for rewriting the history of colonized people by "reclaiming the agency of reinscribing, taking off their inscriptions and reinscribing ourselves" ("Praying for Knowledge," 189). Viramontes reinscribes Chicano history in the face of encroaching colonial erasure, which is, by and in itself, an anti-colonial act.

In *Their Dogs*, Xólotl is not only Viramontes's nagual (represented by the dogs that accompany her characters throughout the novel) but also a metaphor in itself for shape-shifting, from moving from one character's consciousness to another. In doing so, Viramontes employs metaphors, which, like the indigenous dogs that carry the soul of the dead across the river in Mictlán, become bridges through which the reader can, if for only an ephemeral moment, walk in the shoes of the Other, those who are rendered invisible by larger US society: the child, the youth, the gang member, the homeless, the undocumented immigrant, the biracial Chicana/os. Essentially, these are the invisible souls who abound in the underworld of Viramontes's East LA streets.

By looking at the Other, Viramontes's bridges make us look at ourselves, at those individuals that hegemonic oppression makes members of the Chicano community want to disassociate themselves from, hold in disregard, effectively rendering them doubly invisible. By excavating into the colonized imagination of Viramontes's characters, the reader is confronted with the dynamics of interior fragmentation. However, the healing comes from finding a common humanity with those members of the Chicano community who are treated as rabid dogs. Moreover, Viramontes's urban aesthetics in the novel cement a more truthful portrayal of Chicanas and Chicanos; her healing knowledge shows us that the physical, emotional, and spiritual are intrinsically connected.

Perhaps it took Viramontes ten years to complete *Their Dogs* because only she knows that to deconstruct violence, to challenge stereotypical portrayals of the colonized, to undo centuries of oppression, to carefully pick one's words to construct a new decolonized imagination is no simple task. Indeed, one must love language and believe in the power of metaphors to transform the reader, to connect, to love the Other, that is, the Other in us, to heal, to create change . . . to travel to an underworld of a seemingly forgotten past, to venture on a spiritual journey that conjures up from the entrails of the earth the maimed spirits of the invisible who walk among us, to provide us with the vision of the vanquished to be cemented in our material reality so as not to be forgotten, one needs to build bridges to the spiritual.

With *Their Dogs*, Viramontes, a child of the Chicano movement, gives new breath to younger generations. By the very act of chronicling her journey to the East LA of her childhood and youth, she provides us with the decolonial remedy necessary for the cultural survival of Chicanas/os to heal the wounds of colonization.

Notes

1. The Aztecs were a "Nahuatl-speaking group that migrated south from *Aztlán*, 'Place of herons,' which many contemporary Chicanos identify as their US Southwest homeland and which is the origin of the word *Aztec*; they were also known as the *Mexica* (pronounced 'Meshica'), from which *Mexicano* and *Chicano* are derived" (Alarcón, 151).

2. This introduction came to be through conjuring up much of Viramontes's magnetic words in *Their Dogs Came with Them*. In particular, see pp. 9, 33, and 169 for quotations and other references used.

3. *The Broken Spears* is a collection of oral stories told in Nahuatl and translated into Spanish that recount the Spanish invasion of the Aztec empire. I use the 1992 English edition of the book; the original was first published in Spanish under the title *Visión de los vencidos: Relaciones indígenas de la conquista* in 1959. These accounts narrate that upon the arrival of the Spaniards in México, omens that foretold the violent fate of indigenous peoples multiplied: visions of death and of peoples in chains, lakes of blood, comets, and swarms of insects.

4. See Fortier and Rodríguez for a full discussion of what constitutes "cultural memory." In making this statement, I argue that the various experiences of Chicano communities with both Spanish and Anglo colonialism can be considered "historical memories that are so overwhelmingly significant that they define the essence of a people and become imperative for their survival" (121).

5. From this point on, I will refer to *Their Dogs Came with Them* simply as *Their Dogs*.

6. Belinda Acosta, in her review of *Their Dogs*, writes, "The weight of surveillance, the destruction of the old way of life, and the already turbulent political period make up the dynamic canvas from which the characters of *Their Dogs Came with Them* emerge . . . to fully appreciate it [the novel], approach it like a mural. While the grandness of a mural is what first commands attention, the viewer enters through its image details. After which, the viewer can then step back and reflect on the whole. The same is true of Viramontes' startling second novel."

7. In *Their Dogs*, the narrative shifts back and forth in time, spanning three generations, yet most of the action takes place in forty-eight hours. As in "The Cariboo Café," Viramontes's most well-known and anthologized story, the fragmented and interrupted narrative structure reflects "the disenfranchised, the fragmented world, the fragmented way that these marginalized people live" ("Praying for Knowledge," 147). This circular nature of time is more closely associated with conceptions of time found in Mesoamerican cosmology, which undermines Western linear temporality and modern notions of progress. See Bonfil Batalla (38) and Le Clézio (109, 192).

8. See Bonfil Batalla (15, 81).

9. According to Varner and Varner, in an encounter with the Spanish dogs, indigenous people thought they were gods because they had come with Cortés, whom they also believed was the Aztec god Quetzalcoátl (63). The Spaniards used dogs for other purposes, including combat, blood sport, guard duty, hunting, testing food for poison, and the enforcement of Christian principles among "pagan infidels," often regarded as belonging to a species inferior to that of the animals unleashed to them. Among the activities considered most repugnant by the Spaniards were what they considered social deviations such as homosexuality, transvestism, and the practice of pre-Hispanic religion (193).

10. "Quetzalcoatl (Plumed Serpent), God an cultural hero of a central myth and historic legend in Mexico and Yucatan, where he was known by his Mayan name, *Kukulcan*; *Quetzalcoatl* is a compound noun derived from *quetzalli*, 'precious feather,' and *coatl*, 'snake'; he is identified with *Ehecatl*, the God of Wind, and with the planet Venus; as a Toltec cultural hero . . . he promised to return after being defeated by the priests and the new cult of *Tezcatlipoca*; Hernán Cortés was identified with this deity when he first appeared on the shores of the Aztec empire in 1519, the year *Ce-Acatl*, which was the date prophesied for the return of Lord Quetzalcoatl" (Alarcón, 153).

11. The domestication of corn, along with other native plants, gave rise to agriculture in Mesoamerica, which would then eventually lead to a sedentary way of life for indigenous communities. See Bonfil Batalla, 4–5.

12. Praising *Their Dogs*, the *San Antonio Express-News* states, "The novel draws us in with Viramontes' hypnotic prose. Unflinchingly . . . tells the story of the conquered people from the point of view of those conquered and displaced," as quoted in *Their Dogs*.

13. In *Aztlán y México*, the late prominent scholar Don Luis Leal dedicated an entire chapter to discussing lycanthropy among indigenous Mexicans. According to Leal, indigenous nagualism, or the act of shape-shifting into animal forms, was widely practiced in México in pre-Columbian times (158).

14. Anzaldúa gives a firsthand account of *la naguala*, "the feminine form of nagual, the capacity some people such as Mexican indigenous shamans have of 'shapeshifting'—becoming an animal, place, or thing by inhabiting that thing or by shifting into the perspective of their animal companion. I have extended the term to include an aspect of the self unknown to the conscious self. Nagualismo is a Mexican spiritual knowledge system where the practitioner searches for spirit signs. I call the maker of spirit signs 'la naguala,' creative, dreamlike consciousness able to make broader associations and connections than waking consciousness" (Anzaldúa and Keating, 577, n. 4). Anzaldúa's shamanic imagination informs her entire life project. She wrote considerably on the concept of "shape-shifting," which is present in several of her short stories.

15. Unlike in *Their Dogs*, the metamorphosis of a human character to animal form does occur in modern Latin American novels and stories. For more on this, see Nancy Gray Díaz's *The Radical Self* (1988).

Works Cited

Acosta, Belinda. "In Person: Helena María Viramontes." *The Austin Chronicle*, April 20, 2007, http://www.austinchronicle.com/books/2007-04-20/467008/.html.

Alarcón, Francisco X. *Snake Poems: An Aztec Invocation.* San Francisco: Chronicle Books, 1992.

Anzaldúa, Gloria. *Borderlands/La Frontera: The New Mestiza.* San Francisco: Spinsters/Aunt Lute, 1987.

———. "En rapport, In Opposition: Cobrando cuentas a las nuestras." In *Making Face, Making Soul/Haciendo Caras: Creative and Critical Perspectives by Women of Color*, edited by Gloria Anzaldúa, 142–148. San Francisco: Aunt Lute Foundation Books, 1990.

———. "Quincentennial: From Victimhood to Active Resistance." In *Gloria E. Anzaldúa: Interviews/Entrevistas*, edited by AnaLouise Keating, 177–194. New York: Routledge, 2000.

Anzaldúa, Gloria, and AnaLouise Keating. *This Bridge We Call Home: Radical Visions for Transformation.* New York: Routledge, 2002.

Bonfil Batalla, G. *México Profundo: Reclaiming a Civilization.* Translated by Philip A. Dennis. Translations from Latin America Series. Austin: University of Texas Press, 1996.

Cintron, Ralph. *Angel's Town.* Boston: Beacon, 1997.

Díaz, Nancy G. *The Radical Self: Metamorphosis to Animal Form in Modern Latin American Narrative.* Columbia: University of Missouri Press, 1988.

Espinosa, Gastón, and Mario T. García. *Mexican American Religions: Spirituality, Activism, and Culture.* Durham, NC: Duke University Press, 2008.

Fortier, Ted, and Jeanette Rodríguez. *Cultural Memory: Resistance, Faith & Identity.* Austin: University of Texas Press, 2007.

Freire, Paulo. *Pedagogy of the Oppressed.* New York: Continuum, 2000.

Kevane, Bridget A. "Violence, Faith, and Active Miracles in East Los Angeles: *Their Dogs Came with Them* and "The Miraculous Day of Amalia Gómez." In *Profane & Sacred: Latino/a American Writers Reveal the Interplay of the Secular and the Religious*, edited by Bridget Kevane, 11–42. Lanham, MD: Rowman and Littlefield, 2008.

Leal, Luis. *Aztlán y México: Perfiles literarios e históricos.* Studies in the Language and Literature of United States Hispanos. Binghamton, NY: Editorial Bilingüe, 1985.

Le Clézio, J.-M.G. *The Mexican Dream, or, the Interrupted Thought of Amerindian Civilizations.* Chicago: University of Chicago Press, 1993.

León-Portilla, Miguel. *The Broken Spears: The Aztec Account of the Conquest of Mexico.* Boston: Beacon Press, 1992. Reprint of *Visión de los vencidos: Relaciones indígenas de la conquista.* Mexico City: UNAM, 1959.

Markman, Roberta H., and Peter T. Markman. *The Flayed God: The Mesoamerican Mythological Tradition: Sacred Texts and Images from Pre-Columbian Mexico and Central America*. San Francisco: Harper San Francisco, 1992.

Read, Kay A., and Jason J. González. *Handbook of Mesoamerican Mythology*. Handbooks of World Mythology. Santa Barbara, CA: ABC-CLIO, 2000.

Sahagún, Bernardino, Charles E. Dibble, and Arthur J. O. Anderson. *Florentine Codex: General History of the Things of New Spain, Book 10: The People*. Santa Fe, NM: School of American Research, 1961.

Saldívar-Hull, Sonia. *Feminism on the Border: Chicana Gender Politics and Literature*. Berkeley: University of California Press, 2000.

Varner, John Grier, and Jeannette Johnson Varner. *Dogs of the Conquest*. Norman: University of Oklahoma Press, 1983.

Viramontes, Helena María. "The Cariboo Café." In *The Moths and Other Stories*, 65–82. Houston, TX: Arte Público Press, 1985.

———. *The Moths and Other Stories*. Houston, TX: Arte Público Press, 1985.

———. "Neighbors." In *The Moths and Other Stories*, 109–117. Houston, TX: Arte Público Press, 1985.

———. "Praying for Knowledge: Interview with Helena María Viramontes." In *Latina Self Portraits: Interviews with Contemporary Women Writers*, edited by Bridget Kevane and Juanita Heredia, 141–154. Albuquerque: University of New Mexico Press, 2000.

———. "Interview with Helena María Viramontes." In *Communal Feminisms: Chicanas, Chilenas, and Cultural Exile: Theorizing the Space of Exile, Class, and Identity*, edited by Gabriella Gutiérrez y Muhs, 123–137. Lanham, MD: Lexington Books, 2007.

———. *Their Dogs Came with Them*. New York: Atria, 2007.

IV
Interviews

10

Elevated Thinking, Metaphor Making, Aspired Imagining

An Interview with Helena María Viramontes

INTERVIEW WITH GABRIELLA GUTIÉRREZ Y MUHS

Gutiérrez y Muhs: We are all familiar with *And the Earth Did Not Part, . . . y no se lo tragó la tierra* by Tomás Rivera, and can now parallel the young man's experience to Estrella's in *Under the Feet of Jesus*. Your book really addresses the issues of gender, left untouched by previous authors. Even though Rivera's protagonist lives in dire poverty, the protagonist is in a privileged position because of his gender. The attention he's given by his family in trying to get him an education is just a different level of a privileged position than Estrella's situation. Would you like to talk about Estrella's role?

Viramontes: Estrella has what I would call an organic intellect. She's very intelligent, but hasn't been schooled right, and she's a reader of both books and society. Yet who pays attention to her smarts? Here we have Alejo who is allowed to entertain dreams of becoming a geologist. It's a dream supported by his grandmother, and a dream that also allows him to temporarily escape from the cruel fieldwork. He knows this employment is only provisional. Would Estrella have that kind of support? Does Estrella feel that her employment, the unsaid responsibility of caring for her brothers and sisters, is only temporary? Absolutely not, and there lay her sorrow and sorrow for young women like her.

Except for the books providing other worldviews, Estrella doesn't have anything outside of her immediate family, and we all know that families for *mujeres* can be just as suffocating as they may be empowering. To this day, for example, I am still approached by high school students, mujeres who come to me and say, "I want to go to school but my mom wants me to stay home," "I want to take advanced math, but my dad doesn't want me to stay after school." There are those educational policy makers who say our lack of achievement lies in our Chicana/o culture, but to place all blame there is a mistake. Why does a mother want her daughter to stay home—because she has to work to put food on the table. Why does a father want his daughter not to stay after school—because certain hoods are unsafe after dark. So, it's not just cultural.

The difference between my sisters and I was in my love of reading. I was captivated by this whole idea of words. Like Estrella, I experienced both the desire to read *and* the horror of not having books. Coming from a bookless home, I've learned not to take for granted book availability and ownership. In many communities of color, we don't have libraries and we don't have bookstores. There wasn't a bookstore in mine until a self-proclaimed Communist opened one up in East Los Angeles back in the seventies. Combining language and my desire to write about women like me, sisters, made me think about Estrella.

But let's get back to Estrella. Such hunger to read, such eagerness to see beyond the fields, she tries to read discarded newspapers to re-imagine herself. Remember how she learns to read—Perfecto shows her the tools and she becomes transformed in more ways than one. Using language as "tools" for social change, I turned the metaphor inside out. And Estrella marvels at the connection between rebuilding and reinventing and reconstructing both materially and abstractly. Given that incredible realization, do we want to circumvent the Estrellas of the world by not allowing them to exercise their intelligence?

Gutiérrez y Muhs: Do you go into any of the other genres? I know you write short stories.

Viramontes: I wrote a script that got produced by the American Film Institute and directed by Ana Maria Garcia. It was a totally different type of writing, which helped me, in the long run, to write better fiction. But scriptwriting was mostly challenging. You can't reply on dialogue, and you certainly can't use clichés, and it's extremely important to use visuals to reflect a character's interior life. You can't say, "And then he suddenly felt," like you can in fiction. It took me about a year to write a thirty-page script, and I would not have done it, had it not been for my experience with Gabriel García Márquez at the Sundance Institute. His confidence in my work gave me the ovaries to try and script something. And I thought I could write a movie, and I could produce, and I could direct it for sure. [*laughs*] Oh man, let me tell you, I thought I was really hot stuff, and then I started writing, and whoa, it is one of the most difficult art forms, much closer to poetry and I'm not a poet. As soon as I finished it, Ana Maria asked to see it and said, "Can I shoot it?" To this day, Ana and I remain the best of friends over this experience. We did an eleven-day shoot, and working with a whole crew of people who all have different takes on the script, who all gave and took from the script, was also an experience I wasn't used to. After that, I was hired by this production company to do a script for the life of Danny Romo, who's a tattoo artist in LA. He's the one who did all the tattoos for *American League* and for *Heat*. He's a very interesting young man. The producers produced the movie, *The Substitute*, and wanted to do this movie on Romo's life. I'm not a sell-out, believe me. [*laughs*] Is there gonna be a Substitute 2?

Gutiérrez y Muhs: It's not a bad movie.

Viramontes: Have you seen it? But really, this young man Romo, he's for real, a very spiritual man. I met him and I talked with him on two occasions. He's a young gifted man, *todo corazón*. He grew up with six brothers in a rough neighborhood, a murder ensued, and he solely rises out of the ashes, tattoo art rescues him. . . . The whole metaphor of piercing the skin to bleed, to get something out of it, it's really like his life. So I said I would do this script. But life and work got in the way, and I just couldn't commit myself.

Gutiérrez y Muhs: And why do you say you're not a poet?

Viramontes: Well, I'm a failed poet. [*laughs*] I took one creative writing course as an undergraduate and immediately discovered my limitations. You know, as undergraduates, how many of you are writing poetry right now? Oh, come on? I know you are. The rest of you should, it's a wonderful art form. Anyway, I wrote some poetry, and I realized that I couldn't do justice to the form, and being the coward that I was, I abandoned it, then I graduated from college. After graduation, I realized, wait a minute, I've been reading all this literature, and I thought to myself, why can't I try writing a story like *Pedro Páramo*. [*laughs*] See how tall I set the bar? [*laughs*] I love that novella. The beauty of the language, the blending and bending of natural and supernatural worlds inspired me as well as engaged me. I became a participant in forming the narrative, and I found this process fascinating. So I wrote a terrible short story, but it won a prize. The money I received from that prize was pivotal.

In my essay, " 'Nopalitos,' " I wrote about my mother, who thought I was always a little whacked [*laughs*] because she could not understand how a mujer could sit in the living room while the house was a mess, sit there with a pencil and paper, wool gathering [*displaying a gazed thinking face*]. Oh, I could see the *pelitos* rising on the back of her neck. Disturbed by this, she'd immediately interrupt me and request chore doing. And of course I felt very guilty and so couldn't say no. Once I won the first prize and received a check for $25, she came over while I sat wool gathering and asked that I do laundry. I quietly passed her the check. I mean $25 was big money back in '72–'73.

Man, I feel like such an old woman. How many of you were born in that year? Yeah, there you have it. [*laugh*]. So I gave her the check, and she looked at it, and she said, "Where did you get this?" and I said, "I won a short story contest" or something like that. She just didn't say anything, just folded the check and slipped it in her apron pocket, walked away, and then came back with a cup of coffee for me. You know it was then that I realized there was no way I was going to fail with my mother on my side! So what if the world doesn't care? She understands! [*laughs*] But anyway, *este*, going back to your question. I'm sorry, I'm babbling, I swear it was the salad I had for lunch.

Gutiérrez y Muhs: We like your babbling. If this is babbling, just keep going.

Viramontes: But yeah, my poetry was pretty bad. And I still do write poetry. My poems stay between the mattresses.

Gutiérrez y Muhs: But I find that "The Moths" and *Under the Feet of Jesus* are very poetic.

Viramontes: I have such high regard for poets. Poets really do have this beautiful, interesting, intriguing, vigorous worldview. They see moments with great clarity, then steal moments for us to meditate on them. They are the great arbitrators of experience. They force us to listen to our own heartbeats. It's really elevated thinking that I admire, the metaphor-making that I appreciate, the images that I aspire for.

Gutiérrez y Muhs: I wanted to ask you about your spirituality in relationship to writing. Because we've had three other authors go by this room. And it's almost been shocking for us to see what writing represents for each one of them, it's been so different. You know, for one of them it was "puro trabajo," those were the words she used, it was just writing. And for another one it represented the highest spirituality, she had to be in the strands to write. And for the third one it was a combination of the two. Her poetry was spiritual, and her writing was "puro trabajo." And so I wanted to ask about your spirituality in relationship to writing. What is writing for you, how do you write?

Viramontes: I say it over and over that writing is the only way I know how to pray because writing helps me to understand reality.

Writing is resuscitative and empowering in the light of political struggles. For me it reinforces and affirms life. I pay attention to my surroundings and then bring them into that special place of mediation where the faith in my imagination is as important as any religion.

When I sit down to write, I begin with meditation, to pray. First I thank the spirits that I have all this space, that I have this time, that I have this peace whereas in the bigger part of the world bombs fly and children die. Then I plead to my ancestors to help me approach the manuscript with open eyes and an open heart, humbling myself.

If I approach writing without willing to be humble, I may not learn anything. And I believe, sincerely believe, that every time you sit down to write you learn something new about yourself, about another dimension in that limitless world of dimensions. That's why writing is so wonderful, even if you don't publish. To be able to sit down and write and to get in touch with your own mind, to get in touch with this limitless, *limitless*, space that's called your imagination where you find you can envision different worlds, different political views, different solutions. To have that power is incredible. The first thing a real totalitarian government does is to imprison or murder the writers and artists, precisely because of their power.

Imaginative thinking creates hope and isn't it also powerful? And writing is something anyone can do. All you need is pen and paper, not big machines, or fine brushes, or instruments, just a notebook and pencil. We all grow up with the capacity to tell stories. Es la verdad. But you may think, nah, I can't write poetry, because poetry is made for the elite, ivory tower people, or you may think that poetry is not important enough to communicate political ideas. The act of writing has the capability of forming minds, of informing minds, including your own. Whenever you're *chismeando* with someone, you are telling stories. [*laughs*] You think that isn't story telling? For several years I was literary editor of a magazine called *ChismeArte*, gossip art. Our lives are made up of narratives. The mysteries of the world are only mysteries until we see the narrative. Our brains, our memories are narrative forming.

As children we enjoy hearing stories too, until something happens and suddenly you're in high school or college and we lose the capacity to listen intensely. But I always go back to the central issue here: that in order to write, you really do have to have open eyes and an open heart. You have to establish a certain amount of generosity in your spirit. If you don't, you will not see your characters as true human beings—worse yet, they won't reveal themselves to you. It's like a true (to use the cliché) true intervention in the way writing makes you a better human being.

Gutiérrez y Muhs: Can you tell me more about your rituals?

Viramontes: When I first began writing seriously, I would begin by lighting two candles. The candles induce relaxation. I think about gratitude, think about the act before I actually do it. And then I pray for humility. Again, not in a trance-like form, because I am very aware of what I'm doing. But I truly want to see the world through a child's eyes. I truly want to learn something new. And then I turn on the computer, and read what I had previously written, and begin with a sentence. To think of it as a novel, as a whole book, it's too intimidating, too scary. It's like looking at your organic chemistry book and saying tomorrow you're going to have an exam, here, study. [*laughs*] It's too overwhelming. But what I do is select a paragraph, then a sentence, then a word. When you have a word in your hands, you can discover new definitions, and even when that's too scary, take a character's name and write a history of that name, and before you know it you have characterization.

Faith is essential. If I don't write an original word, or an original sentence today, maybe it will come tomorrow, and if it doesn't come tomorrow, maybe it will come Thursday; if it doesn't come Thursday, maybe it will come Friday; and if it doesn't come Friday, maybe it'll come Monday because I take the weekends off. [*laughs*] But, you must trust your imagination. What makes writers different from others is that we will stick it out when the writing is terrible, when we come up short in our reach and we hurt. Glutton for punishment sometimes, and sometimes it takes months. That's where the real work comes in, that's when the real dedication shows. I sometimes experience droughts. I can sit for hours and nothing comes. These droughts come with doubts, and so I have to remind myself why I write in the first place. Love, my source is love. Is there another question? *Por favor?* Yes.

Gutiérrez y Muhs: What have you had to sacrifice, if anything, to get your books published?

Viramontes: Well, there were different issues for different books. As for *Under the Feet of Jesus*, I had to sacrifice sleep [*laughs*] and a healthy relationship with my husband. I've worked on the novel for approximately two and a half years from four in the morning until seven, five days out of the week. I took one week off for one Christmas and then I took two weeks off when we moved from Irvine to Ithaca, New York. And between all those boxes and everything, I continued to work on the novel. I very rarely went out with my husband. He described me as a "ladrillo [brick]," because I'd sleep like the dead [*gestures with her head tipped back in chair, sleeping*]. [*laughs*]

Sleep was one thing, but in between the ten years when I published "The Moths" and *Under the Feet of Jesus*, I had to continuously reinforce the fact that I was a writer, even if I wasn't publishing anything, even if people were not even paying attention to my work. Unless, of course, you're Stephen King, you know, writers are not well respected, nor well paid. How can you possibly say that you're a writer when you don't have a product? Amos Oz, an Israeli writer, once wrote that in Israel, writers are seen as visionaries. Here in the United States they are seen as entertainers.

In those years, I had to remind myself as to why I was doing what I was doing each day. I started two novels, but later abandoned them. For me, it was to get the voices I kept hearing on the page. Periodically I would publish a short story like "Miss Clairol." But anything substantial? Not for years and years until *Under the Feet of Jesus*, and then my personal struggle to write *Their Dogs Came with Them*. Whoa, what a journey that was. The writing of the novel, then my contract broken, and then the intensity of trying to get it published as it was, cheeze. My agent Stuart Bernstein worked overtime to clear the way for *Dogs*, and he found an editor at Atria Books who published the novel.

Gutiérrez y Muhs: The description in the back of *Under the Feet of Jesus* reads like a romantic relationship between Estrella and Alejo. I felt like it was trying to sell the book as a romance novel. But then when I read it, it was less of a romance and more of a political novel. So, I was just wondering where that came from? And how that's tied to the actual contents of the book? [*laughs*]

Viramontes: Marketing is a major element of the publishing world. The editor who actually bought the book was very, very respectful, and only changed a sentence or two here and there. But publishers want to sell books, and once you sign the contract, the book is no longer just yours. However, my editor hooked me up with Simón Silva, who did the cover of the novel. The editor had to also fight for the title, *Under the Feet of Jesus*, because marketing didn't like the word "Jesus." And I had to write up the importance of it. And my editor was very supportive. That is, up until she broke my contract and left *Dogs* without a publisher.

Gutiérrez y Muhs: How did you find someone who understood what you were trying to represent, and be true to it?

Viramontes: Well, this particular editor had periodically worked with Ana Castillo, for example. She understood Chicana writers. Sandra Cisneros and Julia Álvarez proved the marketability of our fiction, and so she didn't need convincing. I was very fortunate at the time. It was 1994, and within a month, I had a few editors interested in talking to me. Having a good editor makes for a special relationship. It's like ice and water, it's like *pan y agua*. There was actually one editor who was very keen on working with me, but she was interested in a different book. Rosemary was the only one who said, "I love this book, and I think there's not much more you can do with it."

I was very lucky. Dorothy Allison, a lesbiana white woman, who wrote *Bastard out of Carolina*, which won the National Book Award, had written a collection of essays about her loyalty to small presses, her loyalty to the feminist community. And for her, it was really a major decision to go to a big publishing company. She wrote of her delight in discovering that there were actually some editors that truly are passionate about literature. They make minimal pay, but they're there because they really love literature.

Gutiérrez y Muhs: I am looking through your acknowledgments, and it reads like a Who's Who of Chicana writers and Latina writers in America. I'm curious, who in particular influenced your work and style of writing? And also who are your favorite writers?

Viramontes: I was a child of the Chican@ movement. At the height of the Chican@ movement, I began to formulate my own political consciousness. I attended this very private four-year liberal arts college, and I received a very radical education by feminist nuns. These nuns gave me Angela Davis, George Jackson, Diedrich Bonhoeffer, and the theology of liberation. They gave me Gabriel García Márquez, Juan Rulfo, Augustín Yáñez, and other Latin American male novelists; they gave me African American writers, women writers of that time, Gwendolyn Brooks, Nikki Giovanni, Tillie Olsen, Grace Paley. We poured our souls into poetry, philosophy, ethics, and literature. I graduated, moved back to the Eastside, and found a job as a beer brewer. But I continued to write. Influenced by *Pedro Páramo*, I wrote my first short story.

I love stories, I love the telling of the story, I love the way the story is told. I am intrigued by the perception of the receiver too. Who's telling the story? Why this story? Why that particular story? And what's under those things that are not said? Fiction is the best way to tell the truth, the best way to offer the reader a complicated view of reality.

Gutiérrez y Muhs: What does your mom think of your work now? Has she gotten any more checks?

Viramontes: The checks? Actually, yes, she has and she's very happy. [*laughs*] No, actually this is fine. It's so funny, none of my sisters have read my book, but they all have it on their coffee table [*laughs*] with the newspaper clippings; it's so cute, they're so cute. But I don't think any of them have read it. [*laughs*] But they're very proud, very proud.

Gutiérrez y Muhs: When you first heard about Arizona SB 1070, the anti-immigrant legislation in the United States, how did you react to it? Have you been writing about it?

Viramontes: Several years ago, I took Pilar and Francisco and my niece Ambrosia to the Museum of Tolerance in Los Angeles. I was so struck by experiential aspects of the museum. Before entering, we were given names of those who entered the labor camps, and we don't know, until the museum end, as to whether they survived the war. We entered a remake of German streets to overhear manikins sitting in cafes discussing the raise of Nazism, and so we became privy to the ways in which the unnamable played out on people's xenophobia and other fears. We entered a room filled with propagandistic children's books. We entered a chamber, and when lights glowed up, we found ourselves inside an ovenlike structure, gasping. We became the six millions by a switch light.

I can't help but make comparisons between the rise of the unnamable and what is happening in Arizona. I'm astonished that more people do not see the parallels here, and more so, I'm astonished that many have chosen to remain absolutely silent on the matter just like millions did during the '30s and '40s. Have we lost it somewhere? This history? Surely, it can't happen in America, right? Xenophobes reduce us to sound bites, untruths, dehumanize us. Literature inflates humanity, complicates it. It is the metaphoric light switch, and in the light, we can see clearly how much we are one and the same.

Gutiérrez y Muhs: Would you mind saying a little bit about living in the Northeast? How has it affected your writing, if at all? What are some of the main differences, especially in terms of being part of Chicano communities from around the United States? Were you initially surprised, at all, by the Chicano communities in the Northeast?

Viramontes: The Northeast has opened doors for me in ways that I would not have imagined, had I not moved here. At first, the move was incredibly difficult to adjust to. My entire support network—sisters, brothers, parents, friends—lived in Southern California.

In addition, Los Angeles is my Yoknapatawpha County, and so I was also worried about how the move would affect my work.

The climate and culture were indeed different, but it wasn't until my mother's death several years later that I actually stopped hoping to return to California. With her, I suppose my desire to return diminished in ways that surprised me, and I slowly settled into a peaceful existence with Ithaca, a city of asylum for writers, a progressive community of artists, farmers, people with alternative lifestyles. We have a small house surrounded by three acres of forest, which is utterly quiet except for a teasing breeze rustling the trees at dusk, a room of one's own. Okay, so the winter is horrific. I'm never warm in winter, and I have to suit up with wool socks, snow boots, and a thick cap in order to simply go out to the mailbox and collect the mail. But I always try and keep things in perspective. How many mujeres cross borders, without monies and without speaking the language, leaving behind everything that felt comforting or familiar? Really. What guts, I think, and so I shouldn't complain and haven't for a while.

I try going to Los Angeles every summer for a prolonged stay where my brother Frank and I hoof the streets for hours, he close by, me in silent conversation with myself gathering notes, impressions. I am a frequent visitor of the main downtown public library, where I spend hours upon hours in the stacks, on microfiche, at a table. I don't think I could find what Flaubert has described as the "divine detail" if I didn't have access to this remarkable library. Being around family and the neighborhood is blood transfusion for the anemic soul, a plasma force. At our own community library, there is a Chicana/o Resource Center, which is walking distance from the house I grew up in with a librarian who is married to a neighborhood friend. To have this center on the very street I write about just fuels the imagination enough to keep me going through the school year. Teaching at a top-tier institution like Cornell University has also made my time in the classroom incredibly rewarding. I love my students very much, and the Latina/o students are like our family. I have awesome Creative Writing colleagues, and our MFA writing graduates continue to contribute to American Letters. Meeting other

Latina/os certainly helped to broaden my horizon, explore similarities, and appreciate differences. Now I have two directions, one west, another east to pull from, a larger region from which to learn. Nonetheless, I often feel a sense of intense loneliness for my community.

Gutiérrez y Muhs: I wanted to ask you about the use of Spanish. Did your editor have anything to do with that?

Viramontes: I could not, not use Spanish. There was some discussion at Penguin as to whether there should be footnotes, glossaries, or even whether the Spanish should be italicized. The only Spanish italicized are those lyrics to a song that Petra is singing. Other than that, not one Spanish word has been italicized; I refused; we don't think in italics, why should we put our words in italics? Several years ago there was this big novel by Cormac McCarthy, *All the Pretty Horses*, about two young Tejanas, in the borderlands. They go to Mexico and they have horses, get into fights and romance. It's a lovely written book. I found it fascinating that there were whole chunks of dialogue in Spanish. Not one reviewer requested glossaries, or translations, and yet when we Chicanas and Chicanos, Latinas, Latinos use Spanish, they ask, why are you doing this, as if we're hiding something from the general public. When an Anglo does it, it's for art's sake, for authenticity. I said hey don't be telling me about marketability. Look at McCarthy.

Works Cited

Allison, Dorothy. *Bastard out of Carolina*. New York, NY: Dutton, 1982.

McCarthy, Cormac. *All the Pretty Horses*. New York: Knopf, 1992.

Rivera, Tomás. *And the Earth Did Not Part*. Berkeley, CA: Quinto Sol Publications, 1971.

———. *. . . y no se lo tragó la tierra (. . . And the Earth Did Not Devour Him)*. English translation by Evangelina Vigil-Piñón. Houston, TX: Arte Público Press, 1987.

Rulfo, Juan. *Pedro Páramo*. Madrid: Cátedra, 1983.

Viramontes, Helena María. "The Moths." *The Moths and Other Stories*, 27–32. Houston, TX: Arte Público Press, 1985.

Viramontes, Helena María. *The Moths and Other Stories.* Houston, TX: Arte Público Press, 1985.

———. "Miss Clairol." In *Chicana Creativity and Criticism: Charting New Frontiers in American Literature,* edited by María Herrera-Sobek and Helena María Viramontes, 101–105. Houston, TX: Arte Público Press, 1988.

———. " 'Nopalitos': The Making of Fiction." In *Breaking Boundaries: Latina Writing and Critical Readings,* edited by Asunción Horno-Delgado, Eliana Ortego, Nina M. Scott, and Nancy Saporta Sternbach, 33–38. Amherst: University of Massachusetts Press, 1989.

———. *Under the Feet of Jesus.* New York: Dutton, 1995.

———. *Their Dogs Came with Them.* New York: Atria, 2007.

II

Faith in the Imagination

An Interview with Helena María Viramontes

INTERVIEW WITH JOSÉ ANTONIO RODRÍGUEZ

José Antonio Rodríguez: Did you always want to be a writer? Was there a specific text that inspired you or was it more a gradual movement toward writing?

Helena María Viramontes: Definitely a gradual movement. My writing career was very serendipitous. I had no idea that one could strive to be a professional writer, and by that, I mean actually surviving the "long, sustained patience" that writing entails to finish a piece, share it with others, and then publish it. One helpful personal element in pursuit of writing was my incredible empathy for people. When I used to see my mother work so hard, I used to feel so sorry for her. I'd see someone eating lunch by his/her self in grade school, and I'd feel so sorry for them. From Dukie, the neighborhood drunk, to the battered woman next door, on and on my sadness for others went, and I knew I wanted to alleviate people's pain.

Not wanting to bring more strife into my mother's life, I became a dutiful daughter. I would do anything for my mother.

I remember being about nine or ten years old when my mother asked me to take a bus all the way to the end of the line, get off and go across the street, pay the phone bill, run right back, and take the same bus back. That was one of the most terrifying experiences that I've ever had. I was petrified, trying to memorize all the streets in case I got lost. But somehow, she knew I'd accomplish the task, and she was right. I came home feeling like a million dollars. Anyway, seeing the inequalities between the genders, the way women and men were treated in our household, where the men were given incredible privilege and the women of course had to do everything . . . From a very early age, I started thinking this wasn't fair.

I also knew I had to get out of the house or go nuts. I was having a conflict with my older brother and with my father. My father was a hard-core Catholic patriarch. He was an incredibly . . . It's hard to describe. He was a very complicated person. He was a husband who would beat up his wife, and who periodically got a hold of one of us for a good whipping. He was as brutal as his life had been as a laborer working to support eleven people. At the same time, though, there were these occasions of great love that he showed us. And he took it upon himself to buy the family a set of World Book encyclopedias, which became my major source of reading. But as I grew older, I had harbored an immense feeling of hostility toward him that I knew wasn't healthy for me or for my mother because she was in the middle of all these arguments. So when this opportunity arose to go to college and live in a dorm, I took it. This was in 1970.

Rodríguez: Did you know what you wanted to focus on?

Viramontes: I had no idea. My second oldest brother Serafín was going to San Diego State at the time. I remember he took our family to his campus, and we toured the library. I was amazed that this is what he did. That he would read books, go to class, and work part time. It wasn't sweeping, throwing out the trash, doing the laundry, but nurturing heart and soul. When I got to Immaculate Heart, I took things one step at a time. I majored in English because it was my second language, not my childhood language, and I felt I was lacking in skills. Remember, I was a product of the Los Angeles school district where the Eastside was basically forgotten and where there were several student "blowouts" to demand a better education. And you know the school system had to be pretty bad if even the students walked out in protest.

Fortunately, I didn't have the college pressures that parents put on their children. If I was to drop out of college, it would have been no big thing. But understand, this was the first time in my life that I was exposed to Anglos my own age, in a setting where I had to interact with them. Now that was a trip. I also didn't understand a word the professors were saying in the classroom, and so would go straight to the library and ask, who's Aristotle? I had a lot of reading to catch up on.

Rodríguez: So at what moment do you think, *I think I can do this?* I imagine it took years.

Viramontes: I guess by my senior year. The English major was a wonderful opportunity for reading the works of Latin American writers, of African American women writers, of socialist writers, of radical theologians. You know, Immaculate Heart was a very radical school in many ways. The nuns and other instructors taught us about being serious citizens of the world. In 1971, we debated abortion, test-tube babies, issues that eventually came to pass. It was an incredible education that the nuns, very radical and feminist, tried to instill in us, not convert us, but make us critical thinkers, singular but important voices that, through a collective, could move mountains. I just ate it all up.

Though I read like crazy, I had read very little of Chicano or Chicana literature because it simply wasn't accessible to us. This would later influence my decision to become literary editor of *ChismeArte*.

Writers say it all the time: first and foremost you have to be a passionate reader in order to become . . . or even to understand how to write passionately. And that's where I was. I was reading everything. I remember the first time I read *One Hundred Years of Solitude*, opening up and reading it in two and a half days and then finishing, and not knowing what time of day it was, looking at the end again, and then starting it all over again. Very exciting time for me. But my first *aha* moment in actually thinking about writing was when I read *Pedro Páramo* by Juan Rulfo. What Rulfo does is that he interweaves reality with non-reality and so you don't know at certain points in the novel who is a phantom and who is not. And he has total control of it. It is the most fantastic novella I have ever heard. I thought: I wanna try this.

Rodríguez: I was thinking of the idea of great writer or great writing giving us license. I suppose for you that was the first time or the beginning of that, where you felt directly empowered by the writing.

Viramontes: Exactly. The fact that Juan Rulfo also makes you work as a reader because he doesn't give you a chronology is thrilling to me. He gives you bits and pieces, and you have to put them together. And once you put them together, you realize how perfectly the incredible puzzle works. I had to read it several times, and each time it feeds you, it allows you to open another door, think about something else. And somehow each time that you read it, it gives you something back. So your imagination is working full force; your intellect is configuring and you are having a splendid time.

Rodríguez: For you, reading entails much more than just reading for aesthetic pleasure.

Viramontes: This is something that I talk about all the time: the engagement of the reader with the writer. Toni Morrison says that half of the art is finished when the book is published, but the other half is the reader. And so they have to work together. And that's how you have the dancing minds. It's a beautiful engagement. I also think literature that challenges allows me to open up other veiled realities. So it isn't just an aesthetic experience. It really is a fundamental exercise in developing my capacity as a critical thinker because it is challenging me to think about things in a certain way through its aesthetics, through its language, through the way Rulfo was able to masterfully put all this together. Even if it was an incredibly challenging read the first couple of times, by the time I felt I could appreciate it fully, I realized what a brilliant writer Rulfo was.

Rodríguez: I'm struck by what you're saying. It reminds me of *Their Dogs Came with Them*, its disjointed nature and the challenge that it presents for the reader.

Viramontes: I came to realize, after all these years, this is the way I think. I think in a very disjointed way, but also in a way that blurs past and present. To a certain extent that's what memory is. A very famous writer once said, "As soon as we begin to remember, we begin to fictionalize." I think that makes perfect sense. I think too that when you start remembering something, it becomes present, so present, the memory begins to embody. So those questions of complexity astonish me and then make me wonder how best to write this out. As a result, a lot of my fiction is experimentation in time, in memory, in storytelling. Some are more successful than others.

But with the *Dogs*, I didn't feel that I was writing a novel to emulate Rulfo. What I was trying to do was trying to see how I could write this novel with an incredible complexity of community and this devastation. How *does* one not only record but recreate trauma and the people who are traumatized by the disintegration of their collectivity? They're traumatized by being isolated and amputated, by being forgotten, traumatized because they can no longer connect. And my gut level reaction in trying to do that was that it had to be disjointed, since I'm trying to capture how the displacement and fragmentation caused by the freeways affected this community. There's no other way that I could have done the *Dogs* than the way I did.

Given that, there are times when I begin to doubt myself because there are so many readers who tell me it's so difficult to read. Of course this is sad. Before I sold the novel to Malika Adoro, at Atria Books, there was another editor who said that a recognizable framework is missing, one that could assist readers. That's precisely what I didn't want; I didn't want me in the narrative. I thought about it a lot, and I just couldn't do it. I had worked on it for so long and so hard. Half of the editors that read *Dogs* said it was too difficult to read, and readers didn't want to read depressing stories anyway; the other half thought it brilliant (their word, not mine), and woe the day they couldn't sell it past the marketing division. I think to myself, was I being a diva? Should I have maybe done another draft and structured it in a way to make it easier for some people to follow or contextualize it a bit more?

If it wasn't for those readers who write to me, others who I meet, people like you José, people like Michael Silverblatt, host of the Bookworm radio show, as well as other radio interviewers and book reviewers who seem to love the novel, I would have shut myself up in more ways than one. Without them, I would be suffering one long writer's block.

Rodríguez: I think the published draft of *Dogs* reflects a great faith in the reader, an incredible belief that the reader will follow, will step up to the challenge.

Viramontes: You're right. I argued with some of the editors too, about readership and some of the difficulty and having the faith in the reader. But you know, what I would like to do is write a novel that my own sisters can read. That's where my doubt comes in. But you're absolutely right. I continue to have faith in readers. Although the pool of serious readers becomes smaller and smaller, I still stake my reputation by *Dogs*, I'm very proud of it.

Rodríguez: The following quote from *Dogs* speaks to one of its central themes: "Turtle sat on the same porch step Cross-eyes had a few hours before. She looked into the endless fields of the construction. By Monday, the earthmovers would be running again, biting trenches wider than rivers; the groan, thump and burr noise of the constant motors would weave into the sound of her own breath whistling the blackened fumes of dust and crumble in her nasal cavities." Could you talk about the relationship between the cityscape and the human body and psyche in this novel?

Viramontes: That's all part of the destruction of the community. It doesn't happen over a week. It happens over years. The destruction is so *there* that it becomes a presence. You can't help but have the dust, the cement, the noise, and it becomes a part of your experience. Even though it's basically dehumanizing you, destroying you, you're slowly becoming a part of it; this is scary because then you become accustomed to that noise and that way of life, the inhaling of the debris; it becomes a natural occurrence, an acceptance to a very unnatural happening.

Rodríguez: There is a common theme in your writing, the idea of the environment resembling the human body that is then traumatized and subsequently traumatizes its inhabitants.

Viramontes: We are wholly connected to the earth. We are its matter, and its salt. We destroy it, we destroy ourselves. As simple and complicated as that. We are at fault for only thinking in the moment, and we will pay dearly for not thinking of the future as our ancestors tried to do.

Rodríguez: Here's another quote that echoes what we've been talking about: "The bulldozers resembled great ships." Can you elaborate on the theme of colonization in this novel?

Viramontes: Before this quote, I begin the novel with an epigraph from Miguel León-Portilla's *The Broken Spears: The Aztec Account of the Conquest of Mexico*. It's a key by which to begin reading *Dogs*. The quote you just read brings to mind another type of colonization in East Los Angeles by the coming of the bulldozers. Like the great ships that landed in Hispaniola, the bulldozers were sent to destroy and reclaim.

How does colonized thinking work to oppress? Like, why is it that the character of Ermila could rarely get out of the Eastside? I mean, she goes to the beach and that's a big thing, but she acquires this knowledge through Big Al who she's fucking. Returning home, she has trials and tribulations. Why is it that we're so isolated as a community, that we can't even begin to imagine ourselves going elsewhere spiritually, outside of our own geographical settings physically?

Rodríguez: And then there's the Quarantine Authority, which is an even more brutal force that creates perimeters, limits people's movements, their bodies, their imaginations. It's a prison environment.

Viramontes: Exactly. And that comes from a very direct experience with having the curfew and the roadblocks right after the Chicano

Moratorium uprising. I mean, you couldn't get into certain areas without showing proof of living there. How horrific is that? How fucked up is that, when you can't freely go into your own home? Or by giving proof, by being forced to give proof, it automatically feels like you've committed some crime and you have to prove your innocence.

Rodríguez: So then these apparatuses or institutions destabilize identity.

Viramontes: Yes.

Rodríguez: If someone questions you enough . . .

Viramontes: You begin to wonder. Exactly. If it's repeated enough times, it holds a level of conviction.

Rodríguez: How did the motif of the roaming dogs and the rabies problem come about? Is it based on autobiography?

Viramontes: I will say that I found out that the city of Los Angeles had a problem with rabid dogs twice and had to shoot them. It's been documented. But I didn't find out until after I wrote the novel. It's cool, you know, fiction ahead of fact.

Also, when you go to third world countries, the first thing you notice are the stray dogs. Here they're domesticated pets. But in other countries, the cultural significance of dogs is totally different. It felt like a good metaphor for this reason: people become cruel because they've been treated so cruelly. And so if you're treated like a dog, you become a dog.

Rodríguez: Your work has been widely reviewed. How well do you think the critics have understood what your aim was with *Dogs*?

Viramontes: Except for a few good souls, it was virtually quiet among the print reviewers. But *Poets & Writers'* Renee Shea did a wonderful job. There was Michael Silverblatt who I mentioned earlier. In an interview with him, I must have spoken about five words total because I was silent struck that he loved the book. I literally lost my voice because I was just so unprepared for his praise. He completely understood from an aesthetic point of view this history, these people. After the paperback came out two years ago, the readership has grown thanks to dedicated professors and their students. *Dogs* will be discussed in two panels at the American Literature Association this year, which pleases me very much.

Rodríguez: That's always good.

Viramontes: And there were a few online outlets that did some wonderful reviews. I think more than anything else, if they didn't catch the structure or the history, at least they caught the stories, the human stories. Linda Martin Wagner, from the University of North Carolina at Chapel Hill, told me that the Ben character was "astounding." And I told her, it's funny because that's about the only character that I modeled after a real person, my brother Frank. Everybody else sort of had seeds of other people that I knew, but for the most part, I let fiction make its mysterious ride.

So I think at least some readers connect with the stories of the characters. But you see, this is the way it was with *Pedro Páramo* and me. I didn't really get it the first time, the second time, started getting it the third time. By the sixth time, the puzzle had been solved. But, you know, I'm not a saint; after working on a novel for close to seventeen years, I wanted big recognition, a parade with confetti. And yet, the world has been, and continues to be, kind to me, so I don't want to sound ungrateful.

Rodríguez: That takes me to another question about the seventeen-year gestation of the novel. Last summer at a reading in Louisville, Kentucky, you said that the difference between you and non-writers isn't so much talent as perseverance, focus, patience to see a project through to the end. Where do you think that patience or that ability to maintain focus come from?

Viramontes: I want to really think about that. Off the cuff, I think it's just the compulsion to find out what's going to happen to these characters, the mystery of it all that you begin to develop and begin to miss if you're not with them for a period of time. Concern for them always pulled me back.

Rodríguez: Can patience be taught?

Viramontes: I have to say, it's been increasingly difficult to teach patience to younger undergraduate writers. Somehow they become the binge writers—write for twelve hours straight and then take four or five days off. Janet Burroway advises *know thyself*, to know what system works best for you. But I think it's like prayer—there always has to be a consistency to commitment which then transforms it into a meaningful practice. If there were no meaning, the motivation to practice (and practice here is essential) would sour any faith. Too, in order to connect with your subconscious, you really have to train it to go into a space of sacredness, because there is nothing more sacred then being in your own imagination. It's like tripping at church, going to mass. When you're at mass, you're not texting, but rejoicing with a collective group to practice the faith, even if you don't agree with the priest or don't think he's knowledgeable. Still and all, when you walk into a church, it's because you want to put yourself in that space.

Rodríguez: It is a push toward compassion for these characters that live in liminal spaces. And ultimately I think the compassion that we are asked to have for others comes back to us because then we can more easily have compassion for ourselves.

Viramontes: I think that's an excellent point. I would also like to say how essential that teaching of compassion is. Because if we . . . you know, this world is getting smaller and smaller and if we continue to have these binary views about issues, where we can no longer even talk to one another or come to some common ground, we're fucked. So one way of finding that common ground is to be able to show something in a compassionate way so that you create empathy. For me, that's almost a political practice: as a writer, this is what I do. This is what I strive for. I want to show these people who you think are totally non-beings, show them to be real human beings. Thank you for bringing up that point.

Rodríguez: You've spoken about your troubles as a young writer with a particular professor devaluing your work because it dealt with the lives of Chicanos. In what ways do you think the situation for writers who come from historically marginalized communities, whether based on ethnicity, gender, nationality, or otherwise, has improved since?

Viramontes: To a certain extent, diversity in literature is now a little more accessible than in the 1970s. That's why I turned to the African American women writers, or the white socialist writers of the 1930s. These are the writers that spoke to me. A lot of us Chicanas were affirmative action babies, first-generation college students, exposed to global literatures back then. We began writing, honing our skills, sharing our work, and I guess we had to wait for the publishing moment in history. I remember exchanging mimeographs with Sandra Cisneros and Lorna Dee Cervantes, being introduced to María Herrera-Sobek, the grandmother of Chicana feminism. The publishing world of the 1970s was very different. Just pick up an American Literature anthology textbook then and one published in 2010 to see firsthand how the literary landscape has changed.

Rodríguez: Sandra and Lorna have been and continue to be part of your community. Would you say community has been integral to your development as a writer?

Viramontes: This was our generation. We were all seeking and writing and hoping to transform society with our art. We were serious about our art just as we were serious about our activism. All three of us ended up doing something with publishing and distribution. Lorna ran Mango Press, while Sandra created the Guadalupe Cultural Center Book Fair [later, she founded Macondo Foundation and remains instrumental in mentoring younger writers]. I worked for *ChismeArte*. We were all in agreement as to what was needed, writers/artists with a mission. Our motivations fed off of one another. Of course we three were only a small part of the Latin@ overall literary production.

Rodríguez: Was this an attempt to establish an infrastructure for the possibility of that tradition?

Viramontes: In the 1970s, these literary productions were for us like spreading the Latin@ gospel according to *US*. The scholars who fought to have our work in the classroom, the small presses who began to publish our work, the cultural events that invited us to read (ok, so they needed something while the band was setting up); nonetheless, slowly we began to make an impact. I guess what I want to say, is that it took a loadful of people at all levels to ring this literature free.

You can go into a Barnes & Noble and look at the Latino literature section. They may only have five or six copies, but at least I'm thankful for the small acknowledgment from the bookstore. In American literature catalogs of some major publishing houses, Latino literature and African American literature or women's literature or gay literature are now subtitled, being there's more than one title. That's not to say that ten years from now the *Heath Anthology* or the *Norton Anthology* is going to continue to include us. Editors change, historical moments regress, politics change, and before you know it, you're back to basically mostly Anglo writers. Look at the Texas school board—history changes with those who are in power to change it.

Rodríguez: So you feel you can't ever rest too comfortably? You have to be vigilant?

Viramontes: Exactly. I like to use Toni Morrison's term: I'm cautiously optimistic. But never take anything for granted, even if you do have a tradition. That tradition can be disrespected and destroyed. Because people will do that, whatever their motives are to devalue, to silence, make invisible through devaluing the literature.

Rodríguez: One last question: your work keeps increasing in page length. What comes next and how long is it going to be?

Viramontes: I have a feeling *The Cemetery Boys* is going to be a very long epic novel. The novel so far deals with six boys who are born in 1945, when the atom bomb is also born. Eighteen years later we have the Vietnam War, and then I jump to 2005 where it's the Iraq War. So far that's the vague thin line.

But writing about wartime Los Angeles . . . well, I have to cover the Zoot Suit Riots and the Boyle Heights Jewish community in relationship to East Los Angeles, not to mention Central Avenue, the number one corridor for jazz, where everyone came together, brown, black, Jewish, Anglo, military men, to dance. You know, it's an amazing history. Wish me luck.

Works Cited

García Márquez, Gabriel. *One Hundred Years of Solitude*. New York: Harper & Row, 1970.

León-Portilla, Miguel. *The Broken Spears: The Aztec Account of the Conquest of Mexico*. Boston: Beacon Press, 1992.

Rulfo, Juan. *Pedro Páramo*. Madrid: Cátedra, 1983.

Viramontes, Helena María. *Their Dogs Came with Them*. New York: Atria, 2007.

About the Contributors

Margarita T. Barceló is a third-generation Chicana originally from the greater Los Angeles area. She holds a joint appointment in the departments of English and Chicana and Chicano Studies at the Metropolitan State College of Denver. She received her BA in English from Santa Clara University, a PhD in English and American Literature from the University of California, San Diego, and she was a UC President's Postdoctoral Fellow, University of California, Berkeley.

Mary Pat Brady is a Chicana professor from Douglas, Arizona. She currently works at Cornell University, and she is the author of *Extinct Lands, Temporal Geographies: Chicana Literature and the Urgency of Space* (Duke University Press, 2002), which was awarded the Modern Language Association's Prize for the Best Work of Latina/o and Chicana/o Literary and Cultural Criticism. She is also an associate editor of the sixth edition of the *Heath Anthology of American Literature* (Cengage, 2008–2009).

Barbara Brinson Curiel is Professor of English and Ethnic Studies Program Director at Humboldt State University. She has published on the work of Sandra Cisneros in the collection *Reading U.S. Latina Writers: Remapping American Literature* (Palgrave Macmillan, 2003), and her essay "The General's Pants: A Chicana Feminist (Re)Vision of the Mexican Revolution in Sandra Cisneros's 'Eyes of Zapata,'" appeared in the journal *Western American Literature*. Her current scholarly work focuses on the intertextual ties between the work of Cisneros and other writers. She is also the author of the poetry collection *Speak to Me from Dreams* (Third Woman Press, 1989).

R. Joyce Z. L. Garay is an associate professor of English at New Mexico State University. She received her PhD from Arizona State University, where she specialized in US literatures. As a scholar, she is interested in the intersections of multiple US literary traditions, attending especially to conversations surrounding cultural, gender, and racial difference within Chicana/o and Latina/o texts. The scope of her teaching interests and commitments ranges from surveys of Chicana, Southwestern, Latina/o, and Black US literary traditions, to the genre of autobiography, and to the theoretical realms of multiraciality, borderlands, girlhood studies, and feminisms. Her publications include the co-edited anthology *New Bones: Contemporary Black Writers in America* (Prentice Hall, 2001) and work on Chicana/o writers Alejandro Morales, Demetria Martinez, and Cherríe Moraga.

Gabriella Gutiérrez y Muhs (MA and PhD, Stanford University, 2000) is an associate professor at Seattle University in Modern Languages and Women's Studies. She held the Wismer Professor Endowed Chair for Gender and Diversity (2007–2009), and she is the 2009–2012 Latin American Studies Program Director. Dr. Gutiérrez y Muhs has also been the director of the Diversity, Citizenship and Social Justice Core Track for several years. She has published literary and cultural criticism in various journals in the United States and abroad. She works on transnational feminisms and has recently presented her research on Latina identity and subjectivity both in Chile and Colombia. Dr. Gutiérrez y Muhs is a renowned and anthologized Chicana writer and poet, as well as a Latina/Chicana cultural worker. She represented the United States as one of three American poets attending the 2011 Kritya International Poetry Festival in Nagpur, India.

Dr. Gutiérrez y Muhs has published multiple papers and encyclopedia entries on Chican@ authors and Latin American authors. Her work on literature and culture appears in national newspapers and journals regularly (*Border-lines, Commonweal, Ventana Abierta, Puentes, MALCS, Hispanic Outlook, NCR*). Her edited book of interviews with Chilean and Chicana authors, *Communal Feminisms*, was published in 2007 by Lexington Books and is being reissued in paperback. Her poetry collection *A Most Improbable Life* was published in 2003 by Finishing Line Press.

Dr. Gutiérrez y Muhs's research interests lie principally in the areas of Chican@/Latin@ and Latin American literatures, cultural studies, and feminist theory, but her intellectual and teaching interests include literary and cultural theory, Latin American Studies, the study of immigration, and the shifting of international positions toward ethnicity and identity.

Juanita Heredia is a scholar of Chicano/US Latino and Latin American cultural and literary studies and currently serves as an associate professor of Spanish at Northern Arizona University. She is the author of *Transnational Latina Narratives of the 21ˢᵗ Century: The Politics of Gender, Race and Migrations* (Palgrave Macmillan, 2009) and co-editor of *Latina Self-Portraits: Interviews with Contemporary Women Writers* (University of New Mexico Press, 2000). She recently published "The Dominican Diaspora Strikes Back: Cultural Archive and Race in Junot Díaz's *The Brief Wondrous Life of Oscar Wao*" in *Hispanic Caribbean Literature of Migration: Literature of Displacement* (Palgrave Macmillan, 2010); "From Golden Age Mexican Cinema to Transnational Border Feminism: The Community of Spectators in *Loving Pedro Infante*" in *Aztlán* (2008); and "Voyages South and North: Transnational Gender Identity in *Caramelo* and *American Chica*" in *Latino Studies* (2007).

Juan D. Mah y Busch is an associate professor of English and an affiliate of Chicana/o Studies at Loyola Marymount University. He is interested in the interplay between ethics and epistemology, especially in regard to questions of agency and consciousness. Through reading Chicana/o literature and Latina/o thought, he retheorizes values (and virtues) in essays such as "Beyond Anticolonial Hope and Postcolonial Despair: A Chicana-Feminist Reconfiguration" and "Writing Honestly: On New Knowledge and Chicana/o Narrative Ethics." He also has written on the principles that unify Gloria Anzaldúa's writings; co-authored an essay with Helena María Viramontes, "Being the Border: A Train of Thought, Imaginative Training"; and written an essay about Viramontes's nonfiction,

"In Sight of a Hummingbird." He lives in Los Angeles with his partner Irene and their children, Izabel, Paolo, and Serén.

Aldo Ulisses Reséndiz Ramírez (a.k.a. @ldo rexéndiz) is a Gates Millennium Scholar and a scholar-activist who holds dual undergraduate degrees in teaching and sociology, with minors in women/gender studies, Latin American studies, and Arabic. Reséndiz self-identifies as a two-spirited Hñhäñhu-MeXican@ immigrant (indigenous Hñähñu-Mexicano-Xican@ mestizo) whose political consciousness has been fostered by Chicana/o mentors in the far-off lands of the Aztlán del Noroeste region. As an activist, teacher, and cultural worker, he has lived in and traveled through the Middle East and Latin America where he has supported and learned from various local and global social movements.

José Antonio Rodríguez was born in México and raised in south Texas. He holds degrees in biology, theater arts, and English from the University of Texas–Pan American and is currently a doctoral student in English and Creative Writing at Binghamton University. *The Shallow End of Sleep: Poems* is forthcoming from Tia Chucha Press. His work has appeared in *Paterson Literary Review*, *The New York Quarterly*, *cream city review*, *The Spoon River Poetry Review*, *Border Senses*, and elsewhere.

Sonia Saldívar-Hull is a professor of English and the founding executive director of the Women's Studies Institute at the University of Texas, San Antonio (UTSA). She received her PhD from the University of Texas, Austin, and earned tenure at UCLA before coming to UTSA in 2001. *Feminism on the Border: Chicana Politics and Literature*, her book on Chicana feminist literature and theory, was published by the University of California Press in 2000. Her publications include numerous book chapters, articles, and introductory essays on Chicana literature, feminism, and the cultural intersections of borderland studies. She was awarded the Distinguished Achievement Award for Literary and Cultural Criticism by the Western Literature Association in 2003. She has been the co-editor of "Latin America Otherwise: Languages, Empires, Nations," a book series with Duke University Press, since 1997. Professor Saldívar-Hull also serves on the National Advisory Board for *Chicana/Latina Studies: The Journal of Mujeres Activas en Letras y Cambios Social*.

Raelene Wyse is currently a Latin American and Caribbean studies master's student and MacCracken Fellow at New York University, and she has been invited to pursue her doctoral degree with a writing fellowship at the University of Massachusetts–Amherst following completion of her NYU studies. Her gratitude for being included in this collection, among such incredible thinkers and writers, is beyond words. She hopes to someday find some way to thank the women responsible for such a truly feminist act.

Yvonne Yarbro-Bejarano is a full professor in the Department of Spanish and Portuguese at Stanford University. She was inaugural director of the Chicana and Chicano Studies Program in Stanford's Center for Comparative Studies in Race and Ethnicity and, after chairing the Department of Spanish and Portuguese, directed the Chicana/o Studies Program again from 2002 to 2008. For several decades now, she has been involved with the critique of dominant heteronormative discourses in Chicana/o Studies, as well as the analysis of cultural representations of Chicana/o queer sexualities, subjectivities, bodies, and desires.

Since 1994 she has been developing the digital archive *Chicana Art*, a database for research and teaching of images and information featuring women artists. Yvonne is the author of the books *Feminism and the Honor Plays of Lope de Vega* (Purdue University Press, 1994) and *The Wounded Heart: Writing on Cherríe Moraga* (University of Texas Press, 2001). She also co-edited *Chicano Art: Resistance and Affirmation, 1965–1985* (Wight Art Gallery, 1991). Her research, writing, and teaching focus on representations of race, sexuality, and gender that interrogate such discourses as home, family, and nation.

As director of Chicana/o Studies, Yvonne and her team organized "Feminicide = Sanctioned Murder: Gender, Race and Violence in Global Context" in May 2007. This international conference examined the extreme gender violence that has assumed epidemic proportions in such countries as Mexico, Guatemala, El Salvador, and Argentina. It brought together leading activists and experts on the subject of feminicide.

Index

African American literature, 246, 253, 261, 262
agency, 147, 148–49, 150, 163
Alarcón, Francisco X., 19
Alarcón, Norma, 36
Alejandro Morales (Gurpegui Palacios), 21n1
Alejo (Estrella's friend in *UFJ*), 238, 245; imagery, 198–200, 204–8, 211–14; migrant collectivity, 69–72, 74, 76, 88–89, 92–93; migrant life, 34–35, 39–41, 45
All about love (hooks), 151, 152
Allison, Dorothy, 245
All the Pretty Horses (McCarthy), 249
Althusser, Louis, 134
America (Baudrillard), 176
American literature, 68, 261, 262. *See also* Chican@ literature
Ana (character in *Their Dogs*). *See* Brady, Ana
Anglo-Americans, 98, 99, 103, 108, 111, 114
Anzaldúa, Gloria, ix, 36, 218, 222–23; *conocimiento*, ix; *la facultad*, 199–200; mestiza consciousness, x, 36, 201; Nepantla, viii; *nepantlera*, ix; spiritual activism, 229. *See also* nagual/a; "othering"
Aptheker, Bettina, 124
Ardener, Edwin, 201

Ardener, Shirley, 201
Aristotle, 149; Aristotelian ethics, 156
Arte Público Press, vii, 16
Aztecs, 110, 126; colonization of, 98–99, 100, 103, 220, 221, 231n3; mythology, 221–22, 231n1, 232nn9–10
Aztlán, 12, 126, 231n1

Banfield, Ann, 73, 74, 93nn3–4, 94n22, 94n26
Barrio-Logos: Space and Place in Urban Chicano Literature and Culture (Villa), 2, 102, 132
Bastard out of Carolina (Allison), 245
Baudrillard, Jean, 176
Beauty Secrets: Women and the Politics of Appearance (Chapkis), 127, 129
Ben (character in *Their Dogs*). *See* Brady, Ben
Bernstein, Stuart, 244
Bhabha, Homi, 201, 215n5
"Birthday" (Viramontes), 123, 125, 133, 137–41
Border Crossings and Beyond (Rivera, Carmen), 21n1
Borderlands/La Frontera: The New Mestiza (Anzaldúa), 218, 222–23
Borderlands of Culture: Américo Paredes and the Transnational Imaginary, The (Saldívar, Ramón), 167–68

271